MAGIC, SCIENCE, RELIGION, AND
THE SCOPE OF RATIONALITY

THE LEWIS HENRY MORGAN LECTURES 1984

presented at
The University of Rochester
Rochester, New York

THE LEWIS HENRY MORGAN LECTURES 1984
Lewis Henry Morgan Lecture Series
Fred Eggan: *The American Indian: Perspectives for the Study of Social Change*
Ward, H. Goodenough: *Description and Comparison in Cultural Anthropology*
Robert J. Smith: *Japanese Society: Tradition, Self, and the Social Order*
Sally Falk Moore: *Social Facts and Fabrications: "Customary Law" on Kilimanjaro, 1880–1980*
Nancy Munn: *The Fame of Gawa: A Symbolic Study of Value Transformation in a Mussim (Papua New Guinea) Society*
Lawrence Rosen: *The Anthropology of Justice: Law as Culture in Islamic Society*

1. Frontispiece A medieval man of many parts and pursuits: the revered and ingenious father Bertold Schwartz of the Franciscan Order, Doctor, Alchemist, and founder of the art of rifle shooting in the year 1380.

Magic, science, religion, and the scope of rationality

STANLEY JEYARAJA TAMBIAH,
Harvard University

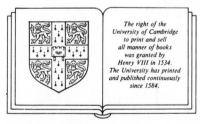

The right of the
University of Cambridge
to print and sell
all manner of books
was granted by
Henry VIII in 1534.
The University has printed
and published continuously
since 1584.

CAMBRIDGE UNIVERSITY PRESS

Cambridge
New York   Port Chester
Melbourne   Sydney

Published by the Press Syndicate of the University of Cambridge
The Pitt Building, Trumpington Street, Cambridge CB2 IRP
40 West 20th Street, New York, NY 10011, USA
10 Stamford Road, Oakleigh, Melbourne 3166, Australia

© Cambridge University Press 1990

First published 1990

Printed in Great Britain at the University Press, Cambridge

British Library cataloguing in publication data

Tambiah, S.J. (Stanley Jeyaraja), *1929–*
Magic, science, and religion, and the scope
of rationality. – (The Lewis Henry Morgan
lectures: 1981)
1. Culture. Anthropological perspectives
1. Title
306

Library of Congress cataloguing in publication data

Tambiah, Stanley Jeyaraja, 1929–
Magic, science, religion, and the scope of rationality / Stanley
Jeyaraja Tambiah.
p. cm. – (The Henry Lewis Morgan lectures: 1981)
Bibliography.
Includes index.
ISBN 0-521-37486-3. – ISBN 0-521-37631-9 (pbk).
1. Ethnology – Philosophy – History. 2. Rationalism. I. Title.
II. Series.
GN345.T36 1989
306.8'001–dc20 89-31436 CIP

Contents

Plates

Acknowledgments Plates 2.1, 2.3, 3.1, 3.4, 3.5, 5.1 and 5.2 from the
Francis A. Countway Library of Medicine; photograph for Plate 3.2
by Deborah Tooker; photograph for Plate 3.3 by author; photographs
for Plates 4.1–4.7 by Jerry Leach.

Foreword

Since Lewis Henry Morgan's day, anthropology has become established as an international enterprise with trained anthropologists on every continent, participants in a generalizing discipline that both includes and transcends local concerns. Professor Tambiah, educated in Ceylon and the United States, taught in Ceylon and England before coming to the United States, where he is now on the faculty of Harvard University. His previous research, based on fieldwork in southeast Asia, has attracted widespread attention, and over the past twenty-five years has earned him an enviable list of honors and awards. The 1984 Lewis Henry Morgan Lectures were delivered by Professor Tambiah on March 13, 15, 20 and 22.

An outline sketch of Professor Tambiah's argument and conclusions could not do justice to the subtle clarity and elegance of his presentation; here it is possible to touch on only a few general points. In this expanded version of his Lewis Henry Morgan Lectures, Professor Tambiah examines several concepts that have been especially important in much anthropological work. "Magic," "science," "religion" and "rationality" are obviously not the exclusive concern of anthropology; the history of thinking about them can be traced very far back. In this book they are examined in a broadly conceived framework, so constructed that not only the use of the terms over the past hundred years or so is considered, they are also placed in the context of work in other disciplines.

It is apparent, on reading these lectures in relation to Professor Tambiah's other publications, that more than twenty years of research and critical thought lie behind them. The discussion goes beyond anthropology's boundaries, making it clear that anthropology has major contributions to offer regarding discussions and debates that have exercised philosophers, historians and others over the years. This work, then, can be read as a contribution to the history of ideas, and as a critical contextualizing of what has been written, in terms of Professor Tambiah's own theoretical scheme.

This way of proceeding permits the author to consider what such major contributors to our thinking as Tylor, Malinowski and Wittgenstein have

ix

said. But it is also necessary, in his view, to offer both careful evaluations of other authors and his own resolution of the problems their work raises. This set of conclusions, especially as developed in the final chapters, will undoubtedly stimulate controversy. It is just as certain, and perhaps more important, that Professor Tambiah's theory makes it possible to move on. He, together with others, can now make use of his conclusions in dealing with particular ethnographic cases.

Interested readers will find much to think about on every page, and will undoubtedly appreciate the stimulating impact Professor Tambiah's lectures and seminars had upon his audiences.

Alfred Harris
Editor
The Lewis Henry Morgan Lectures

Acknowledgments

I thank the University of Rochester, and in particular Professors Alfred and Grace Harris, for inviting me to give the Lewis Henry Morgan Lectures in 1984. They, together with the faculty and the graduate students of the Department of Anthropology, were warm, considerate, and stimulating hosts, and I hope that the revised text of the lectures will please them.

Thanks are also due to the following: to Dan Rosenberg for reading the text in draft form and offering comments for improvement; to Geoffrey Lloyd and Milton Singer for their valuable and encouraging comments in the role of readers; to Richard J. Wolfe, Elin L. Wolfe, and Déla T. Zitkus of the Francis A. Countway Library of Medicine, Harvard Medical School, for their informed and gracious help in choosing many illustrations for inclusion in the book; to Jerry Leach for the wonderful photographs of people of the Trobriand Islands; and to Deborah Tooker for the picture of an Akha spirit priest.

I am very much in the debt of Kenneth Laine Ketner for permitting me to make lavish use of the translation prepared by him and James Eigsti entitled *Ludwig Wittgenstein, Remarks on Frazer's Philosophical Anthropology.*

1

Magic, science and religion in Western thought: anthropology's intellectual legacy

As a Victorian it was natural, in 1877, for Lewis Henry Morgan to give the following subtitle to *Ancient Society*: "Researches in the lines of human progress from savagery, through barbarism to civilization." I feel that it is equally natural for me in 1984, over a century later, to want to affirm this statement of Morgan's: "The History of the human race is one in source, one in experience and one in progress,"[1] not by insisting as he did on the ladder of progress and evolution as the key to that history, but by affirming the continuities in experience and the generality of existential problems that constitute the psychic unity of mankind. If I do honour to Morgan then, I do so by pitting myself against that great evolutionary scheme that he helped construct as the major paradigm of his time.

My presentations are from the standpoint of a social anthropologist who has studied religions and social phenomena in the field, particularly in South and Southeast Asia, and who at the same time is interested in the intellectual origins in Western thought of the concepts of religion, magic and science, and the bearing that that history may have on their valid application as general analytical categories in comparative studies.

Magic, Science and Religion is the title of a famous long essay published by Bronislaw Malinowski in 1925.[2] These three categories or domains, their demarcation, differentiation and overlap, have been the subject of a vigorous polemical dialogue among a number of scholars who are invariably included in any genealogy of anthropological theorists. My genealogy as well as itinerary begins with late British Victorians like Sir Edward Tylor and Sir James Frazer, passes on to the French *Année Sociologique* school of Emile Durkheim and Marcel Mauss, and others who interacted with them such as Lucien Lévy-Bruhl and Maurice Leenhardt, then returns to Britain to its Functionalists, principally Bronislaw Malinowski and Radcliffe-Brown, and finally leads to moderns: E. E. Evans-Pritchard, Robin Horton, John Beattie, Ernest Gellner and many others.

This lively dialogue that has extended for at least eleven decades, since in fact Morgan's time, is interesting for two reasons. Firstly, it accepted the categories of magic, science and religion as meaningful domains prevalent in virtually all societies, and therefore as generally useful analytical categories for comparative study. Secondly, the long dialogue consisted of polemical exchanges in which the theorists took different positions regarding the three domains: their substantive contents, their boundaries, their developmental stages, and the quality of the "rationality" they portrayed. Indeed the debate inevitably led the theorists to ask whether the mentalities and modes of thought of men and women everywhere were the same or different. If the same, what were their common features, and where were we to locate them? If there were universal features, how did we explain cultural diversity? If the mentalities were different, were the differences decisive, qualitative, and discontinuous between "us" moderns, and them "primitives," or were all human societies merely occupants of different positions on a single developmental continuum, whose bedrock was the "psychic unity of mankind"?

In this first chapter I wish to present a few historical backdrops as illustrative of the West's intellectual, epistemological and even ontological legacy, that has influenced, oftentimes unconsciously, the anthropological discourse of the past, and continues to influence it in the present. The anthropological debate which I have mentioned as stretching from the 1870s to the 1980s will derive its maximum value only if we locate it in the stream of Western intellectual history which again was inflected by cataclysmic social, political and economic developments. When we have acquired some appreciation of these historical and contextual circumstances, we shall not only better understand the epistemological and philosophical debates of the past, but also comprehend why we have to confront today the question whether or not the categories of magic, science and religion may be "tendentious" and their analytical value rendered suspect by their historical "embeddedness."

Although Max Weber (and certain others) pronounced that the historical conditions which give birth to certain ideas and concepts need not affect their objective status and truth value, there are powerful questionings and disavowals of this thesis from other directions. Let me mention some. Karl Marx, and his successors, particularly the Frankfurt School of Critical Sociology (Horkheimer, Marcuse, Habermas, et al.), have relentlessly sought the critique of ideology, and to deconstruct "ideology" as serving and legitimizing "interests". Ideology as distorted discourse not only masks the ambitions of powerful interests, it can also actively produce practices and policies that constitute social reality. "Science" too has not escaped this taint of being tarred by interest groups and by political power. Recently, from another intellectual tradition Foucault, in popularizing the equation of Power/Knowledge, has sought to unveil "the political status of science and the ideological functions it could serve,"[3] and the interventions in society that it stimulates. Onslaughts on the universal applicability of the notion of economic man and economy as defined by neo-classical economics, the notion of economy as a differentiated and separate domain of behavior in which individuals act to maximize returns in a price-forming market situation, conceptions perhaps best descriptive of the classical capitalist bourgeois economy, have been mounted by Karl Polanyi and the so-called "substantivists" in economic anthropology.

Louis Dumont, in spirit sympathetic to Polanyi, in his *Homo Hierarchicus* confronts the same problem in a different context. He has striven to convince us that Indian society and civilization are constructed on a conception of hierarchy, in which the domains of religion, polity and economy are arranged and weighted differently from their manner of interaction in modern individualist capitalist societies. In such a hierarchy, moreover, the relevant criterion is how the different parts contribute to the whole rather than how atomistic units as basic reference points add up to make a whole. Similarly, Wilfred Cantwell Smith in *The Meaning and End of Religion* has made suspect the general application of a narrow rationalist definition of religion, born of the European Enlightenment, which has construed it primarily as a doctrine of beliefs and a system of intellectualistic constructs.

Once we raise these comparative epistemological and sociological issues, our discussions will inevitably lead us to the grand problem, which is at the heart of the anthropological enterprise: How do we understand and represent the modes of thought and action of other societies, other cultures? Since we have to undertake this task from a Western baseline so to say, how are we to achieve "the translation of cultures," i.e. understand other cultures as far as possible in their own terms but in our language, a task which also ultimately entails the mapping of the ideas and practices onto Western categories of understanding, and hopefully modifying these in turn to evolve a language of anthropology as a comparative science?

In some measure this task of understanding and translation has been the increasing self-conscious concern of us moderns. To give just one example in the study of religion: the Dutch phenomenologists of religion (such as G. van der Leeuw and W. Brede Kristensen) have been exemplary in urging students of religion to adopt an attitude both of "distancing" and "sympathy" toward alien faiths; to refrain from attempting to judge the ultimate truth value of other religions (the attitude of *epoché*), especially from the standpoint of one's own religion, for this is properly the task of a theologian and not a student of religion; to avoid easy and superficial reductionism of religion to some level of social structure or individual psychic conditions; and not to resort to biased evolutionary schemes by which some forms of religion are considered lower and others superior. These phenomenologists have at the same time held before us the comparative prospect of establishing common meanings and structures in a number of different events and manifestations both within and between religions.

One must see then that the daunting double task of translation of cultures and their comparative study raises not only the question of the mentality of us and other peoples, but also ultimately the issue of "*rationality*" itself, and the limits of western "scientism" as a paradigm.

As a sequel to this preamble, let me now sketch in some historical backdrops. The historical origins and derivation of the concepts of religion, magic and science bear relevantly on the question of using them as general analytical categories for the understanding of the modes of thought and action of non-Western societies.

In order to fully understand the concept of *religion* as taken for granted in the modern West it is necessary to have some idea of its vicissitudes and trajectory in the history of Western thought.

A thumbnail sketch of the history of "religion" as a concept

My main source for this thumbnail sketch is Wilfred Cantwell Smith.[4] Although Smith does not use Kuhn's or Foucault's language, we may construe his account as showing paradigmatic shifts in the European's concept of religion. Since "religion" in English ultimately derives from the Latin word *religio*, we should begin with Roman times. *Religio* carried a double meaning: the existence of a power outside to whom man was obligated; and the feeling of *piety* man had towards that power. By and large, religion as a generic concept still carries these meanings though they do not exhaust it. But in Roman times the reification of a religion as a great objective phenomenon or as an entity of speculative interest did not exist. Religion was something one felt and did, so to say.

In early Christianity the following emphases and attitudes were developed. An integral component of religion was the sense of an "organized community," a *church*. So was the concept of *faith*. The early fathers interpreted the new *faith* as ramifying with every aspect of a believer's life. Religion was all inclusive, a "total phenomenon" to use Marcel Mauss's twentieth-century words, which included both the subjective orientations of the worshippers and the hierarchical organization of the Church. Finally, early Christianity had a definite conception of true versus false religion (*vera et falsa religio*), was strongly exclusive with regard to other faiths and was intolerant of them.

In the Middle Ages, St. Augustine carried further this claim of Christianity as the one true religion. He emphasized the personal relationship to the one and true transcendent God. In the Middle Ages "faith" not "religion" was the great word. *Religio* in fact was a special designation for the monastic life, a heritage we still continue when we refer to the members of the monastic orders as "the religious."

The main message, as it issued during the Reformation from the mouths of Zwingli and Calvin, was that men should not put their faith in any external institution, the Church, or in any religious system as embodying the divine. Instead *religio* designated something personal, inner and transcendentally oriented.

It is essentially in the modern period, since the Enlightenment, that a particular conception of religion that emphasizes its cognitive, intellectual, doctrinal and dogmatic aspects, gained prominence. From the seventeenth century onwards European thought progressively showed interest in the intellectual constructs, systematic and abstract, that were elaborated in the religious realm. As Smith says, the leaders of European thought "gave the name 'religion' to the system, first in general but increasingly to the system of ideas, in which men of faith were involved or with which men of potential faith were confronted."[5] So a century after Calvin, men were calling by the name *religio* not their personal visions of God and their relationship with Him, but all the beliefs and practices that Calvin regarded as vehicles to that end. By the later seventeenth century, the consideration of religion as a system of ideas and beliefs, as a doctrine, had become regnant. (I must here draw your attention to this intellectualistic attitude of the Enlightment to religion, which, as primarily composed of "doctrine" or "beliefs," was a legacy inherited by our Victorian fathers of the anthropology of religion such as Sir Edward Tylor, whose minimum definition of religion was "the belief in Spiritual Beings." Tylor will engage us in detail later.)

It is also relevant to note that the Enlightenment tendency to produce an intellectualist and impersonal schematization of religion was extended and universalized in terms of the concept of *natural religion* as a generic phenomenon. It was claimed that beliefs about God were common to all mankind and were attainable by man by virtue of his natural reason. At the same time, during the seventeenth and eighteenth centuries, the religious wars and conflicts that raged in Europe made the subject of religion a matter for polemical and apologetic labelling and disputation.

So in the nineteenth century, despite the return to the more personal and moral aspects of religion by John Wesley and the Methodists and by the German pietists, the dominant trend in the study and exposition of religion was to infuse the static quality of the Enlightenment's rationalism with an increasing sense of history and historical knowledge. The subject of religion now included the theme of the historical development of religion over the centuries. A comparative focus with an evolutionary framework developed, making use of the new information on other religions reported by travellers and missionaries. This process of "objectification" of religion had by now been taken to its furthest point. Religion had become an object of study and it had been substantialized. Individual religions were regarded as phenomena with their distinctive histories, and scholars sought to compare them, and some even to grade them into higher and lower.

Moreover by the beginning of this century, Western scholars had already labelled the great religions as *isms*: such as Hinduism, Buddhism, Confucianism, etc. In this labelling and delineation the so-called doctrinal texts, the beliefs and tenets, of the religious *virtuosi* and intellectuals were given prominence as the core of the *ism* under study.

One legacy from the Enlightenment's rationalist emphasis that influenced the dominant defence of Christianity by its theologians was the framework of "historical realism," which was seen as entailing the reconstruction of the past "as it actually was" in terms of methods compounded of biblical criticism, Greek rationalism, and the scientific method. The characterization of religion, its "justification" by adherents (or its "denigration" by its opponents), had to be done in a way that took cognizance of the extant scientific discourse and philosophical argumentation. There has been a felt need to provide a cognitive account of religious belief that made the intellectual exercise a parallel to a kind of objectivist scientific description. In our discussions hereafter I shall try to argue that from a general anthropological standpoint the distinctive feature of religion as a generic concept lies not in the domain of belief and its "rational accounting" of the workings of the universe, but in a special awareness of the transcendent, and the acts of symbolic communication that attempt to realize that awareness and live by its promptings.

The early Judaic religion: true religion and false magic

In order to fully understand the current Western conception of magic it is best that we take note of two legacies – one deriving from the early religion of Israel (which became later a part of the broader Judaeo-Christian religious tradition) and the other deriving from Greece, which is usually credited with the origination of systematic "science," and whose principal ideas are said to have influenced later European thought from the Renaissance onwards.

The early biblical religion, say from its beginnings to the Babylonian Exile has, according to Yehezkel Kauffmann[6] who is my principal authority here, made a sharp distinction between the monotheistic worship of YHWH and pagan idolatry, which went as follows:

YHWH was Israel's "living God" as opposed to the pagan gods who were worshipped in the form of images, constructed out of wood and stone by man.

The distinctive feature of Israelite monotheism was not merely that there was one God, but also that there was no realm, primordial or otherwise, to limit his sovereignty. Such a supreme God therefore cannot be the focus of any mythology. There are no myths – indeed there cannot be any myths – about YHWH's origins or his pedigree.

Moreover this monotheistic sovereign God of Israel created the universe *ex nihilo*; there was no pre-existent stuff he used, he simply created it by fiat, and the processes of nature were established by his divine decree.

This means that there is no natural bond between God and nature, for nature did not share in any of God's substance or body (that is, nature was not "iconically" connected with God). Similarly, there was also a great chasm between God and man as his creation. There was no bridge between the God and the created universe.

In line with this absolute divide was the conception that morality was God-imposed. Sin is rebellion against the will of the creator and its punishment is God-willed. There is thus no automaticity or mechanical causality about this conception of man's sinful acts and their results. It follows therefore that the

Bible places a relentless ban on "magic" (as a form of causal action to manipulate God) under pain of death, and that it should also regard prophecy as God directly speaking to a prophet who relays the message to the people. That is, the prophet is not conceived as possessed by God or as being a "vessel" filled by God.

Now in Kauffmann's account the worship of idols is credited with practically all the opposite implications. The Bible describes the idols as bearers of occult powers, and therefore as having powers to act. Pagan worship is directed to appeasing them and receiving benefits from them. It is these attitudes and ritual transactions that are denounced as magic and sorcery. (I am reminded at this point of a famous hymn of Bishop Heber's which expressed the same sentiment in these lines: "The heathen in his blindness/Bows down to wood and stone)." Be that as it may, I must underscore the point that the Bible accepts the reality and efficacy of pagan magic. It however condemns it as false religion not in the sense of its not producing empirical results but in the sense of being anathema to the Jewish people bound to YHWH by a special covenant.

The pagan cosmology in contrast to the early Judaic is pictured as accepting the existence of a primordial realm and primordial stuff anterior to, or parallel with, or even independent of the gods. Thus pagan gods do not transcend the universe but are rooted in it and bound by its laws.

The existence of a primordial realm with its pre-existent autonomous force thus allows for, nay stimulates, the operation of ritual action of the type branded as "magic," and the elaboration of a rich mythology about gods and men. Gods as well as men are subject to the order of the cosmos (Hindu *rita*, Greek *moira*, Persian *asha*). There are no fixed bounds between gods and men so that men can aspire to be gods, and are open to the benefits of apotheosis.

Magic comes into its own in this cosmology as a distinctive kind of ritual action. In its quintessential form – and this is the early Judaic legacy that has coloured subsequent Western thought – magic is ritual action that is held to be automatically effective, and ritual action that dabbles with forces and objects that are outside the scope, or independent, of the gods. Magical acts in their ideal forms are thought to have an intrinsic and automatic efficacy. This is one strand in the Western conception of magic, and a lot of sophistry and special pleading has gone into preserving this definition over time.

Now, I want to suggest to you that the Hindu cosmology, a product of high civilization, has structural features similar to those attributed by early Judaism to early paganism, and that in this Hindu scheme we are able to see some startling implications for comparative study and for the translation of cultures.

Judaeo-Christian monotheism is in spirit totally antagonistic to the cosmology of Hindu polytheism and non-dualism. Judaeo-Christian monotheism is honour bound to declare any conception of a cosmos, in which man and transcendental entities share certain similar properties and capacities, and can have relations of reciprocity, exchange and even coercion, and in which objects and forces that exist apart from and anterior to them can be employed, as not only polytheistic but also magical and pagan.

Moreover the Hindu-type "pagan" cosmology highlights entirely different problems and generates different puzzles to solve from those of early Judaism as its central religious questions, and advances entirely different solutions to general existential problems like the origins of evil and the justification of theodicy (explanation of the distribution of suffering in this world).

Wendy O'Flaherty writes in *The Origins of Evil in Hindu Mythology*[7] these words that are impossible to admit in Judaic monotheism:

"The gods are responsible for the creation of evil for various reasons: in orthodox Hinduism, because *dharma* is only possible, and valuable, when *adharma* also exists to balance and contrast with it; in asceticism mythology because the gods fear that men will become too peaceful and overcome the gods; and in devotional mythology because God wishes to descend to the level of evil, and to participate in it, to help or free mankind."[8]

Thus Hindu mythology in certain contexts entertains these "heresies" and these "magical" activities as judged by the canons of Judaic monotheism: that God is not good or does not wish man to be without evil; that not only is evil inevitable, it is desirable; that men can acquire power through ascetic practices (*tapas*) to challenge the gods. When a sage asked why Brhaspati, the guru of the gods, told a lie, the reply he received was: "All creatures, even gods, are subject to passions. Otherwise the universe, composed as it is of good and evil, could not continue to develop."[9]

The origins of Greek science

In this second backdrop relating to the rise of Greek science (the period up to the fifth century B.C.) we are particularly interested to discern why classicists and Western intellectual historians point to Greece as the womb of "science," in the sense science is recognized today.

If we look at traditional discussions of science we are faced with several definitions among which one has increasingly won out. J. G. Crowther (in *The Social Relations of Science*)[10] defined science as "the system of behaviour by which man acquires mastery of the environment." The trouble with this loose definition is that by this criterion no society whatsoever has lacked the rudiments of science. Another definition that has been advanced (Charles Singer, *A Short History of Scientific Ideas to 1900*)[11] is that science is the "active" process of "knowledge making," and "no body of doctrine which is not growing, which is not actually in the making can long retain the attributes of science." By this criterion we have to acknowledge as science the great developments over stretches of time in medicine, metallurgy, geometry and astronomy in the Near East to which Greece was heir, and also the technical achievements of Ancient China that preceded Greek science.

But the classicists seem to have more restrictive criteria in mind. M. Clagett (in his book *Greek Science in Antiquity*)[12] enumerates these: first "the orderly and systematic comprehension, description and/or explanation of natural phenomena," and second "the tools necessary for that undertaking, including, especially, logic and mathematics."

By far the most useful writing on early Greek science I have encountered is G. E. R. Lloyd's works, who in his *Magic, Reason and Experience*,[13] uses three criteria that establish that Greece produced the first philosopher scientists:

(1) The demarcation of nature as separate from the domain of the supernatural. Together with this go these conceptions: laws of nature, regularity of nature, and causation in a physical and mechanical sense.

(2) The development of the tools of logical argument and of mathematics, and the systematic deployment of them to formulate a mode of demonstration and proof. This discourse is furthered by the practice of rational criticism and debate, the presence and encouragement of lively academies and disputing schools of thought, and a general climate that tolerates a general skepticism.

(3) The increasing guidance of these methods and canons of demonstration and proof by empirical observation and research in order to extend the empirical base of knowledge.

Now, it cannot be said that the early Greeks developed this scientific mentality all at once or in a widespread manner. The Greeks had no conception of "science" that can be considered equivalent to our own notion of science that developed in the seventeenth century (and became current, say, in the Royal Society of London around 1645). But the Greeks in question did possess terms such as *philosophia* (love of wisdom, philosophy), *episteme* (knowledge), *theoria* (contemplation), and *periphyseos historia* (inquiry concerning nature) as in part overlapping with, even rough equivalents of, what came to be labelled later as science. And most interestingly and importantly, early Greece was familiar with the category of magic: μάγοι [*magi*] meant magicians, and μαγεία [*magea*] meant the religion of the *magi*). We ought thus to pay close attention to the contents of these terms and how they related to each other in a semantic field.

Of the many features of early Greek science, I wish to draw your special attention to this point. The first time in extant Greek – indeed, it is claimed, in extant Western literature – when a body of beliefs was explicitly declared to be magical was in a medical text from the latter part of the fifth or the early part of the fourth century B.C. The text in question was *On the Sacred Disease*. It belonged to the Hippocratic Corpus and its subject matter was epilepsy.

The text is a landmark for these reasons: it rejected this disease (and certain others) as being the result of divine intervention; in other words, it rejected a certain kind of explanation and action that was labelled "magical" or occult. It proposed as a substitute explanation a naturalistic explanation of disease, which itself was tied to a doctrine of the uniformity of nature and the regularity of causes (we are tempted to say, using Kuhn's celebrated phrase, that this text represented an intellectual "paradigm switch").

Now, while this text does have some kind of momentous significance, equally significant for us is the fact that the umbrella of "naturalistic explanation" sheltered in early Greece many fanciful explanations, which had a weak empirical base and were grounded in doubtful inferences. It is true that certain empirical studies were being made at the time in the form of astronomical and clinical observations – for instance, all seven books of the Hippocratic Corpus titled *Epidemics* reported case histories (a representative sample of which numbering forty-two cases are to be found in volumes 1 and 3) – and it is also true that the concept of dissection was known before Aristotle's time but only occasionally performed at that time. By and large, however, the medical doctors of the Hippocratic School appealed to naturalist causes without possessing a real positivist methodology or an efficacious technology of curing, including pharmacopeia. Thus we may note that "nature" as the ground of explanation was accepted theoretically before an efficacious medicine and medical technology were developed.

This state of affairs provides an occasion for me to underscore a point which is equally true now in our time as it was then. A commitment to the notion of nature as the ground of causality, of nature as a uniform domain subject to regular laws, can function as a belief system without its guaranteeing a verified "objective truth" as modern science may define it. In other words, the appeal to "nature" or "science" can serve as a legitimation of a belief and action system like any other ideological and normative system. (I need only remind you of how today the laity at large is frequently called upon to use medical drugs, or assent to industrial and chemical and nuclear projects, on the basis of alleged "scientific" reasoning and evidence: medical tragedies such as thalidomide babies and nuclear reactor accidents such as that which happened at Three Mile Island in Pennsylvania, and the horrors of Love Canal in upstate New York, are stark reminders of our victimization on the altars of innocent belief in science, technology and economic growth.)[14]

Next we ought to bear in mind that despite the development of a "scientific" mode of thought in early Greece, early Greece knew the co-presence of many types of healers and healing systems which both competed with one another and also overlapped as regards therapy. Hippocratic doctors, herbalists, temple medicine priests practiced simultaneously, and there was a general belief in the efficacy of drugs, amulets, spells and prayers. Terms like "purification" and "cleansing" carried both "natural" and "moral" meanings, much as they do in many parts of the world today.

Thirdly, we should also bear in mind that both pre- and post- Aristotelian science exhibited mystical aspects. For example, the Pythagorean sects cultivated esoteric doctrines and practices, including a mystical number theory and astrology. Geoffrey Lloyd notes that several of the writers and schools, such as Ptolemy and other astronomers, who were prominent in the development of Greek cosmology and science, combined an interest and belief in magic with their other work in the "inquiry of nature." This coexistence and overlap of actions that were later construed to be incompatible genres is a notable fact. (As we shall see later, a similar point can be made about intellectual activity in the overlap period between the late medieval times and the Renaissance in Europe, and even about the activities of some famous heroes of Enlightenment rationalism.)

Lastly, as regards our three terms *magic, science, religion* as applied to early Greek experience, we see these demarcations and interrelations:

(1) It is clear that the writers of the critical Hippocratic medical texts were able to demarcate a realm called *nature* and to formulate a brand of naturalistic/materialistic explanation that was different from occult, "superstitious" explanations and manipulations. Thus "magic" was demarcated from medicine as a "proto-science." It is not entirely clear how medicine of the Hippocratic school separated itself from *philosophia*, but the polemic between the advocates of the two forms appears to have related to the problem of establishing "certain" knowledge.

(2) But these same philosophers and forerunners of "science" did not rule out "religion" as opposed to or incompatible with their knowledge. Indeed among these Greeks the "divinity of nature" was taken for granted and was not a matter for disputation. They believed that the divine principle pervaded all phenomena. So if the divine pervaded everything, it could not be invoked to explain specific causalities. Thus it may be said that if the early Greeks distinguished between magic and medicine ("science"), they did not oppose "religion" to them as a third category. Religion in any case was not a focus of theorizing, and in the prevailing climate of pluralism, competing doctrines, and even skepticism, the question of the divine, and man's relation to it, did not figure importantly in intellectual debate. Thus we may write the relevant semantic distinctions in Early Greece in terms of this "formula":

$$\frac{magic/medicine\ (\text{``science''})/philosophy}{religion\ \text{(pervasive divinity)}}$$

The historical watershed: Europe of the sixteenth and seventeenth centuries

Developments in Europe during the sixteenth and seventeenth centuries have been decisively important for the demarcation in Western thought between religion, magic and science. (I have already in the preceding sketch of the path of "religion" as an object of study pointed to the Age of Enlightenment in the eighteenth century as constituting a new perspective.) In these two centuries three streams converged, and I shall illustrate the convergence, here and in the next chapter, by reference to some landmark studies.

The Protestant ethic and the spirit of capitalism

This classic work[15] by Max Weber deals with the first issue, namely, the concordance between certain developments in Protestantism, especially the Protestant "ethic," and the values and motivations associated with capitalism as a form of economic activity. Weber's thesis was that the Puritan values such as the doctrine of vocation or work as a "calling" on behalf of God, of engaging in good works and in systematic activity upon nature and its transformation for the glory of God, combined with a personal asceticism as regards the use of material benefits and wealth for one's pleasure. All these were conducive to rational economic activity and to the requirements of profitable capitalism, such as the systematic ploughing back of profits into industry (capital investment), postponement of present consumption and gratification for the sake of future yields, the adoption of systematic accounting and book-keeping in business, and so on. The tensions posed between an "innerworldly ethic" of attaining salvation and a this-worldly imperfection, between a doctrine of predestination, which held that God alone decided men's fates, and an anxiety among the religious whether they will attain salvation and what the outward signs of that grace might be, served positively to motivate and fuel an orientation of transforming this world through rational conduct and good works. Weber was careful to point out that although Calvinism originally rejected the world and its wealth, in due course a transformation took place by which it came to legitimate the creation and accumulation of wealth provided it was combined with personal asceticism. In short, Weber postulated that the Protestant Reformation stimulated systematic conduct in the world in the domains of economy, administration, politics and science.

The scientific revolution and the Protestant Reformation

Thus we come to the second major theme attributed to this period: the relation between the scientific revolution and the Protestant Reformation. Science as a self-conscious activity with its distinctive methods and professional organization comes into its own in the seventeenth century especially with the formation of the Royal Society in London around 1645.

Robert Merton[16] in a remarkable study has advanced the thesis, which we can regard as an extension and elaboration of Max Weber's ideas, that the values and attitudes basic to ascetic Protestantism generally so canalized the interests of many Europeans and New Englanders of the seventeenth century as to constitute one important factor in the enhanced cultivation of science and technology. "The deep rooted religious interests of the day demanded in their forceful implications the systematic, rational, and empirical study of Nature for the glorification of God in His works and the control of the corrupt world."[17] Merton concludes his essay with these words: "The positive estimation by Protestants of a hardly disguised utilitarianism, of intra-mundane interests, of a thoroughgoing empiricism, of the right and even duty of *libre examen*, and of the explicit individual questioning of authority were congenial to the very same values found in modern science. And perhaps above all in the significance of the active ascetic drive which necessitated the study of Nature that it might be controlled. Hence, these two fields [Protestantism and scientific-technological interests] were well integrated and, in essentials, mutually supporting, not only in seventeenth-century England but also in other times and places."[18]

Merton's starting point is a remarkably vivid characterization of the members and activities of the Royal Society. He documents that Thomas Sprat's widely read *History of the Royal Society of London*, published in 1667, correlated point-to-point the principle of Puritanism with the attributes, goals and results of science. Puritanism and the scientific temper were shown to be in most felicitous agreement "for the combination of *rationalism and empiricism* which is so pronounced in the Puritan ethic forms the essence of the spirit of modern science."[19]

The English puritans whom Merton enumerates as leading spirits of the Society include Robert Boyle, John Ray (the botanist), Francis Willughby (the geologist), John Wallis and John Wilkins, one of the leading lights of the "invisible College" which later developed into the Royal Society. "Baconian teachings constituted the basic principles on which the Royal Society was patterned." The combination of Puritan piety with the utilitarianism and empiricism of science as then conceived is illustrated in the hopeful words of Boyle that the Fellows of the Society might "discover the true Nature of the Works of God", and John Wilkins's proclamation that the experimental study of nature was a most effective means of begetting in men a veneration for God.[20] Merton comments that "It is hardly a fortuitous circumstance that the leading figures of this nuclear group of the Royal Society were divines or eminently religious men"[21] markedly influenced by Puritan conceptions. "Among the original list of members of the society in 1663, forty-two of the sixty-eight concerning whom the information is available were clearly Puritan."

Similarly corroborating evidence comes from France, where the Protestant academies "devoted much more attention to scientific and utilitarian subjects than did the Catholic institutions."[22] Merton reports the fascinating statistics compiled by Candolle in his well-known *Histoire des sciences et des savants*: "Candolle finds that although in Europe excluding France, there were 107 million Catholics and 68 million Protestants, yet on the list of scientists named foreign associates by the Academy of Paris from 1666–1883 there were only eighteen Catholics as against eighty Protestants."[23] The same trend is confirmed in the case of foreign members elected to the Royal Society of London in 1869.

The pietists in Germany and elsewhere entered into a close alliance with the "new education", namely the study of science and technology. August Francke and Christian Thomasius helped advance the new education at the University of Halle, and other pietistic universities, such as Königsberg and Göttingen, and the Calvinistic University of Heidelberg, followed suit. The same pietist predilection for science and technology was manifest in secondary school education.

In the New World, the correspondents and members of the Royal Society who lived in New England were trained in Calvinistic thinking. Examples are the younger John Winthrop, and the Puritan, Increase Mather, who founded the "Philosophical Society" in Boston and also served as President of Harvard College from 1684 to 1701.

Merton supplements the thesis which we have reviewed – that the attitudes basic to ascetic Protestantism enhanced the cultivation of science and technology – with another formulation[24] which documents in detail the interest shown by the followers of Bacon's programme, the members of the Royal Society, in the practical arts and crafts. They learned from these applied pursuits and in turn contributed to them in the devising of instruments and procedures. Newton's own work was furthered and influenced by "such practically-oriented scientists as Halley, Hooke, Wren, Huyghens and Boyle; Newton also made considerable use of the astronomical observations deriving from Flamsteed's work in the Greenwich Observatory constructed for the benefit of the Royal Navy by command of Charles II." Merton combats Sombart's thesis that seventeenth-century technology was almost completely divorced from the contemporary science by describing how many of these English scientists – like Wren, Hooke, Newton, Boyle, Halley, Flamsteed – turned their theoretical knowledge to practical account. Both mathematics and astronomy were significantly advanced through research oriented to the solution of problems concerned with better ship building, with better charting of sea voyages and determining longitude at sea, and with the devising of better compasses (which furthered the investigation of magnetism in general). "The finding of longitude was one problem which, engrossing the attention of many scientists, furthered profound developments in astronomy, geography, mathematics, mechanics, and the invention of clocks and watches."[25] It may be concluded that Merton is documenting in the mode of "external history" that on the one hand scientists' interest in the solution of practical problems was integrally related to the economic and commercial and mercantile expansion in seventeenth-century England, and on the other hand the scientists' involvement in applied science directly enlarged the fund of theoretical scientific knowledge.

It must be recorded that Merton's formulations, which are an extension of Weber's ideas of the concordance between Puritan values and the ethic of capitalism, have attracted criticism.[26] Aside from questions of definition and application by Merton of the label "Puritan," some of the new historians of science have claimed that the radical sixteenth- and seventeenth-century theoretical developments in astronomy, mathematics, mechanics and optics owed very little to the new technology, instruments and observations. The novelties in the thought of Galileo, Descartes and Newton were predominantly intellectual and included Renaissance Neoplatonism, a revived ancient Greek atomism and the rediscovery of Archimedes. Moreover, these critics advance the "internal history" view that the contributions of these scientists are best understood as the consequence of the internal dialectic and evolution amongst a cluster of fields which in the time in question were pursued in a new vigorous intellectual milieu.

Kuhn's assessment[27] is that these corrections can only lead to a revision of the Merton thesis, not its rejection. Kuhn says that it could be said of the main branches of science transformed during the sixteenth and seventeenth centuries, such as astronomy, mathematics, mechanics and optics, that theirs was "a revolution of concepts." But in the seventeenth century there were other fields of marked activity – the study of electricity and magnetism, chemistry and thermal phenomena whose roots were more in the established crafts than in the universities, and whose progress was critically dependent on the experimentation which craftsmen helped to introduce. These interests were pursued not so much in the universities but by amateurs loosely clustered round the new scientific societies, like the Royal Society, which were the institutional manifestation of the Scientific Revolution. Subsequent achievements in the following centuries also owed much to these new developments. All in all then the radical Protestant movements in England, the Low Countries and Germany drastically altered the interest in and the locus of much scientific and technological research and applications in the seventeenth century.

2

Anthropology's intellectual legacy (continued)

Protestant cosmology and the new science

Although Merton's study of the general congruence of Reformation values and scientific activity is a major contribution, there were other reasons for the high representation of Protestants in the European science of this time which he has not explored. There appears, for instance, to have been a congruence between the cosmological principles of Protestant theology and the new theories of modern science. This congruence becomes salient when we consider the implications of the shift from a geocentric Ptolemaic scheme to a heliocentric Copernican and Keplerian framework. To substantiate this point I shall mainly rely on Lovejoy's landmark work *The Great Chain of Being.*[1]

Although Calvin was opposed to Copernican astronomy because it conflicted with the literal interpretations of the biblical scriptures, he also rejected the medieval cosmic hierarchy of beings possessing graduated delegated powers. The great Schoolman, Thomas Aquinas, approved the "principle of plenitude" upon which the medieval hierarchy was based by maintaining that the perfection of the universe consisted in the orderly variety of things, and was thus intended by God the creator. In *Summa contra Gentiles* Aquinas asserts: "The perfection of the universe therefore requires not only a multitude of individuals, but also diverse kinds, and therefore diverse grades of things."[2] The doctrine of the plenitude of God together with the closely connected principle of "the continuity of beings" and the wonderful "linkage of beings" (*connexio rerum*)[3] produced a graded universe from the Empyrean through angels to humans and animals, and a cosmography that made God an unmoved final cause of motion and of endeavour in other beings.

Calvin substituted for this chain of being the notion of a truly omnipotent and unimpeded God as designer of the universe who acted according to his Providence. Calvin's insistence on absolutist rule by a cosmic ruler, a radical monotheistic stress, did of course allow for the occurrence of miracles that God might perform if he so wished, but the more important implication of his absolutist cosmology was that it subsequently accommodated the notion of a God who acted according to regular laws of nature, which were designed by him. Thus this new conception of regular laws of nature, which could be understood by man in terms of his empirical experience, was integrally and vitally in accord with the scientific spirit of the time. A further entailment of the conception of a Sovereign God who has promulgated the laws of nature, which man could investigate and affirm empirically through his own senses and ingenuity, was to allow that Sovereign God to recede further and further from view in everyday practice of positive science. (This was the slope that finally led to the "secularization of the world").

The affinity between Calvin, Copernicus and Kepler consisted in the fact that the latter two rejected a similar cosmology of a gradation of material elements, and declared that the earth was similar in its makeup to other planets. At the heart of the Copernican system was the attribution of motion to the earth. The earth moved, like other planets, and this recognition removed it from the scope of Aristotelian physics, which placed a motionless earth at the centre of the universe. Copernicus declared that the sun exercised absolute rule over the solar system as God did over the world (and Kepler even went as far as locating God in the Sun itself).[4]

In *De Revolutionibus* Copernicus wrote with joyous fervor "In the middle of all sits the Sun enthroned. How could we place this luminary in any better position in this most beautiful temple from which to illuminate the whole at once? . . . so the Sun sits upon a royal throne ruling his children the planets which circle around him."[5] There always had been an incongruity between the centrality accorded to the idea of God in medieval metaphysics and the peripheral position of the highest heaven, the Empyrean. In Kepler's eyes the chief merit of his new system was that "it eliminated this incongruity, placing at the heart of the sensible universe the body which could most naturally be regarded as the physical symbol or counterpart of deity, or, more precisely, of the first Person of the Trinity – the orb which was admittedly 'the most excellent of all,' the source of all light and color and heat...."[6] In the heliocentric theory of Kepler's, God is not the unmoved final cause of motion in the Aristotelian manner, but is a generative and self-diffusive energy.

In any event, the angels were declared redundant to the workings of the cosmos, and the idea of natural processes at work as a more economical and effective explanation of them gained ground.

A natural culmination of these trends was the mechanistic philosophy of Descartes in the era of Enlightenment which held that only one kind of power, mechanical motion, governed all physical events.

This accommodation, demarcation, and alliance between Protestant theology and modern science lasted for a century and a half. It represented a major epistemological and ontological agreement regarding the manner in which religion and science both divided and intersected. It broke down only in the latter part of the nineteenth century after the Darwinian theory of evolution demolished the premise that the world was governed by certain and irrevocable laws which gave it an unchanging pattern. The lesson taught by

Darwinian theory was that evolution taking place through the adaptive process of natural selection manifesting at the level of the individual member of a species was an open-ended process, not a pre-ordained pattern, and sometimes fortuitous and not always maximally functional. (And we know today that it did not necessarily entail a theory of progress either.)[7]

The gist of what I have said so far is this: The concept of rationality that characterizes the new science is that of natural laws governing the universe – laws amenable to mechanistic interpretation, inferred through both empirical observation and the application of mathematical thought. The concept of rationality that characterizes the new economic order that came to be labelled capitalism was of an instrumental kind in which a formal matching of scarce means to chosen ends was sought. Both these endeavors, economic capitalism and modern science, on the one hand found stimulation in Protestant ethical values, and on the other hand, shared a common orientation to this world, which is one of incessant acting upon the world so that it will approximate some idea of imagined unfolding of reason and increasing perfection.

Religion and magic

The fourth important development of the sixteenth and seventeenth centuries, which aided in the demarcation this time between religion and magic, is most conveniently discussed in relation to Keith Thomas's classic: *Religion and the Decline of Magic.*[8]

The story that Keith Thomas tells us is contained in these quotations. The first relates to his baseline, and goes thus: "The line between magic and religion is one which is impossible to draw in many primitive societies; it is equally difficult to draw in medieval England."[9]

The second quotation relates to the situation at the end of his period of study, the second half of the seventeenth century: "At the end of our period we can draw a distinction between religion and magic which would not have been possible earlier."[10]

This religion, explains Thomas, was one which had outlived its magical competitors and had triumphed over magic. But it was a religion with a difference: it did not try to associate misfortune with guilt, but recognized the authenticity of the (Cartesian) mechanical philosophy.

During the late sixteenth and early seventeenth centuries, English Protestant thought confronted and moved away from medieval Catholic theology as well as Catholic rites and indulgences. If the distinction between magic and religion had been blurred by the medieval Church, it was strongly reasserted by the propagandists of the Protestant Reformation.

These Protestant propagandists attacked the rites of the Catholic Church, including the doctrine of transubstantiation, as sacramental magic.

They emphasized the notion of God's sovereignty and of divine providence and omnipotence which were reflected in the daily happenings of the world, and which in turn gave continuous manifestation and evidence of God's purpose. They even went so far as to deny the possibility of chance or the possibility of events that could occur outside of God's purpose. Moreover, as Thomas remarks, "A religious belief in order was a necessary prior assumption on which the subsequent work of the natural scientists was to be founded. It was a mental environment which made possible the triumph of technology."[11]

It was inevitable and logical given this formulation of God's sovereignty that Protestant theologians would hammer out the distinction between religious acts as primarily intercessionary in character, and magical acts as being coercive rituals ambitiously attempting to manipulate the divine. "Magic postulated forces of nature which the magician learned to control, whereas religion assumed the direction of the world by a conscious agent who could be deflected from this purpose by prayer and supplication."[12] For these Protestant theologians then there was a fundamental distinction between prayer and spell, the former belonging to true religion, the latter to false religion. Moreover, all in all, these same theologians evinced a characteristic Protestant rationalism that saw religion first and foremost as a system of beliefs.

It is my submission that this emphasis on religion as a system of beliefs, and the distinction between prayer and spell, the former being associated with "religious" behaviour and the latter with "magical" acts, was a Protestant legacy which was automatically taken over by later Victorian theorists like Tylor and Frazer, and given a universal significance as both historical and analytical categories useful in tracing the intellectual development of mankind from savagery to civilization.

The Protestant legacy of course harks back to Calvin, and even earlier to the core monotheistic ideas of early Judaism, just as the attitude to magic harks back on the one hand to the Greek legacy and on the other to early Judaism. Against this extended background let me underscore the relation between Protestant and early Judaic ideas on magic.

When we recall my earlier discussion of the early Judaic distinction between true religion and idolatry, we are struck by the fact that these Protestant theologians of the late sixteenth century seem to be resurrecting or repeating the dichotomy already constructed in early Israel.

There is however a basic difference, despite the similarity. As I have remarked before, in early Israel, while the worship of idols and the propitiation of them was condemned as pagan fetishism, yet the Bible did not disbelieve in magic and did not deny that the idols might have had occult powers. (As Kauffman puts it: "Biblical writers are aware of the pagans' belief that their idols have the power to act . . . It is as such that YHWH the God wreaks his judgments upon them.")[13]

But the Protestant reformers have now gone one step further: they not only declare magic to be false religion, they also declare it to be inefficacious action, for the true God cannot be so manipulated. (In part this formulation overlaps with the attitude of early Greek medical science, that magical and occult theories of causation of diseases (like epilepsy) are fallacious because they appeal to the intervention of divine and spiritual agents whereas the diseases in question have natural causes.)

On providence and the laws of nature

The Reformation saw a new insistence on God's sovereignty and providence, which, as we have seen, went so far as to deny the possibility of chance or accident, and to affirm that God could work miracles. (It is interesting that the doctrine of predestination that eliminated the possibility of magic, found it necessary to champion the triumph of miracles.)

This inevitably raised the conundrum: Did God work through nature or was he above it? Despite Calvin, who held fast to the omnipotence of God and his ability to act as he wanted even if this meant his enacting miracles, many seventeenth-century theologians came to hold that God had bound himself to keep the laws of nature. "God's sovereignty was thought to be exercised through regular channels, and the natural world was fully susceptible of study by scientists seeking causes and regularities."

No doubt the mechanical philosophy of the later seventeenth century – the model of the universe as a great clock – subjected the doctrine of God's special providence to a good deal of strain. By 1700, however, the doctrine that the world was a purposive one, responsible to the wishes of its creator, was adjusted to the notion of laws of nature on the one hand, and the idea of "sanctified affliction" (i.e. that sickness was God's visitation and that medicine worked with God's permission) on the other. This second theme of how moral behaviour was related to the occurrences of worldly adversity or prosperity was especially plausible to the actors of that time in the context of extreme visitations of plague, epidemics and venereal diseases. Keith Thomas concludes from these tendencies that the idea of obedience to God's commandments and the idea of providence were conducive to the development of an ideology of action and self-help and to achieving prosperity and safety in the world. Since "belief in providence was compatible with self help" it was only a matter of time before the rational regulation of capital and nature combined in profitable ways.[14] This, of course, is much the same as Max Weber's conclusion that no religion did as much as Puritanism to identify economic achievement with spiritual success. After the mid-seventeenth century it became unfashionable in historical writing to explain events in terms of God's providence, although as a minority view it persisted among certain evangelicals and sectarians.

The problems and issues raised by the Keith Thomas analysis are many for those engaged in comparative anthropology.

(1) If the distinctions between religion and sacramental magic, between

prayer and spell, between sovereign deity and manipulable divine being, were the product of a specific historical epoch in European history and its particular preoccupations stemming from Judaeo-Christian concepts and concerns, can these same categories (embedded in and stemming from an historical context) fruitfully serve as universal, analytical categories and illuminate the texture of other cultures and societies? This major question will engage us continually when we study the writings of Tylor, Frazer, Mauss, Lévy-Bruhl, Malinowski and Evans-Pritchard.

(2) While Keith Thomas (like Max Weber or Robert Merton) asserts that although the chief reasons for the rejection of magic were in general the scientific and philosophical revolutions of the seventeenth century, which resulted in the triumph of the mechanical philosophy, yet he also recognizes – but does not do justice to – the issue of the coexistence and overlap of occult and scientific perspectives at that time. (This question is best raised *vis-à-vis* the writings of Frances Yates, to which I shall return in the next section.) For instance, Thomas notes more or less in passing that at the beginning of the seventeenth century an intelligent contemporary could not have predicted the outcome, because magic and science had originally advanced side by side, and because mystical-magical theories and preoccupations advanced the formulation of those theoretical systems that would later be seen as the triumphs of the new science: examples are heliocentrism, the infinity of the worlds (essential ideas in the Copernican-Keplerian systems), the circulation of blood (the Harvey contribution), and certain applications in mathematics. We also should remember that astrology influenced astronomical observations. Yet Thomas fails to deal with these overlaps and coexistences in terms of a historical writing in both retrospective and prospective terms; he also fails to consider the possibility of "occult" and "scientific" intellectual schemes coexisting in terms of a hierarchical scheme of evaluations. His preference seems to be for an explanation in terms of a revolutionary shift in paradigm in the styles of both Karl Popper and Thomas Kuhn. In any event, according to Thomas, by the later seventeenth century the partnership between magic and science had collapsed. Boyle, for example, had destroyed the assumptions of alchemy, the botanists those of the doctrine of "signatures." (I may digress to remark that Foucault in *The Order of Things* gives us a vivid picture of the doctrine of signatures whose chief concept of "resemblance" maintained that words and things were one, that the name of a thing was an essential part of it, its signature, and a system of resemblance held everything together. The seventeenth century developed a different view of language in terms of "representation" in which language related to the world in an arbitrary way.)[15] The epistemological demand for certainty of demonstration by experiment and dissection was eroding magic. In this decisive account Thomas invokes a Popper-type falsification test: "Magic, unlike science, never learned from failure but simply explained it away." Thomas is here perilously close to Tylor and Frazer in the spectacles he wears, as we shall see later.

(3) One of Thomas's most interesting and intriguing statements relates to

his rejection of a hypothesis regarding magic attributed to Malinowski – that magic ritualizes man's optimism when there is a hiatus in man's knowledge, that magic is invoked and practiced to fill in the gap of anxiety and uncertainty when the limits of technological control are reached.

Thomas remarks that the sixteenth and seventeenth centuries provide only an apparent confirmation of Malinowski's thesis. There were technical accomplishments: improvement in agriculture, control of the plagues (which disappeared altogether after the 1670s), better communications, establishment of banking and insurance (against marine accidents and against fire), and so on. But in actual fact magic declined before the technological revolution, and was rejected before the discovery of new remedies to fill the gap. Despite the scientific findings of Harvey, Boyle, Hooke and others there was little actual progress in medical therapy. Real medical innovations belonged to a much later age. (In rejecting the so-called Malinowski hypothesis, Thomas also in a sense confirms a conclusion reached by Geoffrey Lloyd – that a naturalistic mode of explanation was adopted in early Greece when in fact the empirical practices in that mode were based on false or inadequate empirical knowledge, and therefore did not necessarily bear more efficacious fruits than the occult arts.)

Be that as it may, to account for the invalidity of the Malinowski hypothesis, Thomas now reverses an earlier concession that magic and science, when they coexisted, did feed each other at least in the earlier part of the seventeenth century. He now champions the view that the magic practiced was conservative in subject matter as well as technique, it inspired no new elaborations, and therefore it was potentially "one of the most serious obstructions to the rationalization of economic life." (At this point, Thomas in fact alludes in his support to Weber's postulation that Protestantism led to the increasing manifestation of the process of rationalization and the corresponding "disenchantment" of the world.)

Whatever the rough edges in Thomas's reviewing of the Malinowski thesis in terms of the seventeenth-century English context, it is decidedly a challenging thought that there was (and can be) a mental or theoretical revolution before an applied technological one is in place. This proposition serves as a foil to a simplistic utilitarian and functionalist logic. The difference between the sixteenth and the eighteenth centuries, says Thomas, lies not in achievement but in aspiration. The openness to the idea that solutions had to be technical found commitment before actual achievements were made. The change which occurred in the seventeenth century was thus not so much technological as mental, and it was the scientists who embodied best the new aspirations.

(4) But this very singling out of the scientists as the holders of these new views, and other statements by Thomas to the effect that there was a notable gap between the learning and intellectual horizons of the upper classes and of the lower strata in mid-seventeenth-century England, and the undermining

admission that the common people of the sixteenth and seventeenth centuries never formulated a distinction between magic and science – all these raise the serious question of the validity of Thomas's general conclusion that by the end of his period of study a distinction between religion and magic had occurred, and that magic was doomed to decline.

Is it possible that Thomas has overdrawn the generality of the distinction between religion (that is associated with an organized church) and magic (regarded as a collection of miscellaneous recipes) because he has been misled by Reformation thought (and by modern anthropological theorizing that was unaware of its historical legacy)? Has Thomas employed the polemical categories of certain theological circles that spearheaded the Reformation as actually valid categories that explain the historical process? In a critique of Thomas's book, Hildred Geertz provocatively comments that "It is not the 'decline' of the practice of magic that cries out for explanation, but the emergence and rise of the label 'magic'." Thomas "takes part in the very cultural process that he is studying" by accepting the categories of the actors and using them "as analytical categories to develop his own causal hypothesis of decline."[16] To say that Thomas conflates "phenomenological" and "causal" approaches is one thing; to say that he is also possibly only portraying the views of a minority of the English people of that time is another thing.

In a sharp critique of Thomas's book E. P. Thompson,[17] the English historian, introduces the class dimension, and questions whether in fact during the late seventeenth and eighteenth centuries the intellectual views of the scientists and intelligentsia seeped through to the masses at large and the illiterate. He suggests that the populace may have reacted to the polite sermons of the Enlightenment by withdrawing into a vivid symbolism of their own. There was the strong possibility that a counter-culture would develop among them combining the doctrines and rituals of the official Church and pagan ritual into an amalgam more appropriate to their own life experience. According to Thompson, Wesleyanism was a "movement of counter-enlightenment" in which there was a return to pastoral duties amongst the poor, and this missionary vocation incorporated and affirmed popular ritual practices such as bibliomancy, exorcism by prayer, and ritual acts that involved the hand of providence.

Thompson remarks that Thomas's work is weakened by a reluctance to draw on "literary" sources such as fiction, novels and essays of that period, and this is a pity because religion, magic, astrology, prophecy "operate in a language of symbolism, which when translated into rational argument, loses a portion of its meaning, and all its psychic compulsion." The symbolic and "poetic" meanings will always have been powerful at the popular level.

I might round off this critique with a couple of observations of my own. Thomas provides no analysis of the symbolism of magic and witchcraft, and is equally insensitive to the performative features of ritual acts that are familiar to students of the linguistic philosophy of J. Austin and his followers. A narrow yardstick of "rationality" misses the rhetorical and illocutionary aspects of ritual performances.

Thomas also falls short in his methodology from an anthropological viewpoint. The book is packed with a conscientious but redundant accumulation of instances and occurrences, but nowhere is there a micro-analysis in depth from beginning to end of an astrological consultation or a magical rite performed in its context. There are no extended case studies, or descriptions of incidents traced through time from their moment of instigation to their denouement. Thompson reflects the same disappointment when he says: Thomas's procedure "again and again, by the accumulation of instances presented in rapid sequence" takes a toll: "he denies himself the space for micro-study, and for exploring the inwardness – and the irregularities as well as the regularities" of the evidence.[18]

The challenge to orthodox historiography: the Renaissance philosophers and magi

This mainstream historical and sociological account of how the economic order of capitalism and the institutionalization of science strove towards a systematic and rational understanding and transformation of the world which I have outlined in previous sections, was what Max Weber labelled the process of "rationalization" as a world historical process. The world-view relegated certain other kinds of orientations and activities, such as the so-called "pagan religions" and their magical rites, to an inferior position, condemned to be superseded. Was this account tendentious, in that it represents an Enlightenment and "whig" reading of the march of science and rationality? We have already reviewed E. P. Thompson's critique of this as an elitist thesis.

There is no doubt that the confidence of this crystal-clear story of linear progress with the Renaissance being the first leap forward towards modernity has been to some extent punctured and muddied from a different direction by that kind of recent scholarship represented by Frances Yates. The Middle Ages and the Renaissance we now know were complex times when the cosmologies, belief systems and intellectual aspirations of scholars simultaneously traversed the domains of astronomy and astrology, chemistry and alchemy, medicine and curative incantations, mathematics and number mysticism.

The careers of Renaissance figures such as Marsilio Ficino, John Dee, and Giordano Bruno are crucial for mounting a revisionist account. Marsilio Ficino was counted in the Enlightenment accounts as a Neoplatonic scholar but it was not mentioned that he was also a Neoplatonic magician. Ficino's theories on magic and his use of talismans has been the discovery of recent twentieth-century scholarship.[19] Ficino's astral medicine drew on *Asclepius*, the magical treatise attributed to "Hermes Trismegistus," who was "mis-

dated" as having been coeval with Moses. John Dee (1527–1608), interested in
the mathematics of Copernicus, was astrologer to Queen Elizabeth, and his
commitment to the occult science of "Hermes Trismegistus" is seen in his
attempts to change the world by using the "influence" or radiation of the sun
and other planets by focusing them in talismans, and other objects sympathetic to the heavenly power. This "angel magic" consisted in invoking the
in-dwelling spirits of stars in order to influence the lower human world. But
note that Dee championed the belief that the conquest of nature was to be
attained through the methods of pure mathematics. The most illustrious of
our cases is Giordano Bruno. As Frances Yates has established, Giordano
Bruno was presented some decades ago as an enlightened Renaissance
philosopher who defended Copernicanism against reactionaries. But it
transpires that Bruno also quoted at length from the *Asclepius* on magical
reform, and that his defense of heliocentricity was influenced and inspired by
"Hermes Trismegistus" on the sun.

It is therefore apposite that I report some features relevant to our discussion
contained in Yates's landmark book *Giordano Bruno and the Hermetic
Tradition.*[20]

"The great forward movements of the Renaissance," writes Yates, " all
derive their vigour, their emotional impulse from looking backwards." But
one of these retrospective movements of the Renaissance, "the return to the
golden age of magic, was based on a radical error in dating."[21] This error
related to the works that inspired the Renaissance magi, the writings
attributed to "Hermes Trismegistus," which were thought to be of profound
antiquity, going back to Moses. The literature in question in fact was probably
written much later, between A.D. 100 and 300, and actually contained elements
of "popular Greek philosophy of the period, a mixture of Platonism and
Stoicism, combined with some Jewish and probably some Persian influences."
This extensive literature in Greek, developed under the name of "Trismegistus," was "concerned with astrology and the occult sciences, with the secret
virtues of plants and stones and the sympathetic magic based on knowledge of
such virtues, with the making of talismans for drawing down the powers of the
stars."[22] Besides these recipes there also developed a philosophical literature
in the hermetic framework, of which the *Asclepius* and the *Corpus Hermeticum*
were the most important.

The *Asclepius* purports to describe the ancient religion of the Egyptians,
particularly the rites and procedures through which Egyptian priests drew
down the powers of the cosmos, and animated the statues of their gods. The
Pimander (the first of the treatises in the *Corpus Hermeticum*) was translated
by Ficino around 1463–64, and gives an account of the world that is in parts
reminiscent of the biblical Genesis. "Man, though mortal through his body is
immortal in essence, and this singular double nature gives him a special
destiny. Other features describe the ascent of the soul through the spheres of
the planets to the divine realms above them, or give ecstatic descriptions of a

process of regeneration by which the soul casts off the chains which bind it to the material world and becomes filled with divine powers and virtues."[23]

The writers of the second and third centuries who composed the Hermetic treatises revered the old, especially the alleged traditions of the Egyptians, as pure and holy. And in turn these Hermetic writings fostered the illusion that the Renaissance magus had found a "mysterious and precious account of most ancient Egyptian wisdom, philosophy, and magic."[24] And Giordano Bruno, ignoring Augustine's condemnation of the claims of the treatises (though Augustine as well as other leading Fathers of the Church accepted their great antiquity and their authentic authorship by Trismegistus as a real person) went so far as to maintain that "the magical Egyptian religion of the world was not only the most ancient but also the only true religion, which both Judaism and Christianity had obscured and corrupted."[25]

So what kind of intellectual mood did the Renaissance Neoplatonic philosophers like Ficino, Dee and Bruno represent? Whereas the ban of the medieval Church on magic had forced it into dark corners, "where the magician plied his abominated art in secrecy . . . Renaissance magic, which was a reformed and learned magic and always disclaimed any connection with the old, ignorant, evil, or black magic, was often an adjunct of an esteemed Renaissance philosopher."[26] And the reigning philosophies were tinged with occultism.

Ficino claimed that Hermes Trismegistus was the source of a wisdom that led in an unbroken chain to Plato, thereby implying a historical connection. Ficino was a physician (like his father) as well as a priest. His first book published in 1489 was a treatise on medicine. His orphic magic, which drew down stellar influences by musical incantations and by a sympathetic arrangement of natural objects and talismans, was a return to Trismegistus. The magic he practiced was a combination of incantations and invocations on the one hand and, on the other, the manipulation of objects grouped according to their characteristics. Queried as to how a Christian priest could dabble with astral medicine and astrology, Ficino justified his practice on two grounds – that in ancient times priests always practiced medicine, and that what he was practicing was natural magic, both useful and necessary and not illicit and demonic.

John Dee (1527–1608) was "a genuine mathematician of considerable importance, intensely interested in all mathematical studies, and in the application of mathematics to produce results in applied sciences."[27] He was a practiced scientist and an inventor. But "he was still more interested in the use of numbers in connection with Hebrew names of angels and spirits in the practiced Cabala which he did with his associate, Edward Kelley." Dee's wanting to learn the secrets of nature from the angels was his "way of prosecuting science at a higher level."[28] A recent biography of Dee by Peter French underscores the point that John Dee the prosecutor of "angel magic" championed the belief that the conquest of nature was to be attained through the methods of pure mathematics, and that therefore "the revival of Hermeticism marks the dawn of the scientific age because it unleashed the driving spirit that inspired man to compel natural forces to serve him to an extent never dreamed of before."[29] This judgment is also confirmed by Yates, who says that John Dee, the Renaissance magus pursuing operational power, "is a very clear example of how the will to operate, stimulated by Renaissance magic, could pass into, and stimulate, the will to operate in genuine applied science."[30]

Before we deal with Giordano Bruno, a prefatory reminder of some features of Copernicus's thought expressed in *De revolutionibus orbium caelestium* is relevant in order to evoke the proper context. Although Copernicus's breakthrough hypothesis of the earth's revolution round the sun was the result of a pure mathematical calculation, yet he did not fail to adduce the authority of *prisci theologi* (amongst them Pythagoras), and Hermes Trismegistus, to lend weight to his heliocentric system. Yates is emphatic that Copernicus was living in the world of Neoplatonism, Trismegistus, and Ficino, whose cosmos was intensely heliocentric. It is possible that their framework provided "the emotional driving force which induced Copernicus to undertake his mathematical calculations on the hypothesis that the sun is indeed at the centre of the planetary system"; or that presenting his theory in terms of it was a strategy followed by Copernicus to make his discovery acceptable. "Perhaps both explanations would be true, some of each."[31]

To return to Giordano Bruno: He advocated Copernicanism in the belief that the Copernican sun had a close affinity with Ficinian sun magic. But while Copernicus was completely free of Hermeticism in his mathematics, "Bruno pushes Copernicus' scientific work back into a prescientific stage, back into Hermetism interpreting the Copernican diagram as a hieroglyph of divine mysteries."[32]

Bruno, born on the foothills of Vesuvius in 1548, had entered and left the Dominican order in 1576 over an accusation of heresy, and reached Paris in 1581. From there he visited Oxford two years later. In him two strands met: Renaissance Hermetic philosophy and the classical art of memory as a form of Hermetic magic.[33] In Bruno the ambition of achieving knowledge and powers through talismanic memory images reached a peak.

The later years of the sixteenth century were the time when religious Hermetism of all types reached the summit of influence. Bruno, who espoused the Egyptians as being earlier than the Greeks and Hebrews, and said they had the best religion and magic of them all, thereby placed himself beyond the pale of Christian Hermeticism. His magical Hermetism appealed to "sub-Catholics, discontented intelligentsia, and other secretly dissatisfied elements in Elizabethan society."[34] He was burned at the stake in Counter-Reformation Rome in 1600.

It was some years later, with the dating by Isaac Casaubon in 1614 of the Hermetic writings as not the work of a very ancient Egyptian priest called

Trismegistus, but written in post-Christian times, that the stage was set for the shattering of Renaissance Neoplatonism as a framework not only for a Hermetic–Cabalist magic but also for a natural theology. The exposure of the forgery did not altogether undermine the subsequent pursuit of Hermetism. For example, in 1617 Robert Fludd dedicated a work based on religious Hermetism to James I. And the Rosicrucians have been unveiled by Yates as an underground seventeenth-century movement with Lutheran connections and the tendencies of Renaissance Hermetism.

Other examples of the continuing presence of Hermetic philosophy and magic can be pointed to. Perhaps the most dramatic is the case of Isaac Newton himself, who has been sanitized by the post-Enlightenment hagiographers as a model of scientific reason. But it seems that "one of Newton's motives in beginning his work in mathematics was to investigate whether judicial astrology had any claim to validity." The official eulogy of Newton composed by his successors ignored this evidence, because the occultist traditions, including alchemy, magic, divination, no longer demanded or evoked a serious interest. The point of this story is that although there is documentary evidence "that Newton attached equal, or greater importance to his alchemical studies than to his work in mathematics," modern science in its victorious march has "blotted out the immediate past,"[35] and one generation's conscious omissions become the next generation's genuine amnesia.

But perhaps this retrospective rewriting of history in terms of a linear march to modernity in which the great intellectual figures of the sixteenth and seventeenth centuries, including Ficino, Copernicus and Bruno, have been placed in clear-cut niches in the Pantheon of Progress, was bound to win in the long run because the mystical framework of Renaissance Hermetism was fundamentally shattered in the seventeenth century (though not destroyed), and because there were other bodies of opinion, both Catholic and Protestant, which opposed Renaissance magic during the period in which it flourished. One such was the Humanist tradition, a most notable exemplar of it being Erasmus, whose secular humanism showed no interest in metaphysics or natural philosophy but leaned towards a "polite learning, good letters, good Latinity."[36]

So, in taking stock of the revised historiography presented by Yates and others of her persuasion regarding the true proportions of Renaissance Neoplatonism, what can we say about its contributions to the growth of science in the sixteenth and seventeenth centuries?

It is clear from the aspirations and activities of personages such as Ficino, Bruno and Dee that the Hermetic philosophy and magic of the Renaissance turned to number symbolism and mathematics as the key to operations, and the subsequent trajectory of both theoretical and applied sciences has vindicated mathematics as one of the master keys by which the forces of nature can be manipulated and harnessed. (Incidentally even the art of making animated statues used applied mechanics and employed pulleys and weights and pneumatic and hydraulic machines, and thereby contributed to the growth of applied science. Similarly playing with number symbolism and systems of universal harmony prepared for mathematics proper.)

The real contribution of the Renaissance magus in relation to the modern world, asserts Yates, was that he changed the will of man, and conveyed to him the motivation that "it was now dignified and important for man to operate," that "it was also religious and not contrary to the will of God that man, the great miracle, should exert his powers."[37] This psychological reorientation was neither Greek nor medieval in spirit. The Greeks with their many mathematical and scientific discoveries did not take the momentous step of crossing the bridge between the theoretical and practical and of going all out to applying knowledge to technical operations, while the Middle Ages sustained the same attitude "in the form that theology is the crown of philosophy and the true end of man in contemplation; any wish to operate can only be inspired by the devil."[38]

In sum Yates's thesis is that the new operational attitude in Renaissance Europe was ignited by the excitement caused by the discovery of the *Hermetica* and their attendant magico-religious techniques, and that "it is magic as an aid to gnosis which begins to turn the will in the new direction."[39] It seems to collide head on with Keith Thomas's submission that in England in the late sixteenth and early seventeenth centuries it was Protestant thought that hammered out the distinction between intercessionary religious and manipulative magical acts, and in due course would align notions of providence with laws of nature (and an omnipotent God who had willed to work through them). It also seems to collide with the further thesis that Protestantism provided the ethical and emotional motivation for systematic understanding and transformation of the world, a thesis that is a master-key in Merton's account of the development of science in England and to Weber's grander theme of the efflorescence of the spirit of capitalism.

The safest course for us is not to adjudicate these differences in terms of true and false, but to suggest that all these currents and influences fed into the river of history and their cumulative action cannot be reduced to a simplistic linear view of progress. Moreover, the more we confront the latest discussions of the philosophy of science of our time and contemplate the theoretical and speculative flights of fancy in astrophysics and theoretical physics regarding the origins of the cosmos or the fundamental particles of matter, the more our modern sensibilities are able to be tolerant of the possibility that advance in the application of science can live happily with paper and laboratory manipulations of imagined, even metaphorical and fanciful cosmologies and mathematical explorations.

There is also another lesson to contemplate concerning the danger of reifying such phenomena as "astrology", "alchemy", "magic" and so on as well-defined bounded systems, whose contours and motivations and propensities can be delineated ahistorically and universally in a context-free fashion. Whatever position we may take towards the contributions of Yates and her associates, this much is incontrovertible. The Renaissance Hermetic philosophies and magical systems were, in their time of elaboration and ascendance, ambitious and creative and puzzle-solving in their aspirations and outcomes. The Occultism of that time was tied to imaginative cosmologies of universal harmonies and systems of correspondences. They aimed to be rationalist syntheses, and if these syntheses were premature, they were nevertheless compelling and attracted the curiosity and fired the imagination of Copernicus, Kepler and Newton.

Therefore a criterion that Kuhn proposed for declaring "astrology" as not science proper becomes problematic if it is taken as a general formula. *Contra* Popper's ahistorical condemnation of astrology that "by making their interpretations and prophecies sufficiently vague they [the astrologers] were able to explain away anything that might have been a refutation,"[40] Kuhn argued that "the history of astrology during the centuries when it was intellectually refutable records many predictions that categorically failed . . . Astrology cannot be barred from the sciences because of the form in which its predictions were cast."[41] It was only after astrology itself became implausible that criticism of the way it explained failure (to use Evans-Pritchard's words, its "secondary rationalizations") came to seem question-begging. After all, failures in medicine and meteorology were explained in much the same way, and of course normal science itself resorts to defensive strategies of a similar kind.

However, for Kuhn the dividing line between astronomy (as science) and astrology is that when the astronomer's predictions failed he could hope to set the situation right by new measurements, by posing "calculational and instrumental puzzles," and by reformed techniques. "For more than a millennium these were the theoretical and mathematical puzzles around which, together with their instrumental counterparts, the astronomical research tradition was constituted. The astrologer, by contrast, had no such puzzles." Particular failures were explained, but they did not give rise to research puzzles, and the astrological tradition was not revised.

"Though astronomy and astrology were regularly practised by the same people, including Ptolemy, Kepler, and Tycho Brahe, there was never an astrological equivalent of the puzzle-solving astronomical tradition."[42]

In the face of the literature we have examined that described the theoretical philosophical and operational ambitions of Renaissance Hermetism at its height, can we confidently claim as Kuhn does that the astrology and magic of that time had no puzzles to solve or mathematics and mechanics to experiment with? It is possible that Kuhn's view applied to seventeenth-century Europe is not so much a "presentist" view (that is, dealing with the intentions and orientations of the actors in their contemporary contexts) but a "retrospective" view, which knows that in time astronomy did separate out as a science from astrology. What Keith Thomas has to say about England at the end of the seventeenth century may be largely true – that the occult arts there had by then become stereotyped and formulaic, and were mechanically applied, and lacked a secular and critical attitude that is the guarantee of open-ended scientific knowledge.

Thus having taken all these corrections and modifications into account, we may reiterate these conclusions from earlier discussions:

(1) Seventeenth-century Protestant thought contributed to the demarcation of "magic" from "religion," magic being a class of acts ranging from sacramental ritualism to false manipulations of the supernatural and occult powers, and true religion being a "rational" belief system in a sovereign providence. In the eighteenth century, Enlightenment rationalism carried this tendency further and proposed an intellectual conception of religion as an object of study.

(2) The relationship between Protestant and Puritan doctrines on the one hand and scientific activity on the other was one of complementary stimulation as well as increasing separation of domains. Religion and science increasingly inhabited different provinces in peoples' lives. The Puritan ethic had stimulated scientific activity and the active transformation of the world. The carving out of a domain of nature and of regular natural laws pertaining to it helped to move God further and further away from the ideas of causality in empirical science, such that positivist science came to define itself as an autonomous realm with its own rules of verification and testing that required no religious underpinning. As Max Weber pointed out, the capitalist economic ethic became disconnected from religion and became traditionalized and routinized as secular orientation.

(3) In plotting the history of the demarcation between magic, science and religion in Western thought we ought to remind ourselves all the time of the necessary gaps between the elite conceptions of the intelligentsia – scientists, theologians, dogmatists – and the masses at large for whom intellectual hairsplitting was less important than the tasks of practical living and of everyday realities. We must also bear in mind that for the discipline of intellectual history it is the thought categories of the ruling elites and intelligentsia that have constituted the dominant paradigm and legitimating ideology of a society. Finally, we may note that Thomas's major account of the decline of magic in England in the seventeenth century is in line with the mainstream historical and sociological accounts (such as these provided by Weber, Merton, and Lovejoy) of the critical changes in cosmological schemes and religious values initiated by the Reformation and their affinity with developments in economic and scientific activities.

Plate 2.1 Anatomical dissection. Frontispiece from Andreas Vesalius's *De humani corporis fabrica*, Basle, 1543.

Plate 2.2 William Hogarth: The Reward of Cruelty (*c.* 1750). Hogarth sketched Four Stages of Cruelty as a moral tale of which this is the final representation (fourth stage) showing Tom Nero's corpse being dissected at Surgeons' Hall. The stages begin with Tom Nero, as a boy from the Charity School of St. Giles (at that time a parish of low repute), teasing and tormenting cats and dogs, and depict his further progress in crime as he gets older, culminating in his arrest for the murder of Ann Gill (third stage).

Plate 2.3 The doctor gives up treatment on account of the seriousness of the illness. The patient is healed through spiritual blessing. From Pietro Lorenzetti, *Storie della Beata Umilte*, detail from a predella. Pinakothek, Berlin.

ANDREAE VESALII
BRVXELLENSIS, INVI-
ctissimi CAROLI V. Imperatoris
medici, de Humani corporis
fabrica Libri septem.

CVM CAESAREAE
Maiest. Galliarum Regis, ac Senatus Veneti gratia &
privilegio, ut in diplomatis eorundem continetur.

BASILEAE, PER IOANNEM OPORINVM.

Plate 2.1

Plate 2.2

Plate 2.3

Specialists at work

Plate 3.1 Photograph of the eminent Spanish scientist, Santiago Ramón y Cajal, at his table with scientific equipment taken in Barcelona in 1894. His work on the human nervous system and the brain in the late 19th and early 20th centuries earned him a Nobel Prize in medicine in 1906. The photograph was taken by himself.

Plate 3.2 A spirit priest among the Akha, a hill tribe in Northern Thailand, with his paraphernalia laid out next to the main house post. He is performing a soul-calling ceremony. The device on the left is a trap to capture the soul. Other items include a sacrificed pig and chicken, a bowl of pig's blood, and a tray with bowls containing different types of rice and liquids.

Plate 3.3 The Buddhist abbot of a Bangkok *wat* sprinkling sacralized water on lay devotees at the *kathin* festival held after the end of the monks' rainy season retreat in 1973.

Plate 3.4 "Goldmaker and Blacksmith": Alchemists and their assistants in their workshop. The original engraving was by Jan van der Straet (1523–1605), done *c.* 1570, and this engraving is a copy "after" Straet by Ph. Galle.

Plate 3.5 Two medical scientists at work *c.* 1900 in a laboratory at the Harvard Medical School.

Plate 3.1

Plate 3.2

Plate 3.3

Abb. 96. Goldmacher und Schwarzkünstler. Kpfr. von Ph. Galle nach Joh. Stradanus, ca. 1570.

Illustrationsprobe aus E. Reich, Der Gelehrte

Plate 3.4

Plate 3.5

3

Sir Edward Tylor versus Bronislaw Malinowski: is magic false science or meaningful performance?

The genealogy of anthropologists who during the last eleven decades have concerned themselves with the demarcations between magic, science and religion is long. Within the bounds of certain parameters these various theorists have held diverse views in various mixes. I have chosen today to discuss in detail two celebrated theorists who held two maximally contrasting positions while sharing some common ground. They are Sir Edward Tylor and Bronislaw Malinowski (I shall also briefly refer to Sir James Frazer as a footnote to Tylor).

The common ground that Tylor and Frazer on the one side and Malinowski on the other shared was not only the use of the categories of magic, science and religion to organize their materials, but also the appeal to the needs and mental aptitudes of the individual actor, i.e. to individual psychology and biology as providing the ultimate explanation of human thought and action. Tylor in the fashion of the philosopher Mill attempted to derive the laws of social phenomena from those of individual life; Malinowski sought explanation in terms that one commentator (Edmund Leach) has likened to the individualist pragmatism of William James.

But beyond this shared ground, not only a generational gap but also a vast difference in theoretical ambitions and personal experience separated them.

Tylor and Frazer, securely placed in the British Victorian intellectual establishment, living at the height of British imperial expansion and presence, excited and intrigued by a flood of missionary accounts and travellers' tales of exotic peoples and remote cultures, and fired by the ambition to discover the key to all mythologies and to unravel the story of human progress from the dark ages to Victorian heights, sat in their comfortable armchairs to arrange the received information according to a tree of evolution and ladder of progress.

Malinowski, a Polish *emigré* to England at the turn of the twentieth century, displaced once again by the events of the First World War to engage in first-hand field observation of life in the Melanesian fringes of Australia, was stimulated and excited as well as shocked by his intimate and long encounter with the Melanesian natives, and dreamed in his tent, pitched on island beaches, of telling the world about Trobriand exotic life in the round, and of making the Trobriand Islands a microcosm of human life in general, and thereby winning enduring fame for himself. On December 2, 1917 on his second trip to the Trobriands from Australia, Malinowski wrote these words in his diary as his boat in the early afternoon arrived near the island of Gumasila, within sight of his destination: "Rapture over the beautiful formes, Joy: I hear the word Kiriwina. I get ready... Feeling of ownership. It is I who will describe them or create them."[1] Again, in his diary, he remarked later on about another island: "Joyful feeling of recognition. This island, though not 'discovered' by me, is for the first time experienced artistically and mastered intellectually."[2]

The intellectualist, rationalist and evolutionary theories of Tylor

In the history of anthropological thought, Sir Edward Tylor and Sir James Frazer, two eminent Victorians, are the most dogged of the theorists who attempted to arrange the categories of magic, science and religion in developmental schemes.

Tylor's life was a long one, spanning some eighty-five years (from 1832 to 1917), and it is said by some that his longevity was linked to the influence he wielded. Tylor's *Primitive Culture* (two volumes), the text in which we are primarily interested, was published in 1871: we may note in passing that Charles Darwin's *The Origin of Species* was published in 1859, and his *The Expression of the Emotions in Man and Animals* in 1872, though it seems that Tylor was not so much influenced by Darwin's model of science as by Lyell's uniformitarian geology.

Tylor regarded himself as a professional anthropologist; he was a distinguished member of the Ethnological Society and of the Anthropological Society in the 1860s and as Burrow remarks: "His appointment in 1884 to the newly created Readership in Anthropology at Oxford was a proper reward for such professional zeal as well as for his writings."[3] R. R. Marett who studied with him at Oxford acclaimed him as "the Father of Anthropology."[4]

Before I describe Tylor's conception of science as he tried to practice it, it is relevant to mention his non-conformist Quaker parentage and background which gave him a strong aversion to religious ritual of the kind displayed in Anglicanism and Roman Catholicism. He had no feeling for what religion, particularly public, organized, ritualized religion, meant to the worshippers themselves. A Quaker background, a non-sectarian bent, belief in the individual as the basis of social and cultural phenomena, a commitment to moral progress, and faith in the explanatory value of science: these were the components of Tylor's intellectual orientation.[5]

Tylor combined science and reform; he was a social evolutionist with a profound commitment to the science of social development. He concluded his second volume of *Primitive Culture* with these words:

"To the promoters of what is sound and reformers of what is faulty in modern culture, ethnography has double help to give. To impress men's minds with a doctrine of development, will lead them . . . to continue the progressive work of the past ages . . .

"It is a harsher, and at times even painful, office of ethnography to expose the remains of crude old cultures which have passed into harmful superstition, and to mark these out for destruction. Yet this work, if less genial, is not less urgently needful for the good of mankind. Thus, active at once in aiding progress and in removing hindrance, the science of culture is essentially a reformer's science."[6]

At the same time Tylor held that the study of human life is a branch of natural science; indeed he held that there can be only a single unified science. He therefore conceived evolution in deterministic, nomothetic and naturalistic terms, i.e. as capable of description in terms of general laws of nature. His scientific method[7] involved the sorting of phenomena into "species"-like groupings, and then arranging these social species in levels or grades. This scientistic ambition borrowed from geology and biology was hard to fulfill in regard to the study of social life, as many a theorist has found out. "Culture or civilization, taken in its wide ethnographic sense," according to Tylor's celebrated catch-all definition, "is that complex whole which includes knowledge, acquired by man as a member of society"; and he asserted that "the first step in the study of civilization is to dissect it into details and to classify these into their proper groups." These proper groups were "weapons, textile arts, myths, rites and ceremonies, in that order."[8]

Now culture, as Tylor defined it, was a unitary phenomenon characteristic of mankind as a whole. Closely related to this generic conception of culture was Tylor's affirmation of the psychic unity of mankind, evidenced by the parallelism or independent occurrence of the same inventions around the globe. (Tylor was no advocate of the theory of diffusion of discoveries from centers of civilization to the uninventive but receptive peripheries.) Yet at the same time, Tylor held that there was a mental evolution and a ladder of progress in mankind's history, which were the results of differential adaptation to circumstances. The establishment of the ladder was enabled, as he saw it, by the evidence of survivals. The doctrine of survivals had three propositions. Today's primitive customs of simpler peoples are the same as, or comparable to, those of antiquity; higher civilizations have preserved certain primitive features or customs as survivals which are paradoxically testimonies to their progress; the behavior of our (European) infants and children today illuminate the conduct of adult savages in the non-European world, that is to say, ontogeny (the history of individual development) recapitulates phylogeny (the "racial" evolution of mankind). Thus the yardstick of survivals was employed to plot an evolutionary scheme from savagery through barbarism to civilization. Tylor's scheme of progressive development also employed the notion that since early or primitive man was closer to "nature," his technology as well as his cultural creations were also closer to the natural state. Thus stone tools are merely modifications of natural things. Similarly, primitive languages, developed by imitating sounds in nature, still show evidence of their beginnings. But as culture and technology advanced mankind was less constrained by natural limitations and associations and thus they developed in a more diversified, freer and more creative and conventional manner. In line with this, Tylor, as we shall see, adopted this same distancing logic from natural to metaphorical or conventional to postulate the development of religion from a lower natural to a higher "revealed" state.

On magic and the occult sciences

Tylor interestingly never attempted in *Primitive Culture* to directly compare and contrast magic with religion (though he compared magic with science in an indirect way). He merely separated in space magic from religion – his discussion of magic was in volume I and his discussion of religion was in volume 2.

Unlike his relatively neutral discussion of religion, Tylor viewed the "magical arts," witchcraft and the "occult sciences" (as he called them), whenever they were encountered in the civilized European societies, as *survivals* from a barbarous past, from which these societies were necessarily becoming estranged, and which they were destined to discard altogether. He therefore regarded the magical arts as "one of the most pernicious delusions" that ever vexed mankind. There was no truth value at all in "the whole monstrous farrago."

What was the intellectual basis for this phenomenon? Tylor asserted that magic was based on a general human intellectual propensity, namely the principle of "association of ideas." But magic was a product of an erroneous application of these principles of association, especially the relations of analogy. The error, he said in a celebrated phrase, consists in mistaking "ideal connexions for real connexions." The false or mistaken application of the "argument of analogy" consists in contingent associative relations being taken for causal relations and then being inverted in the magical act. For example the primitive notices that the cock crows with the rising sun; he then infers that if the cock is made to crow the sun will rise. Similar associations are noted between the appearance of the sun and the behaviour of the heliotrope, so that the latter is mistakenly manipulated in an effort to control the sun.

Tylor, as far as I can see, asked two critical questions about magic, which in a sense have acted as primary puzzles or conundrums which his successors, most notably Evans-Pritchard and Lévi-Strauss in our time, have felt compelled to answer.[9] One question is: if magic and the occult practices are a false art, does then a magician, sorcerer, diviner hypocritically and falsely exploit a credulous public? The second question is: Why does magic persist if "the evidence was indeed against it," in the sense that frequently the promised results are not obtained? We might call this, borrowing a phrase from Sir Karl Popper, the falsification riddle: if indeed magical acts are frequently decisively falsified why do they continue to be enacted?

Tylor's discussion of these issues is complex and equivocal. He concluded that magic does not have its origin in fraud though the practitioner may be "a dupe and a cheat". And magic may persist even if the empirical evidence is against it for several reasons. A large number of successful outcomes effected by natural means are either disguised or misconstrued as results of an efficacious magic. And although a large number of failures occur, the magician prevents them from counting by adopting various stratagems. The magician is extraordinarily resourceful in the use of conjuring skills, sleight of hand, rhetoric and impudence (i.e. he has the communicative skills of an impresario). He deals in ambiguous phrases, vague diagnoses and predictions, such that most outcomes can be retrospectively interpreted as fulfillments. Or again, he blames failure on the non-fulfillment of difficult conditions essential to the magical performance and to various "interferences" human and non-human (i.e. he invokes secondary rationalizations). He is incapable of appreciating negative evidence which therefore happily allows one success to outweigh half a dozen failures (i.e. it is a common feature of optimism to forget failures and to point only to the successes).

Looking forward to our own times, we may say that Tylor's list of answers partially foreshadows, and through certain shifts in focus has enabled, advances in interpretations suggested by phrases that are in vogue today such as "self-fulfilling prophecy," "psychosomatic efficacy," "psychodrama and sociodrama," "secondary rationalizations," "negotiated cures" between doctor and patient, "impression management," "placebo effect," and so on.

Be that as it may, it may have been noticed by some of you that Tylor's answers relating to the practice of magic as "pseudo-sciences" correspond in part with Thomas Kuhn's description of the manner in which "normal science" is conducted, especially how the majority of respectable scientists working under the umbrella of a paradigm are willing to tolerate anomalies and may resort to *ad hoc* explanations and additions and apologetics to save it. (We may at the same time note that Tylor's notion of positive science is a simple version of Karl Popper's idealization of it: that at the heart of the sciences is the search for decisive falsifications.)

In any case, since Tylor saw the magical and occult arts as superstitions having no basis in truth in terms of a positivistic conception of science, in the last resort he could only attribute their practice to wrongheadedness and conservatism on the part of humanity, even though he saw their analogical basis in man's natural reason.

The Tylorian paradigm inevitably ruled out seeing witchcraft beliefs, for instance, as a "projective system" or a "symbolic system" (or to use an impressive Marxist phrase, as "alienated objectivations") dialectically related to the social order, and that the techniques of witchcraft may be functionally related to the grappling with and amelioration of tensions and conflicts in social relations.

One wonders how far Tylor could have gone with his doctrine of "survivals" if he was set the problem of explaining the European witch-craze that occurred in the sixteenth and seventeenth centuries precisely in the effervescent and turbulent years of the Renaissance and Reformation, which many scholars have regarded as ushering in the dawn of modern rationality and civilization. Trevor-Roper poses the intellectual challenge in this way in his book: the puzzle of the witch-craze was the inflammation of already existing unsystematized beliefs, the "incorporation of them by educated men, into a bizarre but coherent intellectual system," and their use by men of learning in high places to direct a dreadful persecuting force and to perpetrate wholesale purges that took a toll of thousands of lives. At no time in the Dark Ages of Europe was a "witchcraze" of this malignant order manifest. "The years 1550–1600 were worse than the years 1500–1550, and the years 1600–1650 were still worse. Nor was the craze entirely separable from the intellectual and spiritual life of those years. It was forwarded by the cultivated popes of the Renaissance, by the great Protestant reformers, by the saints of the Counter-Reformation, by the scholars, lawyers and churchmen of the age of Scaliger and Lipsius, Bacon and Grotius, Berulle and Pascal."[10]

We see from this example that a doctrine of survivals and of misapplication of the laws of association of ideas cannot cope with these features of the phenomenon of a witchcraft craze that raged for two centuries: The systematization of witchcraft beliefs as a body of knowledge and its integral position in a total cosmology, the periodic reactivation and intensification of the craze, because of a continuity of pressure generated by the social order in which the beliefs were grounded, or because of a longitudinal recurrence of similar patterns of social, political and religious tensions in a whole continent. These interpretive frames and hypotheses were not open to Tylor on account of his evolutionary perspective, compounded of ideas of progress and of archaic survivals, and a commitment to an individualist psychology.

Tylor on religion in *Primitive Culture*

Tylor is remembered in anthropology, aside from his catchall definition of culture, for his minimum definition of religion (and animism) as "the belief in Spiritual Beings." Tylor's treatment of religion is remarkably different from Robertson Smith's sociological treatment of it in *Religion of the Semites* (1899) which appeared some 28 years after *Primitive Culture*. While Robertson Smith would see *totemism* as the earliest manifestation of religion, in which the religion of the group or clan dominates individuals, and in which rite precedes belief, Tylor's conception of religion put belief before rite, and saw its original basis in individual psychology. It is an example of his perspective that the laws of social phenomena are derived from the laws of individual life.

It seems that in terms of subject matter, Tylor was an innovator in focusing on primitive religion when his contemporaries like Maine were interested in legal institutions and Spencer in social structures and their functions.[11] This change of direction in the substantive interests of evolutionary theory was to reach its apogee in Frazer's *Golden Bough.*

Evans-Pritchard has dubbed Tylor's individualist psychology intellectualist speculation of the "if I were a horse" variety. Tylor "imagined" himself into the savage's mental condition and deduced that the first animistic projections were the doctrines of the soul and spirit. Primitive man by virtue of his natural reason postulated the notion of soul on the basis of his dream life (in which his phantom was seen as engaging in action while the dreamer slept); these same souls were transformed into spirit beings existing in their own right, after human beings who possessed souls died.

From these basic premises and features of early religious life, Tylor with an impressive skill built up his scheme in evolutionary terms. Thus lower natural religion was transformed into higher revealed religion, distinguished by morality and ethics. Take the trajectory of sacrifice as an example of his theorizing: its earliest manifestation was in the idiom of "gift" (*do ut des*) reciprocity, modelled on human relations between chiefs and ordinary persons, in which the worshipper stands to benefit because he strikes a bargain; sacrifice then develops a higher form which is based on the notion of homage to a deity: the sacrificer does something to gratify the deity as his superior; finally we reach sacrifice which expresses abnegation, in that the sacrificer voluntarily parts with a part of himself, and this intentionality represents an ethical conception appropriate to high religion.[12]

Tylor systematically built up other progressions: from the belief in souls to belief in spirits after death, on which was predicated the cult of ancestor worship on the one hand and spirit cults (exorcism and oracle possession) on the other. By means of these progressions Tylor constructed his (hypothetical) developmental scheme from animism to polytheism to monotheism, the last being the highest form.

There are many valid criticisms made of Tylor's evolutionary hierarchies in the sphere of religion. For our purposes, the most damning one is that the evolutionary scheme actually never postulated the actual mechanisms and connections by which humanity passed from level to level or cultural "species" to cultural "species" (as contained, for example, in Darwin's notion of "natural selection"). The scheme then has only an illusory magnificence, without hinges to support the edifice. As George Stocking has penetratingly remarked: "Tylor's central problem as a 'uniformitarian' evolutionist was to fill in the gap between 'Brixham Cave and European Civilization' without introducing the hand of God. Yet he produced no specific processes and mechanisms by which cultural evolution took place, so that anthropologists are ill advised to look for a dynamic in either 'technological determinism' or "cultural Darwinism'."[13]

The magic/culture distinction in primitive culture

As I have remarked earlier, Tylor never directly compared magic with religion (though he does compare religion with science in an indirect way).

Those phenomena Tylor identified as examples of magic and religion could be arranged in two columns as follows:

"Magical arts" and "occult sciences" (pseudo-sciences)	Religion
Sorcery Witchcraft Astrology	Animism. Doctrine of the soul and doctrine of spirits with which are associated sacrifice and soul loss ceremonies.
Divination with bones (haruspication) Chiromancy (palmistry)	Ancestor worship, the quintessential elementary form of primitive religion. Possession cults, such as oracle possession (usually benevolent) and exorcism of evil spirits. Fetishism (the belief in spirits in material objects; image worship).
All the magical arts are based on a mistaken association of ideas: the mistaking of "ideal connexions for real connexions."	Religion over time develops from "natural" lower religion to higher "revealed" religion. The typical rites associated with higher religion are prayer and sacrifice, which over time elaborate into several forms.

The following are the implications of this grouping.

(1) We should note first of all that Tylor saw animism, the earliest form of religion, as *coexisting* with magic in primitive societies.

(2) However, this coexistence, while possibly a plausible state of affairs, causes difficulties with regard to rigorously separating them. If magical acts are seen as acts to get practical things done in a causal mode, Tylor also sees in the lower forms of religion, such as divination and sorcery, the occurrence of dealings with spirits and deities to gain favours and get practical things done. So if animism deals with manipulation of and causation in spirits how can its objectives differ from "magical arts" and "occult sciences," which also traffic with spiritual agencies and forces in the same mode? (Evans-Pritchard

remarks that Tylor, faced with this issue, recognized that magic and religion "must continually overlap since there is often a notion of animism in the *materia medica* of magical rites."[14]

(3) Thirdly we see clearly how Tylor is importantly an heir to Reformation thought. He separates out a higher revealed religion in the Christian mode, which is characterized by the intercessionary forms of worship such as prayer, and by ethics and morality. Tylor's revealed religion is belief in one God, who is creator and sovereign governor in relation to whom a belief in moral retribution is appropriate. Lower religion by contrast, according to Tylor, pursues personal advantage, and is even devoid of morality and ethical content, as may be expected of a religion that is directly projected on the logic of self-interested human interpersonal relations.[15] (We may note here the directly antithetical position to that of Tylor's that Durkheim held, as he did on other issues: For Durkheim religion is importantly, from its very beginnings, concerned with the regulation of the moral life of the community or society, and "the real function of religion is not to make us think, to enrich our knowledge . . . but it is to make us act, to aid us to live.")[16] As Talcott Parsons put it, Durkheim held not so much that religion is a social phenomenon but that society is a moral phenomenon.

The role of science *vis-à-vis* magic and religion

Tylor asserted, as we have seen, that the magical arts were "pseudo-sciences." He also maintained that "natural religion" is a theory of personal causes, because it construes spirits to be real beings who act upon the universe. Tylor further argued that the role of science in civilization was to change ideas from notions of personalized force to impersonal force; science therefore necessarily dissolved animism. Let there be no mistaking Tylor's position: animism as a "personalized causation theory" is opposed to "impersonal causation" concepts of science. The source of change in the educated world, he said, "is the alteration in natural science, assigning new causes for the operations of nature and the events of life. The theory of the immediate action of spirits has here, as so widely elsewhere, given place to ideas of force and law."[17]

Here we see a curious lacuna in Tylor's thought (also present in Frazer's flamboyant prolixity) that can perhaps be taken to be linked to his belief in the claims of positive science as the source of all truth and his reluctance at the same time to engage directly with high religion's – that is Christianity's – truth claims *vis-à-vis* science.[18]

Let me explain. While Tylor tells us why science dissolves animistic ideas of spiritual forces actuating on the universe, he fails to explain why higher religion with its ethical retributive monotheism should persist in the face of science, or what moral–causal space it occupies such that it does not collide with science. He takes refuge in the indirect formula that "Barbaric philosophy retains as real what civilized language has reduced to simile." Tylor in any case seems to be innocent of the Christian theological maneuvers by which the will of God and laws of nature were brought into correspondence in the seventeenth century. All in all the Victorian cultural evolutionists exhibit a blockage – that can be seen as a failure of nerve or as the action of cultural blinders – when it came to the question of pushing their brand of cultural evolution into the provenance of the established church of their time.

There is one contrast to be made between Tylor's implicit position and Durkheim's remarkable suggestion. While Tylor sees the elementary religious ideas of causation in a personalistic mode as antithetical to scientific ideas of force and laws, Durkheim proposes in *The Elementary Forms* that elementary religious ideas are the precursors of scientific ideas of force, causality, and connection. In other words while Durkheim proposes an "historical" continuity between early religions and later science, Tylor proposes a discontinuous shift in paradigms.[19]

Perhaps one of the most devastating criticisms levelled against Tylor (that is equally appropriate to Frazer) is his never posing the question why primitives would mistake ideal connections for real ones in one domain when they do not do so in their other activities. As Evans-Pritchard puts it, and in this he and Malinowski stand together: "The error here was in not recognizing that the associations are social and not psychological stereotypes, and that they occur therefore only when evoked in specific ritual situations, which are also of limited duration . . ."[20] This idea of the relevance of contexts of thought and action which apply to all human beings in all societies is a seminal idea that I shall exploit in this book. Moreover, as we shall see later, this observation accords with Lévy-Bruhl's position that it is not differences in innate mental processes but differences in the way collective thought impinges on the individual that better explains differences between so-called primitive and modern mentalities.

The twilight relevance of Sir James Frazer (1854–1938)

To many laymen it may seem strangely disproportionate that I should here treat Frazer as a postscript to Tylor. For Frazer in his long professional career of some fifty-four years – his productive period began around 1884 – dominated the field of classics and archaeology, and was seen by his contemporaries as exploring the unitary experience of the human race. He was seen as the great teller of the story of how humanity from its remotest and darkest beginnings gradually developed its manifold relations and its understanding of its place in nature and in the cosmos. This story was seen as having a compelling contemporary significance because it was these primitive intimations and understandings that later culminated in the emotional power and uplifting beauty of the great religions of the world. Yet "Nothing matches the greatness of Frazer's fame so well as the completeness of its eclipse among anthropologists today."[21] The eclipse of Frazer is as much due to his ornate style and his prolixity (he has been accused of being a "mere miser of facts" and a voraciously diligent library mole) as to the untenability of his major thesis. Mary Douglas has suggested that Frazer's decline in our time may be attributed in part to a creative misunderstanding between the "styles" of two adjunct generations, and refers in this respect to certain remarks of Wittgenstein which I shall quote shortly.[22]

On the positive side, one of Frazer's contributions was the sorting of Tylor's principles of association in magical thought into two basic types, namely the principle of similarity or resemblance (homeopathic) and the principle of contagion or contiguity. (Frazer thus subdivided magical systems into two sorts: "sympathetic magic" and "contagious magic" though he was aware that they overlapped in practice.) Frazer, much in the vein of Tylor, declared that these two are general or generic laws of thought, which were misapplied in magic. Magic, he declared in a stronger tone than that adopted by Tylor, was in some ways a precursor of science, but it was its bastard sister.

Frazer pushed the similarity and contrast between magic and science to a point which Tylor in his wisdom did not. For instance, Frazer maintained that the fundamental conception of magic is "identical with modern science," namely the "uniformity of nature." The magician believes that the same causes will always provide the same results, and as long as he performs the ceremony in accordance with the rules laid down, the desired results will inevitably follow. Thus the similarity between magical and scientific conceptions of the world is close: "In both of them the succession of events is perfectly regular and certain, being determined by immutable laws, the operation of which can be foreseen and calculated precisely, the element of chance and of accident are banished from the course of nature." It is because Tylor did not insist on, indeed did not exaggerate, the magician's commitment to the uniformity of nature and to a faith in determinism, that he could open up what we today label as the problem of secondary rationalizations and conventional strategies by which anyone committed to a "belief system" strives to save it from anomalies and falsifications. Moreover, as we have seen, Tylor in a sense shielded his separation of "magic" from "animism" by not directly confronting them, and by his equivocations when he described empirical data. But Frazer's confident and strident confrontation of magic with a positivistic conception of science makes his caveats seem obvious tortuous stratagems whenever they are proffered. Thus Frazer did concede that magic often dealt with spirits, but that when it did so, it treated them exactly as "inanimistic agents," that is, it coerced and constrained them instead of propitiating and conciliating them in the manner of religion. But there is a *non sequitur* here. To coerce another person or being is not to make that entity "inanimate." Frazer resorts to this assertion precisely because he has decided that the magician and scientist share the same presuppositions concerning "the uniformity of nature" and impersonal causation. In making this equation Frazer, as well as Tylor in a less naive way, have both introduced a distinction which was alien to medieval or Renaissance magic in Europe predicated on the mediation of angels and planetary spirits. It is the uncomplicated resort to the Protestant formula that magic is to religion as spell is to prayer, that also leads Frazer to the melodramatic and unsustainable pronouncement about the "relentless hostility" between priest and magician, and their opposed technologies, for such statements can be easily disproved empirically.[23] Frazer could easily have made his point by the moderate phrasing that as ideal types "magician" and "priest" may be described as emphasizing different techniques and procedures depending on the kind of relation they postulate between supernatural agent and man, but that empirical cases frequently show a mixing of the two modalities.

But there is some molten gold in Frazer's volcanic overflow. For example, the associational principles of similarity and contiguity as general features of the human mind have since Frazer's time found an elaborated use in other interpretive frameworks stripped of their "causal" connotations as applied to magic. Roman Jakobson has fruitfully exploited the terms "metaphorical and metonymical associations" in his linguistic and literary studies, and after him Lévi-Strauss has popularized them in the study of savage thought, particularly in the realm of mythology. In my own essay on "The Magical Power of Words" I apply them (I hope productively) in the analysis of Trobriand ritual.[24]

Frazer also extended Tylor's more nuanced discussion in unacceptable ways. He made nonsense of Tylor's categories by arranging without qualifications magic, religion and science in an evolutionary linear scheme, with the unsupportable assertion that magic preceded religion in time, and with the inescapable inference – which he however evaded – that science must inevitably dissolve religion in our time. In Frazer's evolutionary scheme, magic is older than religion in this history of humanity – indeed at this earliest stage the functions of priest and sorcerer were often combined. The age of magic corresponds to the age of stone, and a case in point are the Australian "races," according to Frazer, the lowest in mental and social development among contemporary humanity: "all men in Australia are magicians, but not one is a priest." What then led from the Age of Magic to the Age of Religion?

It was the tardy recognition of the inherent falsehood and barrenness of magic that led the more thoughtful of mankind to cast about for a truer theory of nature. Man came to realize that he had been pulling at strings to which nothing was attached. So it dawned on him that superior beings control the universe, and he assumed a humble dependence towards them and propitiated them for favours. Frazer defined religion as the "propitiation or conciliation of powers superior to man which are believed to direct and control the course of nature and of human life."[25] But if this change of tack became necessary, why did not intelligent man – who must have existed at all times – detect the fallacy of magic sooner? Why did magic persist in the face of falsification, a modern Popperian might ask? Frazer's reply given in passing was as follows: "The answer seems to be that the fallacy was far from easy to detect, the failure by no means obvious, since in many, perhaps in most cases, the desired event did actually follow, at a longer or a shorter interval, the performance of the rite which was designed to bring it about . . . Similarly, rites observed in the morning to help the sun to rise, and in spring to wake the dreaming Earth from her winter sleep, will invariably appear to be crowned with success, at least within the temperate zones."[26]

Here indeed Frazer in his stilted fashion does illuminatingly touch on an important interpretive possibility concerning the performative context of certain kinds of ritual, particularly of the calendrical type. Durkheim remarked in his *The Elementary Forms of the Religious Life* that religion accounts for the regularity of nature rather than its extra-ordinary nature. Nadel made a similar point when he suggested that many rites are efficacious because nature is regular.[27] These comments make eminent sense concerning the widespread celebration of rites linked to changes of seasons, rites of rainmaking or harvesting, and other calendrical cosmic rites. In respect of these Suzanne Langer, in *Philosophy in a New Key*, made the dramatic point that these rites do not so much instrumentally "cause" rain or good harvests in a narrow sense as they complete a course of events, the results being the last accompaniments of ritual or the rersults following upon its performance. I may perhaps illustrate the "anticipatory" nature of these rituals that are geared to regular astronomical or calendrical changes by relating a story told me by Meyer Fortes. He once invited a rainmaker to perform the ceremony for him for an attractive fee, and the officiant in question replied "Don't be a fool, whoever makes a rain-making ceremony in the dry season?" There are, of course, many other anticipatory and expressive and performative features to such magical rites that become possible to envisage once they are extracted from the net of positivistic causality. On the whole, Frazer's simplistic evolutionary scheme and his overall characterization of magic as "bastard science" smothered other insights[28] which even when they occurred to him he managed to clothe them in a theatrical garb that robbed them of a general significance.

Wittgenstein's encounter with Frazer

Frazer's immense but bookish learning, and his Victorian preoccupations and fantasies indefatigably reiterated in his mannered and embroidered prose, are said to have riled some great twentieth-century thinkers, his contemporaries in time but not in thought. William James, who happened to meet the Frazers in

1900 at a *pensione* in Rome, remarked that Frazer was "a sucking babe of humility, unworldliness and sightlessness to everything but *print* . . ."[29]

Another luminary who met Frazer only in print but has left us a much longer and more searching record of his impressions is Ludwig Wittgenstein, and since these impressions seem to touch on issues that are central to my book I have decided to reproduce them in detail.

For scholars of magic, science and religion, it is remarkably felicitous and rewarding that Ludwig Wittgenstein, arguably the greatest analytic philosopher of the twentieth century, who first championed "logical positivism" and then repudiated much of it in favour of "ordinary language philosophy," should have dipped into Frazer, the great Victorian story teller of man's remote beginnings in dark superstition and his passage to civilized thought and action. Though Wittgenstein experienced immense irritation with, and scorn for, Frazer's explanation of divine kingship and rainmaking and so on under the rubric of false "sympathetic and contagious magic," he was stimulated by the ritual and religious phenomena themselves described by Frazer to search for a different meaning of them.

Wittgenstein made some notes around 1931 upon reading the abridged one-volume edition of *The Golden Bough*, but the full translation of them into English from his papers has only recently become available, although some scholars in the past have had access to partial versions.[30] Wittgenstein's notes were made at the end of certain specified portions of Frazer's text, and should be read as a running commentary, which though sometimes repetitive is on the whole cumulative in effect. The notes themselves, made *ad hoc*, and never put together as a coherent and consistent critique of Frazer, nevertheless give us most valuable glimpses of Wittgenstein's spontaneous criticisms which no doubt embody his phenomenological reflections and anticipate his later conceptions such as "forms of life" and "language games." These features of Wittgenstein's later thought either foreshadow or are integral to my subsequent discussions of Malinowski, Winch and others.

I propose to reproduce those parts of his reactions that I find most pertinent, and I have divided them into five parts. Each part will begin with a reference to the contents of the passages in Frazer that prompted Wittgenstein's ripostes, followed by my own comments highlighting some themes. Then follow Wittgenstein's own remarks expressed in characteristically allusive, condensed and reflexive style. *I shall italicize certain words that seem to be particularly effective.* My comments will lengthen as we proceed in response to the cumulative implications of Wittgenstein's observations.

(1) Wittgenstein first reads Frazer's elucidation of the "laws of similarity and contact" in magical thought, and Frazer's examples of "rain kings" and the rites in which they figure. He immediately notes the significance of the timing of the rainmaking operations of the rain kings: that they occur during the season of rain and not the dry season. Wittgenstein then intimates his

dislike of the "intellectualistic" appeal to opinions/beliefs to explain ritual acts. He also – and here he goes in a different direction from the criterion of deriving meaning from contexts of use – appeals to a general human psychology which he can recognize both in himself and in the "primitive man," to describe hitting with a stick on the ground as an "instinctive" expressive act.

> I believe that the characteristic of primitive man is that he does not act out of *opinions* (in opposition to Frazer).
>
> I read in many similar examples, of a rain-king in Africa to whom people beg for rain when the rainy season comes. But that surely means that they don't really think that he could make rain, otherwise they would do this in the *dry periods* of the year when the country is "a parched and arid desert." For if one supposes that the people once instituted this office of the rain-king out of stupidity, then it is certainly clear that they had already had the experience that the rain begins in March and that at that time they ought to have the rain-king function for the rest of the year. Or also thus: towards morning when the sun wants to rise, the rites of dawn are celebrated by the people, but not in the night, rather there they simply burn lamps.
>
> When I am angry about something, I sometimes hit with my stick on the ground or a tree, etc. But certainly I don't believe that it is the fault of the ground or that hitting can help. "I can release my anger." And all rites are of this kind. Such actions *one can call actions of instinct.* – And a historical explanation, perhaps that I formerly, or my ancestors formerly, have believed that hitting the ground might help something, these are shadow-boxing bouts, for they are superfluous assumptions which explain nothing. The similarity of that act with an act of punishment is important, but more than this similarity cannot be established.
>
> If such a phenomenon is brought into contact with an instinct which I myself possess, then just this is the desired explanation; that is, that which resolves this special puzzlement (this special difficulty). And an observation on (further inquiry into) the history of my instincts now moves on other tracks.

(2) Frazer's examples of the worship of the oaktree (or oak god) by "all the branches of the Aryan stock in Europe" evoke Wittgenstein's brilliant and amusing aphorism about the flea and the dog, which suggest that the logic of selection of symbols in a rite consists in their "association" in an environment on the basis of symbiosis as well as difference (figure and ground). However, his suggestion that this establishing of similarities and differences (contrastive relations) between entities in the environment is also the awakening of ritual action is, as it stands, an incomplete suggestion, lacking a developed theory of "value" differentiation and "marking" in the form developed by Saussure and other linguists, and subsequently exploited by Lévi-Strauss.

> There could have been no trifling reason, that is, there could have been no *reason* whatsoever why certain human tribes worshipped the oak tree; instead it is simply that they and the oak were united in an environment (symbiosis), not out of choice, rather they united in their development like the flea and the dog. If fleas were to develop a rite, then it would refer to the dog.
>
> One could say, not their union (of oak and man) but, in a certain sense, their separation, has given *occasion* to these rites. Therefore, the awakening of the

intellect *proceeds* with a separation from the original *ground*, from the original basis of life. (The origin of *choice*.)
(The form of the awakening spirit is worship.)

(3) Frazer's fanciful account of the priest king of Nemi, a grim figure prowling in the sacred grove, carrying a drawn sword, and waiting for his stalking assassin; and Frazer's search for the *origins* of this barbarous custom in the motives of the human mind of antiquity; and Frazer's discussion of the "*fallacy* of magic" – as a "mistaken application of the very simplest and elementary process of the mind, namely the association of ideas by virtue of resemblance or contiguity" – these evoke a long response by Wittgenstein.

This response combines a powerful skepticism of the Frazerian attempt to apply criteria of truth and error to magical (and religious) views with a sensitive reaching into the human condition which evokes religious mysteries and seeks emotional solace. Neither metaphysical nor ultimate value commitments, or for that matter a broken heart, are amenable to, or assuaged by, positivist reality testing. Wittgenstein suggests that sometimes a *description* without adding anything is more meaningful than a forced search for an "explanation," which concept belongs to a framework of "hypotheses" deriving from "theory," and their testing for error or truth as "opinions." He also rejects a forced evolutionary search for origins of magical/religious views and practices, preferring if necessary to suggest a basis in a universal or general and timeless human propensity. Finally, he rejects the attempt to *derive* rites from beliefs.

> *Again and again I must dive into the water of doubt.*
> Frazer's presentation of the magical and religious views of mankind is *unsatisfactory*: it makes these views appear as *errors*.
> Thus, was Augustine in error when he invoked God's name on every page of the Confessions?
> However – one can say – if he was not in error, then indeed it was the Buddha – or whoever – whose religion expresses entirely different views. But neither of them was in error, except where he stated a theory.
> Even the idea of wanting to explain the custom – such as the killing of the Priest King – seems to me to be mistaken. All that Frazer does is to make plausible people who think as he does. It is very remarkable that all these customs finally, so to speak, are represented as stupidities.
> It will, however, never be that people do all these things out of pure stupidity.
> If, for example, he explains that the King must be killed in his prime, because according to the views of the savages, his soul would not be preserved, then indeed one can only say: where that custom and these views go together, there the custom does not originate from the view, they are just both there.
> It is possible, and it often occurs, that a man gives up a custom after he has recognized an error upon which that custom depended. However, this is the case only when it suffices to make a person aware of his error in order to change his behavior. But that is not the case with the religious customs of a people, and therefore it is not a question of error.
> Frazer says, it is very difficult to discover the error in magic – and therefore it

survives so long – because for example, a conjuration which is supposed to bring about rain sooner or later seems to be effective. But in this example it is peculiar that the people don't see earlier that it does rain sooner or later anyhow.

I believe that the undertaking of an explanation, therefore, already misses the point, because one must only put together correctly what one knows, without adding anything, and the satisfaction which is sought through the explanation results from itself.

And the explanation here is not what satisfies. When Frazer begins and tells us the story of the Forest King of Nemi, he does this in a tone that shows that he feels, and he wants to let us feel, that something strange and terrible is happening here. But the question "Why does this happen?" is really answered: because it is terrible. That is, whatever we find in this event to be terrible, grandiose, ghastly, tragic, etc., anything but trivial and meaningless, that has brought this event to life.

Here one can only describe and say: human life is this way.

The explanation is, in comparison with the impression which the above writings give us, too insecure.

Every explanation is indeed a hypothesis.

But for whomever might be disturbed by love, a hypothetical explanation will be of little help – it will not calm him.

If one compares the former story of the Priest King of Nemi with the phrase "the majesty of death", then one sees that they are both one.

The life of the Priest King represents that which is meant by that phrase.

Whoever is deeply struck with the majesty of death can express this thought through such a life. – This is also, of course, no explanation; rather it substitutes one symbol for another. – Or: one ceremony for another.

A religious symbol is not based upon opinion. And error is relevant to opinion only.

One would like to say: this and that event has taken place; laugh if you can, friend.

Religious actions, or the religious life of the Priest King, is of no other sort than any genuinely religious action *today*, perhaps a confession of sins. This can also be "explained" and cannot be explained.

(4) A reading of the North American Indian rites which involve pricking effigies or shooting them with arrows in the alleged belief that the real human foe would suffer, stimulates these comments by Wittgenstein which try to replace Frazer's representation of "homeopathic magic" as false causal action with expressive action, where the representation itself *is* the fulfillment. This is an anticipation of John Austin's (a follower of the master) notion of "performative" acts. Wittgenstein's reaching towards the role of language in ritual acts would be more amply realized by Austin, Burke, Searle and others. Wittgenstein uses the same anticipatory (expressive–performative) ideas to interpret benevolent "imitative" rites that are enacted to facilitate childbirth or procure offspring for barren women. In reminding us that the same savage who stabs an effigy also "really" builds his hut and shapes his weapons, Wittgenstein voices the caution that Malinowski, who developed his ideas on magical language independently of Wittgenstein, also makes much of (see next chapter): that the primitive who indulges in "magic" gives evidence of practical reasoning in his technology and mastery of agriculture and crafts.[31]

To burn in effigy. To kiss the picture of the beloved. This is naturally not based upon a belief in a certain effect on the object which the picture represents. It aims at a satisfaction and also obtains it. Or rather it aims at nothing at all; we act in such a way and then feel satisfied.

One could also kiss the name of the beloved, and here the substitution would be clear because of the name.

The same savage, who stabs the image of his enemy, apparently in order to kill him, really builds his hut out of wood and cuts his arrows skillfully and not in effigy.

And magic always depends on the idea of symbolism and of language.

The representation of a wish is, eo ipso, the representation of its fulfillment. Magic, however, brings a wish to life; it manifests a wish.

Baptism as washing. – *An error only arises when magic is interpreted scientifically.* When the adoption of a child takes place in such a way that the mother pulls it through her clothes, then it is crazy to believe that there is some error here and that she believes she has given birth to the child.

(5) Further reading of Frazer, especially his description of savages regarding their names as vital parts of themselves as an instance of their attributing "a real and substantial bond" between a name and the person, or their regarding their acts of drinking and eating as attended with special danger, and then his use of these examples as evidence of savages' "mistaken application of the two fundamental laws of thought," finally drives Wittgenstein to an explosive denunciation of Frazer.

But we should shake off this shock and pay close attention to Wittgenstein's appeal to *general* human reason and imagination, which he, you, and I can employ to devise by thought experiment the range of primitive customs. This is possible because the principle according to which these customs are ordered is "much more general" than the one by which Frazer explains them, and they being "present in our souls" we would be able "to think out all the possibilities ourselves."

This appeal to general human imagination and reason, Wittgenstein artfully combines with another feature of symbolization familiar to Saussure and the later structuralists, that metaphorical and metonymical associations are "arbitrary" or "conventional" as well as "meaningful" and "rational": a king's sacred state is conveyed as much by his confinement from view as by his public display. Thus seemingly "opposite" enactments could signify or exemplify a single state of mind. Indeed, in human constructions anything in our "environment" could be selected and made to represent something else; also diverse entities can be made to represent the same thing and the same thing can signify polyvalent meanings. Moreover, language and other sign systems could be combined to produce complex messages in the service of human constructions of meaning.

These comments by him also raise the issue whether by appealing to a general human reason, Wittgenstein falls prey to the same intellectual fallacy Tylor and Frazer committed: to hypothetically thinking themselves into the state of mind of the "primitive." I think Wittgenstein's mental exercise is different; whereas Tylor and Frazer, fully conscious of being "civilized," attempted to "regress" to the primitive's condition, Wittgenstein is claiming that "civilized" man has within him the same symbolizing and ritualizing tendencies as the "primitive." This is synchronic and not an evolutionary posture.

How narrow is the spiritual life for Frazer! Thus, How impossible to understand another life in terms of the English life of his time! Frazer can imagine no priest who is not basically an English parson of our time, with all his stupidity and dullness.

Why should it not be possible for a person to consider his name to be holy? It is on the one hand the important instrument that is given to him, and on the other, like a *piece* of jewelry that is hung on him at birth.

One sees how misleading the explanations of Frazer are when one sees – I believe – that one could very well devise primitive customs oneself, and it would have to be an accident if they were not really to be found anywhere. *That is, the principle according to which these customs are ordered, is a much more general one than the one Frazer explains, and present in our own souls, so that we would be able to think out all the possibilities ourselves.* That, by chance, the king of a tribe is guarded from anyone's view, we can very well imagine, but also, that every man of the tribe should see him. The latter will certainly not be allowed to happen in some more or less accidental way, but he will be shown to people. Possibly no one will be permitted to touch him, though perhaps they will be required to do so. Remember that after Schubert's death his brother cut Schubert's musical scores into small pieces and gave little pieces of some of those measures to his favorite pupils. This action, as an indication of piety, is just as understandable to us as the other. And had Schubert's brother burned the musical scores, even that would be understandable as an indication of piety.

Yes, Frazer's explanations would not be explanations at all, if they did not appeal ultimately to a certain tendency in ourselves.

That the shadow of a man, which has the appearance of a human being or his mirror image, that rain, that a thunderstorm, the phases of the moon, the changing of the seasons, the similarities and differences between animals and people, the phenomena of death, of birth and of sexual life, in short, everything that a person perceives around him year after year, connected with one another in the most diverse ways, that these will appear (play a role) in his thinking (his philosophy) and his customs is obvious, or is precisely that which we actually know and which is interesting.

How could fire, or the similarity of fire with the sun, have failed to make an impression on the awakening human soul [?] But perhaps not "because he cannot explain it to himself" (the stupid superstition of our time) – for he does it become less impressive through an "explanation"?

I don't mean that specifically fire must make an impression on Everyone. Fire no more than any other phenomenon, and the phenomenon to One, the other to Another. For no phenomenon is, in itself, especially mysterious, but every one can become so to us, and just this is characteristic of the awakening spirit in man, that for him a phenomenon becomes meaningful. *One could almost say that man is a ceremonial animal.* That is perhaps partly false, partly nonsense, but there is also something correct about it.

That is, one could begin a book about anthropology like this: When one observes the life and behavior of men on the earth, then one sees that men, with the exception of the actions which one could call animal-like, the absorption of food, etc., etc.,

etc., also *carry out actions which have completely different (unique) character and which one could call ritual actions.*

Now, however, it is nonsense to proceed so that one would say, as characteristic of these actions, that they are actions which originated from mistaken views about the physics of things. (Frazer does this when he says, magic is essentially false physics, or else false medicine/art of healing/technology, etc.)

On the contrary, that which is characteristic of ritual action is surely not a view, or opinion, whether it is now correct or false, although an opinion – a belief – itself also can be ritualistic, can belong to the rite.

If one holds it to be self-evident that man is gratified by his fantasy, then one must consider that this fantasy is not like a painted picture, or a plastic model but a complicated construction of heterogenous components: words and images. Then one would not place operations with written and spoken signs in opposition to operations with "mental images" of events.

We must plow through the complete language.

(6) Upon reading instances of taboos laid upon warriors returning to their villages after slaying enemies – sometimes even bringing their heads – and Frazer's tedious insistence that these taboos are grounded in "superstitious fears" "dictated by fear of the ghosts of the slain," Wittgenstein's patience once again gives way.

In the following comments Wittgenstein raises the acute question of "translation between cultures": if Frazer uses the English words "ghosts" and "gods" to represent savage concepts, does this not imply that he is equating these terms with those familiar to him in his own cultural experience as a modern European? If this correspondence is made, then Frazer should have realized that there is something in him that "speaks for those modes of action of the savages." (The major issue of "translation of cultures" and "commensurability" between them will engage us at the end of my book.)

Secondly, Wittgenstein makes more explicit the difference between Frazer's arranging of data to seek and support an "evolutionary" explanation in terms of "historical" development, and his own preference for a "cognitive schema" that is synchronic, and sees the significance of "interconnecting links" in a configurational context. Wittgenstein's interpretive methodology is familiar to us in the schemas proposed by "structuralists" (and "structural-functionalists"),[32] including the notion of transformation in a "formal" sense. He leaves us with the intriguing thought that the evolutionary hypothesis is also "a disguising of a formal relationship" (I take it he means that the evolutionary schema also implies a change from one imputed or constructed system or stage to another constructed system or stage).

Frazer: ". . . that these observances are dictated by fear of the ghost of the slain seems certain . . ." *But why does Frazer use the word "ghost"? Therefore, he very probably understands this superstition, since he explains it to us with a superstitious word which is easy to him. Or better, he would have been able to see from it that something in us speaks for those modes of action of the savages. – If I believed (which I don't) that there are human-superhuman beings somewhere that one can* call Gods – if I say: "I fear the revenge of the Gods," then this shows that I (can) mean something by it, or can give expression to a sentiment which has nothing to do with that belief (. . . which is not necessarily bound up with that belief).

Frazer would have been in a position to believe that a savage died out of error. In public school text-books, we read that Attila has undertaken all his great military campaigns because he believed that he possessed the sword of the thunder-god.

Frazer is much more savage than most of his savages, for they would not be so far removed from the understanding of a spiritual matter as an Englishman of the twentieth century. His explanations of primitive customs are more barbarous than the meaning of these customs.

The historical explanation, the explanation as a hypothesis of development, is only one kind of summary of the data – their synopsis. It is equally possible to see the data in their relations to each other and to combine them together into a general schema without doing it in the form of a hypothesis about temporal development.

Identification of one's own Gods with the Gods of another people. Thereby one convinces oneself that the names have the same meaning.

"And so expounds the chorus upon a secret law" one might say to the Frazerian collection of facts. This law, this idea, I can now express (represent) by a developmental hypothesis or even, analogously to the diagram of a plant, by the pattern of a religious ceremony, or even by the grouping of the factual materials alone, in a clearly arranged cognitive schema.

The concept of a clearly arranged cognitive schema is of fundamental importance for us. It signifies our form of representation, the way in which we interpret things. (A kind of "Weltanschauung", as it apparently is typical for our time. Spengler.)

This clearly arranged cognitive schema brings about understanding, which exists just in that we "see the connections." *Thus the importance of the discovery of interconnecting links.*

A hypothetical connecting link, however, should do nothing in this case other than to call attention to the similarity, the connection, of the facts. Like when one *would want* to illustrate (would illustrate) the internal relationship of the form of a circle to the ellipse by this means, that one gradually transforms an ellipse into a circle; but not in order to assert that a certain ellipse had actually, historically, originated from a circle (evolution hypothesis), but in order to *sharpen our eye for a formal relationship.*

But I can also see the evolutionary hypothesis as nothing more than the (a) disguising of a formal relationship.

(7) Wittgenstein's reading about contemporary peasant beliefs and customs in Germany concerning the competition between the reapers and the binders not to be the last to finish because "the wolf sits in the last sheaf," followed by his reading of the Badigas of the Nilgiri Hills of South India laying the sins of their deceased upon a buffalo calf (an act reminiscent of the Jewish scapegoat), stimulates him to contemplate the whole mythology embodied in "our language" and how such knowledge should help in interpreting "their customs and speech forms." (Wittgenstein acknowledged that he took the phrase "The mythology in the forms of our language" from the Austrian writer Paul Ernst, who used it in his preface to an edition of Grimm's *Märchen*.)

Reviewing the points he had made so far, we can say that Wittgenstein has advanced two strategies for interpreting religious/magical views and ritual acts (including ritual speech acts):

(1) Try and identify tendencies, inclinations, motivations in general (universal) human reason and imagination, and in general human existential circumstances, that make man a "ceremonial animal" and give rise to "ritual actions."

(2) Reflect on our own (Western) *cultural heritage*, and the mythological and ritual conceptions embodied in *our own language*, and the fusion in it of "written and spoken signs" and "mental images," and you will see implicit affinities in all ritual actions, whether enacted by the primitive or the modern. Here I think Wittgenstein draws our attention to similarities in the collective cultural representations of humans as social and historical beings.

> In the old rites we have the use of an extremely developed language of gestures.
> And whenever I read Frazer, I would like to say at each point: *all these processes, these changes of meaning, we still have before us in our language of words.* Given that what is concealed in the last bundle of grain, yet also this bundle itself, and also the man who binds it, is called the "Corn Wolf," we recognize in this a language process which is well known to us.
> I would like to say: Nothing shows our relationship with the former savages better than that Frazer has at hand a word that is familiar to him and to us, such as "ghost" or "shade," to describe the views of these people.
> (This is of course different than if he were to write, for instance, how the savages imagined (imagine) that their head falls off when they have killed an enemy. Here there would be nothing superstitious or magical about our description.)
> Yes, this peculiarity is related not only to the expressions "ghost" and "shade" and we have made much too little fuss over the fact that we count the word "soul," "spirit" as part of our own educated vocabulary. *In comparison to that*, it is a *trifle* that we don't believe that our soul eats and drinks.
> *In our language a whole mythology is laid down.*

Final comment

There is a latent tension in Wittgenstein's remarks. Irritated, even angered by Frazer's relentless and condescending attribution of both superstitious fears and reasoning errors to the primitive, Wittgenstein takes the opposite course of trying to demonstrate how we "civilized," both in human endowment and in our linguistic and cultural constructions, are like those "savages."

In proposing this unity of mankind, Wittgenstein reveals a truth that some of our contemporary philosophers have been trying to articulate: that translation of another culture's conceptions into our linguistic categories necessarily implies a "shared space," a "bridgehead of understanding" between the two.

But Wittgenstein is famous for his notions of "forms of life" and "language games", which if pushed in a certain direction also argue for the particularity and contextual nature of historically formed culture complexes and linguistic genres, with their special emphases and centres of gravity. The particularity of forms of life and language games warns against the committing of "category mistakes" by equating and comparing that which is not comparable, and against the too facile assimilation of the conceptions of other peoples' conceptions to our own contemporary Western ones.

Wittgenstein's statements in another text, *On Certainty*, which belongs to the last year and a half of his life (*c.* 1949–51) but contains unmistakable allusions to his reflections on Frazer's *Golden Bough* made almost twenty years previously, might help us to see what he means when he associates explanation with hypotheses and theory, and why he accuses Frazer of misplaced reasoning. A mistake is something which can be tested and shown to be wrong. But the idea of testing already implies some particular system which has as its foundation a set of presuppositions and propositions which cannot themselves be tested or doubted. These propositions make the activity of questioning possible by determining what will count as evidence for arguments and verification. Therefore in order to speak of a mistake, the observer must share the actor's epistemological starting point. Says Wittgenstein: "Whether a proposition can turn out false after all depends on what I make count as determinants for that proposition." "The *truth* of certain empirical propositions belongs to our frame of reference." "All testing, all confirmation and disconfirmation of a hypothesis takes place within a system . . . The system is not so much the point of departure as the element in which arguments have their life." "In order to make a mistake, a man must already judge in conformity with mankind." "When we first begin to *believe* anything, what we believe is not a single proposition, it is a whole system of propositions." "Knowledge is in the end based on acknowledgment."[33] Can we say that Frazer in Wittgenstein's eyes was violating the canons of commensurability, and was making a category mistake?

The tension between the two modalities of universality and particularity contained in anthropology's aspirations to translate as well as compare cultural and social forms is the subject of the concluding chapters of this book. Wittgenstein's remarks on Frazer appear to revolve around these two modalities whose implications are still being explored and articulated in the 1980s.

4

Malinowski's demarcations and his exposition of the magical art

Bronislaw Kaspar Malinowski,[1] born in Cracow, Poland in 1884, died in New Haven, Connecticut in 1942, is instructive for us as a kind of negation of the Tylor–Frazer points of view (of seeing science, magic, religion in a developmental perspective, and of seeing magic and religion as phenomena that had to be tested against the yardstick of scientific rationality). Interestingly enough, the early part of his career was in the sciences: his doctorate was in physics and mathematics, and it is alleged that during an illness, which prevented his continuing his scientific studies, he read Frazer's *Golden Bough* and was filled with such enthusiasm that he became an anthropologist.

It is intriguing then that, like the Father of American Anthropology, Franz Boas, another emigrant, from Germany this time, who was also first trained as a scientist and at the end of an intellectual odyssey founded the science of culture, Malinowski found his way to London (to the London School of Economics), and thereafter to New Guinea partly at least owing to the constraints and accidents of the First World War, and founded the self-proclaimed school of Functionalism, whose basic point of reference was an anti-Durkheimian individualistic pragmatic psychology.

It is intriguing, but not altogether mystifying in an expatriate who had taken to a new country (he is said to have had an exaggerated respect for England and things English) and a new discipline, that Malinowski *qua* anthropologist rarely referred to his Polish intellectual cultural and political antecedents and how they may have contributed to his "functionalism." And it is somewhat remarkable that Malinowski's British disciples also seemingly evinced little interest in their guru's past, and tended to see his anthropological perspective as cut out of whole cloth.

In recent years, interesting information has surfaced concerning the intellectual influences and contexts to which Malinowski was exposed in Poland quite early in his career, and which helped to shape his later scientific and ideological positions as a professional anthropologist.[2] Malinowski's father, Lucjan, was professor of Slavonic Philology at Cracow University. Malinowski's studies at the same historic Jagellonian University in Cracow were chiefly in physics, mathematics and philosophy, and there he read and was influenced by the writings of Ernst Mach, Richard Avenarius, Wilhelm Wundt and others. Indeed Malinowski's doctoral dissertation, entitled "On the Economy of Thought", was centrally concerned with the ideas of Ernst Mach, who was an exponent of a certain type of positivist scientific methodology.[3]

Some of Mach's ideas that are thought to have influenced Malinowski are as follows: Mach launched "a sustained critique of any philosophy of science which fails to take account of the observer and his position relative to the object of observation, or which fails to take account of the cognitive structure of the human mind in its account of scientific method."[4] Mach's positivism which entailed the "concept of 'field' and holism in the physical sciences" is possibly reflected in Malinowski's insistence that the "empirical ethnographic fact must always be evaluated in the context of the whole."[5] Machian positivism included a biological interpretation of knowledge: "It sees ideas as serving a total organism, and as vindicated by constituting the most 'economical' way of serving the organism's needs . . . This leads, in a very natural way to Malinowski's functionalism, and to his holistic attitude to culture."[6]

Evidence provided by Malinowski's daughter[7] shows that Malinowski was developing interests that presaged his later career. After his doctorate in 1908, he studied at Leipzig University until 1910, and there attended courses on Völkerpsychologie taught by Wilhelm Wundt, and worked in economics under Karl Bücher. Indeed by 1908 he had already developed his new interest in anthropology from reading German and English anthropological literature. We should also keep in mind that Malinowski was possibly influenced by the ethnographic and linguistic work of his father and his colleagues.

Between 1910 and 1914 Malinowski studied at the London School of Economics under Seligman and Westermarck, read at the British Museum, and began to make his mark in British anthropology. In 1924 he became Reader at the L.S.E. and in 1927 he rose to the top as Professor of Social Anthropology.

It is interesting that Edmund Leach is one of the few students of Malinowski who have probed Malinowski's philosophical and scientific presuppositions. Being unaware of the details of Malinowski's intellectual antecedents in Cracow, Leach imaginatively surmised that Malinowski's functionalism showed affinity with the philosophy of Pragmatism of William James, which was influential at the time of Malinowski's transplantation to London.[8] We may view Leach as analogically supplementing and deepening our understanding of Malinowski, even if there is no direct proof of the latter's debt to James.

William James's Pragmatism (which in turn owed much to the ideas of Charles Peirce whose semiotics enjoys high fashion today) had its maximum vogue around 1910, the year Malinowski arrived in London and began his studies there. William James argued that the main function of thought was to satisfy certain interests of the organism, and this criterion constituted a measure of truth. James's Pragmatism, while appreciative of the evidence of directly observable facts, and while recognizing that strict logic cannot lead to or be involved in metaphysical judgments, yet supposed metaphysical judgments to have a psychological basis in reason. Thus he argued that it is reasonable and valid to believe and to embrace whatever thought (and behavior) can be shown to be biologically satisfying to the individual, even though such a consequence cannot be verified by experiment or rational argument. Malinowski's perspective, which constituted the heart of his functionalist position, was that certain kinds of behaviour are entirely reasonable because they are based in psychological or organic needs. His interpretation of magic and religion in particular was formulated from this vantage point. It was a dogma for Malinowski that all human beings were reasonable, that is, sensibly practical individuals, and as Leach has remarked, Malinowski's biggest guns were directed "against notions that might be held to imply that, in the last analysis, the individual is not a personality on his own possessing the capacity for free choice based in reason."[9]

Malinowski left for Australia in 1914 to embark on his fieldwork, and he returned to England in 1920. The circumstances of the First World War that forced him to stay down under, and the details of his adventurous field trips in New Guinea and to the Trobriand Islands, interspersed with trips to Australia to write, to recuperate and to conduct his ardent courtship, have been documented in some detail.[10] I therefore only need to draw attention to the inspiration and legitimation that this experience provided for his anthropological assertions. Unlike the Victorian armchair theorists, Malinowski pioneered the techniques of fieldwork, especially participant observation, that have become the distinguishing badge of the profession. Frazer, ensconced in his study at Trinity College, Cambridge, is alleged to have replied to William James's query about his undoubted personal knowledge of some of the savages about whom he wrote so profusely, "God forbid that I should encounter a savage in the flesh!" By comparison, Malinowski preened like a peacock about his live experience and first-hand observations of the primitives. He once remarked "Rivers is the Rider Haggard of Anthropology: I shall be the Conrad."[11] This comparison with another great expatriate Pole is suggestive. But his vanity also participated in a Frazerian universalist ambition: Malinowski it is said jumped from the Trobriand Islands (tiny specks off the New Guinea coast) to humanity at large, of which he too spoke in grandiloquent terms.

Malinowski's demarcations between magic, science, and religion

Malinowski sharply separated off science from magic. Science was a "profane" activity, while magic grouped with religion belonged to the "sacred" domain. (This demarcation is basically opposed to Tylor's and Frazer's scheme, which grouped magic with science as "pseudo-science".)

Malinowski's characterization of "science" was both simplistic and generous when he actually credited the Trobrianders with the possession of scientific knowledge. It is simplistic when judged in terms of the delineation of science by contemporary philosophers and historians of science as a self-conscious, reflexive, open-ended process of knowledge construction. Said Malinowski with a flourish: "If by science be understood a body of rules and conceptions, based on experience and derived from it by logical inference, embodied in material achievements and in a fixed form of tradition and carried on by some sort of social organization," then even the lowest savage has science however rudimentary. He went so far as to claim that even judged against a more rigorous definition of science – for example, the formulation of explicit rules open to experiment and critique by reason – the Trobrianders possessed sciences, as instanced by the grasp of hydrodynamics in canoe building.

Comparison of religion and magic

Malinowski did not address in any significant way in his actual ethnographic works – such as *Argonauts, The Sexual Life of Savages, Coral Gardens and their Magic* – the question of how he would distinguish between religion and magic. I surmise that he did not do so principally because the Trobrianders themselves did not have an indigenous category term for "religion" or its analogue, and Malinowski would therefore have found it difficult to make the demarcation stick. Whereas "magic" and "garden work" (practical activity) were Trobriand categories, there was no local notion that he might have translated as "religion."

But he did try to demarcate religion from magic in his *Magic, Science and Religion and Other Essays* (1948). There he first makes the sacred/profane cut, and lumps religion and magic with the sacred, and science with the profane. The sacred he defined as traditional acts and observances regarded by the natives as sacred and carried out with reverence and awe, and hedged around with prohibitions. Such acts are associated with supernatural forces. The profane he related to arts and crafts (hunting, fishing, tilling, woodwork and so on) which were carried out on the basis of careful empirical observation of natural process and a firm belief in nature's regularity.[12]

While we may declare Malinowski unduly loose in his "demarcation" and comparative use of the concept "science," what makes him unusually interesting is that he, more than any anthropologist up to that time, insisted that a primary issue to address was how, within the confines of a single society or culture, "symbolic" activities like ritual and magic were linked to and interacted with activities of a practical or "pragmatic" character.

In other words, he raised the question how we are to understand man's participation in at least two modes of reality, man's readiness to shift from one context to the other, and also how we are to see them as complementary in relationship. Before we tackle this important topic, let us dispose of Malinowski's general pronouncements on religion.

Every organized religion, says Malinowski (in his famous "Magic, Science and Religion" essay), "must have a dogmatic system backed by mythology, a developed ritual in which man acts on his belief and communes with the powers of the unseen world; there must also be an ethical code of rules which binds the faithful and determines their behaviour towards each other and towards the things they worship."

Although he was capable of this kind of inclusive definition of religion, Malinowski essentially distinguished religion not in the famous Robertson-Smith and Durkheim mode of associating religion with *collective* organizational forms, especially a church and its congregation (and magic with individual self-interested practice) or in the Tylorian modes in terms of animistic beliefs in spiritual beings and the cults associated with them. Instead Malinowski defined religion by function, primarily psychological and secondarily sociological, and in terms of a means (instrumental) and ends (ultimate purposes) distinction.

Religious action was not like magic a means to an end, it was an end in itself and it celebrated ultimate values, such as Providence and Immortality.

The subject matter of every religion is the twin beliefs in Providence and Immortality. The first implies a supernatural agent or essence who is in sympathy with man's destinies and with whom man feels he must communicate. The second deals with the question of continuance after death whether it be reincarnation or some form of after-life. "Religion is rooted in human life" – for the individual it answers to spiritual needs, for society it provides social integration. Again: "Religious development consists primarily in the growing predominance of the ethical principle and in the increasing fusion of the two main factors of all belief, the sense of Providence and the faith in Immortality."

Providence meant for Malinowski the importance attributed to God as the provider for man's biological and psychological needs, and this dependence is manifest in the rules for handling food and the values placed on sacrifice and communion and on exchanges of food gifts. Totemism too expresses man's natural selective interest in nature as provider: as Lévi-Strauss has said, this view comes close to giving a utilitarian explanation by which animals are sacred because they are good to eat. Death and mortuary rites are quintessentially religious: They express the force of emotive attachments and reactions to loved ones, and spring from a spontaneous attitude of horror of death and love for the deceased. Religious acts are in such contexts acts of faith – the belief in immortality is a voice of hope. In religious rites, means and ends are one. Initiation rites and marriage rites are not meant to "cause" the end in question, they are in themselves this transformation, heralding lasting attitudes and stable relationships. (Here one can compliment Malinowski as anticipating the Austinian notion of a "performative" act: more of this later.) Again, once again attempting to illustrate his means–ends relation, he contrasted initiation rites, which are religious because their function is the inculcation and maintenance of collective traditions valued for themselves, with childbirth rites which are magical because they are directed to the practical aim of safe child delivery.

Although Malinowski as a good individualist and pragmatist maintained that society was merely a vehicle for enacting religious beliefs based in individual psychology and reason (such as the notion of immortality), he was well aware of the implications of religious rites as public and collective enactments, and documented the social functions deriving from this public aspect. (He went so far as to say, however, that the public aspect and publicity of ritual are a matter of technique.)

In sum, it is difficult to maintain that Malinowski was an important thinker on religion. His views on it were a mixture of derivative Christian theology and pragmatist considerations akin to the doctrines of William James that however threatened to deteriorate into crude utilitarianism. It has therefore been rightly said that Malinowski's view of religion comes close to Plato's notion of the "noble lie." It is however upon his analysis of Trobriand magic that he expended his imaginative energies, and deployed his linguistic skills and observational powers. It is on the subject of magic that he excelled and scintillated, even though he sometimes overdid the rhetoric and overworked his narrow psychology.

The sacred and the profane

Malinowski adopts the Durkheimian dichotomy – sacred versus profane – but his demarcation only bears a superficial resemblance to Durkheim's partition.[13] Malinowski identified the domain of the profane with practical and technical activity (agriculture, canoe building stripped of the ceremonial features), which he associated with the Trobriander's "rational mastery" of his surroundings, and this again, as we have seen before, he over-enthusiastically assimilated to "science."[14] The sacred therefore embraced all those types of thought and action manifest in religion and magic, and which were concerned with metaphysical relations. Thus Malinowski's partitioning would not admit any such proposition as that made by Durkheim in *The Elementary Forms of the Religious Life* that religion (and magic) was the forerunner of science, especially as regards the concept of force and necessary connections between things.

The disaggregation and interlacing of magic and practical/technical activity in Trobriand life

I consider as one of Malinowski's foremost contributions – and this is related to his demarcation between the sacred and the profane – his descriptions of how the separate strands of magic and practical activity were interlaced to form the braid (or double-helix as I am tempted to say) of Trobriand life. For example, consider this passage from *Coral Gardens*[15] in which Malinowski, using somewhat different language from mine, speaks of ritual and technical sequences as being "parallel":

The association between technical pursuit and its magical counterpart is, as we know, very close, and to the natives essential. The sequence of technical stages, on the one hand, and of rites and spells, on the other, run parallel. The place of a magical act is strictly determined. There are inaugurative rites such as *yowoto* or *gabu*, there are concluding rites such as *vilamalia* and the last act of *kaytubutala*.

Malinowski's most ample and colourful ethnography relates to the widespread and ramifying role of magical rites in every aspect of Trobriand life, and in my essay *The Magical Power of Words* (which was first delivered as the Malinowski Memorial Lecture at L.S.E. in 1968)[16] I came to the conclusion after a close analysis that indeed an important and problematic question was being posed: how are we to describe and interpret the interlacing of magical and technical acts to form an amalgam or, if you prefer, a total activity, which we may label as Trobriand "yam cultivation" or Trobriand "canoe building", activities that covered long stretches of time and combined multiple modalities?

The issues posed by the Malinowski ethnography constitute puzzles for us even to this day: In almost all societies there are on the one hand rites that are set apart and take place as special enactments removed from the doings of everyday life. Examples are cosmic festivals (e.g. Festival of Lights in India or Visākha Pūjā in Thailand, which commemorates the birth, death and enlightenment of the Buddha); rites of passage such as baptism, or wedding or funeral rites; and rites of affliction such as exorcism ceremonies. These enactments are eminently analyzable in terms of the Van Gennep tripartite scheme of separation, liminality, and (re)-aggregation, which among modern anthropologists Victor Turner above all has brilliantly exploited in his discussion of the ritual process.

But these same societies also conduct all kinds of ritual cycles or intermittent rites that are interlaced with practical activities like agriculture, or crafts, or fishing, and here both kinds of action, technical and magical/religious, constitute amalgams and, though often internally distinguished, in a sense occupy the same space such that a simplistic disaggregation into technical aspects and expressive aspects is not possible.

The art of magic

By far the most significant and innovative part of Malinowski's ethnography in *Argonauts, Coral Gardens,* and *The Sexual Life of Savages* speaks to, what in contemporary jargon I would call, a dramatistic and performative view of the magical performance, and a special sensitivity to the role of language in magical acts.

But before I treat this issue, I have to separate the dross (of which there was a generous amount) from the gold, and I also have to argue that the nuggets of gold frequently lie not where Malinowski explicitly said they were (though he implicitly knew deeper truths).

A basic assertion of Malinowski's was that magic serves two functions, one psychological the other sociological, and of these the former was primary and the basic source of inspiration.

But as it turns out his psychological thesis was both naive and easily falsified in terms of his own data. Magic comes into play, he said, whenever primitive man "has to recognize the impotence of his knowledge and of his rational technique." In other words magic is resorted to in those contexts where man's technical control of nature has reached its insufficient limits. Magic is thus directed towards the uncontrollable agencies which affect the success of its practical activities. This is a species of explanation that one may label as "anxiety reduction" and "compensatory action."

In the form it is stated – that magic begins where technology ends – it is easily refuted. Malinowski's famous example was that in the Trobriands lagoon fishing is safe and invites no magic, but deep-sea fishing is dangerous and the uncertain elements of the ocean are not easily controlled, so magical rites are resorted to. But in this comparison Malinowski fails to inform us that unlike the products of lagoon fishing, deep-sea fishing yields shark, which had a high ritual valuation in the Trobriand scheme of things. And therefore there may be other considerations than sheer danger that may have surrounded deep-sea fishing with ritual.

But gardening provides us with an internal test. In Trobriand agriculture the cultivation of yams and taro is surrounded with profuse magic while the cultivation of coconut and mango is not. Trobriand interest in, and control of, yam and taro cultivation techniques was impressive and a matter of great pride, and the good yam and taro gardener enjoyed prestige. So the technical criterion does not yield an answer as to why Trobriand yam gardening is suffused with magic, while coconut gardening is not.

A different kind of answer to this puzzle is suggested by the facts that the Trobrianders lay great stress on the obligations of *urigubu* payments (by which a man has to make annual payments of yams to his sister's husband), and the fulfillment of this obligation is tied to the high social valuation of a good gardener. Moreover, the fact that these gifts of yams were exhibited in yam houses for all to see until they rotted simply underscores the social valuations of generous gifts and conspicuous display which illuminate the social concerns surrounding the magic rather than the technological in-adequacies. In other words, we have to look more at the social valuations and social imperatives which indicate which of a society's economic activities are important to it, and to relate that society's rituals and ceremonials to its anticipations and anxieties in the realization of social values rather than to insufficiencies presented by raw nature or by technology. Malinowski himself coined the felicitous expression "anticipatory affirmations of prosperity and plenty" which inspired magical ritual, an expression that throws more light on

Trobriand psychology than the thesis of reduction of anxiety caused by technological insufficiency.

Moreover, as our previous case studies have shown, both in early Greece and in seventeenth-century England – as described in the works of Geoffrey Lloyd and Keith Thomas – "magical" explanations and practices (consisting of the attempted manipulation of occult powers and agents for achieving practical benefits) were rejected in favour of "naturalistic" explanations before these latter could provide better practical and technological results. There is also evidence against the reverse implication in Malinowski's hypothesis: that if man developed adequate technical procedures for dealing with a task, then any previous "magical" ritual connected with that task ought automatically to disappear.

Malinowski's discovery of the sociological function of magic is then of far greater import than his psychological theorizing. He saw how the calendar of magical rites inaugurated, marked out, phased out, regulated and carried through to a successful conclusion activities such as gardening, and fishing and canoe building and overseas *kula* expeditions. He saw how the ritual expert and specialist, by conducting imperative ceremonies, actually thereby mobilized manpower and resources and that the rites served as triggering mechanisms for the sustained conduct of practical operations. All these insights were exploited and elaborated by Raymond Firth in his masterly work, *Primitive Polynesian Economy*.

How does magic work?

Malinowski had two specific insights into the internal structure and constitution of Trobriand rites. The first was that they exploited simultaneously both words and acts, both speech and the manipulation of objects and substances, thereby posing the problem of the logic of use of multiple media in ritual for his successors to ponder over. Secondly his so-called 'ethnographic theory of the magical word" proposed some illuminating insights which foreshadowed and anticipated in England Austin's "linguistic philosophical" notions of performative force carried by speech acts, that is, how speech acts created both illocutionary and perlocutionary effects by virtue of being conventional acts; and in this country, Kenneth Burke's discussion of the "rhetoric of motives."

For Malinowski there were three elements or constituents of the magical performance: the *formula*, the *rite* and the *condition of the performer*. We may quickly enumerate these as the distinctive features of Trobriand ritual he never tired of expatiating:

(1) The dramatic expression of emotion, the essence of the magical act, through kinesic gestures and movements.

(2) The use of objects and substances, which were "impregnated" with the recited words, and to which through a "rubbing effect" were transferred

certain potencies. The techniques by which the power of the spell is transferred to the charmed object he vividly portrayed.[17]

(3) But above all, Malinowski selected the spell as the most critical component of the Trobriand magical system, and dissected its tripartite structure (the foundation [*u'ula*], the body [*tapwana*], and the tip [*dogina*]), and the various powers it radiated as magical word. The components that generated these powers were: phonetic effects including onomatopoeic words; words of an imperative kind that evoked, stated and commanded certain feeling states and certain consequences; constructions that retrospectively referred back to myths of origins and the pedigrees of ancestors, thereby serving as pragmatic charters for present practice; and strings of words that prospectively looked forward to anticipatory effects. He coined the phrases "verbal missile" and the "creative metaphor of speech" to convey the efficacy of magical words. It is pertinent to note that Malinowski in expounding the creative power of sacred words compared their significance to the binding character of "legal formulas," and comes very close to explaining their efficacy in Austinian terms – that "saying is doing" under the appropriate conventions and conditions.

The ethnographic theory of the magical word

Malinowski expounded at length his ethnographic theory of the magical word in volume 2 of *The Coral Gardens and their Magic*. He reported that the Trobrianders themselves made a distinction between the language of magic (*megwa la biga*) and the language of ordinary speech (*livala la biga*) – a distinction that brings to mind another we discussed earlier between the road of magic and the road of gardening. He attributed the special character of Trobriand ritual speech to such features as these:

(1) Their intrinsic character such as their being sacred and set apart from ordinary linguistic uses, their containing distinct prosodic features including even "meaningless" words which are supposed to exercise special influence.

(2) The context of native belief, which included the native belief in a world pervaded by sympathetic affinities and powerful forces (*mana*); but more importantly the belief that magical speech, man-made, existed from the very beginning as primeval text coeval with reality, and could be launched as "breath" and transformed into magical missiles by accredited magicians.

(3) The "coefficient of weirdness" that magical speech contained (as compared with the higher "coefficient of intelligibility" of ordinary speech), and this was indexed by strange and archaic grammatical forms, condensed structures, words containing esoteric meanings, and strange mythological and metaphorical references and allusions which have to be laboriously tracked by ethnographic inquiry. (As he said: "Weirdness yields to treatment as soon as we place the spells within their context.")

On the basis of this evidence Malinowski came to the conclusion that there

From garden cultivation to harvest distribution and festivals in the Trobriand Islands in the 1970s

Plate 4.1 A Kiriwinan man planting yams with traditional stone tool in the 1970s.

Plate 4.2 A Kiriwinan woman weeding around new yam shoots. A new yam shoot is being trained to grow up a pole in foreground.

Plates 4.3 and 4.4 A group of girls bringing in yams from the gardens during harvest, and building a display before loading them in the yam houses.

Plate 4.5 Loading the ample decorated yam houses of a chief at harvest time.

Plate 4.6 A competitive "long yam", about four feet long, grown through the combined use of skill and magic.

Plate 4.7 Men dressed in skirts and cockatoo feathers performing a harvest dance called *bisila*.

Plate 4.1

Plate 4.2

Plate 4.3

Plate 4.4

Plate 4.5

78

Plate 4.6

Plate 4.7

79

are two crystallizations of language in all societies – the language of technology and science versus the language of "magic and persuasion." In expounding the nature of the latter he drew upon examples from our own contemporary Western world and thereby helped to bring some of the esoteric and mystifying features of magic within the scope of understanding of a modern (Western) man's experience. One example he gave was the language of advertising and the "beauty magic of Helena Rubinstein and Elizabeth Arden." (Trobriand beauty magic by which young men hoped to seduce young women or ambitious men their *kula* partners becomes more comprehensible for contemporary Americans when viewed in terms of the T.V. advertisements that continually bombard us daily, nay hourly, nay every few minutes: such as that if you use a particular deodorant or soap you might make it with your date and so on.) I ask you therefore: how is it that many of us "moderns" are prepared to accept Madison Avenue advertising labelled as "selling costs" as an essential component of rational economics and of the rational theory of the firm, and not grant a similar compliment to Trobriand *kula* magic? Another example, indicated by Malinowski, is the rhetoric of political speeches and the public orations of politicians. In this country when in 1984 the Presidential race was staged, and in 1985, when President Reagan and Gorbachev were grooming themselves for the arms control meetings in Geneva, we were saturated by the rhetoric of these alleged "great communicators."

A third example is the binding character of "legal formulas" which is "at the very foundation of order and reliability in human relations."[18] It is for these reasons that I say that Malinowski's expositions come close to – even anticipate – the notions of performative speech expounded by Austin and other linguistic philosophers – that "saying is doing," when done by the properly accredited persons according to proper conventions under the right conditions.

Pointing to marriage vows Malinowski said that whether they were treated as sacrament or as mere legal contract, they portray "the power of words in establishing a permanent human relation"; the average man he argued must have "a deep belief in the sanctity of legal and sacral words and their creative power" if social order is to exist. There is thus "a very real basis to human belief in the mystic and binding power of words."[19]

The unsettled issues

It would be foolish to claim that Malinowski – whatever his superiority to Tylor and Frazer – has explained to us beyond doubt how to construe Trobriand magic, let alone magical ritual elsewhere. One unsettled issue on which he vacillated, and argued on both sides, is the question whether magical speech – or as I prefer to say ritual speech – is a different genre from ordinary speech or is an intensification of ordinary speech like poetic diction. While in certain contexts he argued for their difference, he also at other places affirmed that ritual speech was in important respects like common language because of its purposive objectives. Magical speech thus "presents significant speech under the guise of esoterica and mysterious forms," it is "but part of the universal, essentially human attitude of all men to all words" (p. 233).

Indeed in characteristic fashion he resorted to an ontogenetic or biographical approach to explain the origins of magical speech, and laid it at the door of infantile experiences. When the child's early cries and babbling evoke the mother's services the child has its first experiences of the power of words. Citing Piaget, Bühler and Stern (p. 233) Malinowski traced the origins to this early experience: "The child actually exercises a quasi-magical influence over its surroundings. He utters a word, and what he needs is done for him by his adult entourage." And he concluded with a flourish – just as when he tried to explain kinship terminology by the same argument – "The development of speech in humanity must have its fundamental principles, being of the same type as the development of speech within the life history of the individual" (p. 232). Thus while Malinowski's origins of magical speech remind us also of Freud's tracing of the child's illusory sense of omnipotence to its infantile wishes and experience, we have to concede that the biographical approach does not decisively settle the problem of the relation of magical speech to ordinary speech.

The second unsettled issue is whether we can unambiguously elucidate the character of the efficacy (or lack of efficacy) of Trobriand magical ritual. Malinowski's answer, when he was pushed to it, was that magic was "objectively" false but that it was "subjectively" true to the actors. But it was also true in the sense of being a "pragmatic" truth, that is in a sense that we may find stated in William James's Pragmatism. It was psychologically true in that it was "reasonable" in terms of addressing certain psychological needs of the individual, and it was sociologically true because its practice raised the optimism and hopes of the human beings, who heard and saw it performed, and because it had multiple positive social consequences. A magician's spell and manipulations may not objectively, causally and directly affect the processes of nature (the garden soil and the plants growing on it could not respond to the magical words and acts), but these words and acts did influence the human witnesses and through them produced consequences by affecting their intentions and their motivations and their expectations. So Malinowski's answer would be that magic was pragmatically effective by creating a change of state in the human actors.

A digression on Kenneth Burke

Since in my earlier writings I have used some aspects of the linguistic philosophy of Austin, Searle and Grice, and some features of Charles Peirce's semiotics, to expound the performative features of ritual,[20] but have never referred to Kenneth Burke, let me take this opportunity to include him in my pantheon.

Kenneth Burke in his *Rhetoric of Motives* explicitly refers to Malinowski, who may be taken to have anticipated some features of his theory of rhetoric, and Burke himself may be included among those who would wish us to move away from seeing magic as "bad science" to seeing it instead as "rhetorical art."

Burke has stated that the basic function of rhetoric is "the use of words by human agents to form attitudes or to induce actions in other human agents."[21] Magic therefore is "primitive rhetoric," "it is rooted in an essential function of language itself, a function that is wholly realistic, and is actually born anew; the use of language as a symbolic means of inducing cooperation in beings that by nature respond to symbols."[22] This attribution of a "real" linguistic function to magic thus appeals to a "reality" of a different kind judged by science to be true or false.

Burke is essentially in accord with Malinowski when he asserts that "The 'pragmatic sanction' for this function of magic lies outside the realm of strictly true-or-false propositions; it falls in an area of deliberation that itself draws upon the resources of rhetoric; it is itself a subject matter belonging to an art that can 'prove opposites'."[23] By "proving opposites" Burke is referring to rhetoric that tries to persuade you to accept the truth of tendentious advocacy; for example, the assertion that U.S. commercial investment in Saudi Arabia is truly good because it will help transform that country's unsavoury feudal structure, whereas the true intent of that speech may be to persuade the American public to approve its country's expansionist policy. The present-day U.S. involvement in El Salvador and Nicaragua can be subject to similar analysis.

But the theory of rhetoric does not completely solve our puzzle about the form and intentions behind Trobriand magical acts. When the chips are down, Burke in effect agrees with Malinowski that though magic may be a false technical act it is a true social act (i.e. it acts upon the human actors rather than upon nature). Burke's formulation reads: "The realistic use of addressed language *to induce action in people* became the magical use of addressed language *to induce motion in things* (things by nature alien to purely linguistic orders of motivation)."[24] This transposition in the use of language implies then that magic, whatever its social efficacy, has an aspect of "distorted" communication.

So it would seem that we cannot yet completely exorcize the ghosts of Tylor and Frazer. Let us therefore for the present leave aside the puzzle posed by magic by virtue of its "duality" or dual structure. On the one hand, it seems to imitate the logic of technical/technological action that seeks to transform nature or the world of natural things and manifestations. On the other hand, its structure is also transparently rhetorical and performative (in that it consists of acts to create effects on human actors according to accepted social conventions). Tylor and Frazer fastened exclusively on the first equation and said it was bad science; Malinowski appreciated the force of the second equation and said that magic was constituted of speech acts in a performative and persuasive mode, and that therefore they were pragmatically reasonable. My own feeling is that one of the most fruitful interpretive developments in recent anthropology, a development that has still to be completed and exhausted, is that kind of exegesis begun by Malinowski, and taken further by recourse to Wittgensteinian and Austinian linguistic philosophy, Peircean pragmatics and Burke's theory of rhetoric. The now puzzling duality of magic will disappear only when we succeed in embedding magic in a more ample theory of human life in which the path of ritual action is seen as an indispensable mode for man anywhere and everywhere of relating to and participating in the life of the world.

5

Multiple orderings of reality: the debate initiated by Lévy-Bruhl

On Lévy-Bruhl (1857–1939)

Lévy-Bruhl was first and foremost a philosopher. He was nominated to the chair of the history of modern philosophy at the Sorbonne in 1904. His first published writings were in philosophy, of which the most important was a work of "refined and skeptical positivism" (as Gurvitch put it) entitled *Ethics and Moral Science* (1903). It was followed by some six volumes on the subject of "primitive mentality."[1]

Already in his first philosophical work on morals he had come to the conclusion that the search for universally valid "theoretical moralities," or a universal science of "theoretical ethics," was doomed to failure, and that since moralities do vary with time and place they should be studied objectively as social formations. Thus in this book Lévy-Bruhl made a frontal attack on the postulate of the unity of human nature and was laying the foundations of his relativistic and pluralistic sociology.[2] Lévy-Bruhl became interested in primitive mentality because by comparing with it the mentality of civilized man, which was the furthest removed from it, he could prove his pluralistic and relativistic thesis.

It is important to realize that Lévy-Bruhl posed the antithesis to the Tylor–Frazer position in that he was not speaking from the point of view of individualistic psychology or the laws of universal individual endowment but, like Durkheim, was referring to collective representations and the influence of collectivities on individuals. Secondly, while of course importantly taking into account the ideas of Durkheim and Mauss with whom he debated, Lévy-Bruhl deviated from them by not entertaining any thesis of continuous development from primitive thought to modern thought. Lévy-Bruhl would not accept Durkheim's thesis that ideas of force contained in (primitive) religion were the precursors of the idea of causality in modern science. Needless to say, Lévy-Bruhl therefore also had no sympathy for the evolutionary ladder of progress from savagery to civilization preached by Tylor and Frazer, though he did advance his own view of the transition.[3]

Now it has to be acknowledged that Lévy-Bruhl's earlier ideas were radically modified, in the face of criticisms, in his later works, especially in that work posthumously published as his notebooks, *Les Carnets de Lucien Lévy-Bruhl* (1949). His mind was in constant evolution and by the end of his life he had made the shift from a skeptical positivism to the sociology of knowledge and a phenomenological interpretation of the primitive's experience.[4] In his earlier phase he had proposed the challenging thesis that the primitive mentality is not to be considered an earlier, or a rudimentary, or a pathological form of the modern civilized mentality, but as manifesting processes and procedures of thinking that were altogether different from the laws of modern logical rational scientific thought.

He unfortunately chose to describe primitive mentality as "prelogical mentality," in opposition to the modern "logical mentality," but he also dubbed it "mystical mentality" which was a less problematic label. But it is not the labels that should interest us but his substantive characterization of this mentality as suffused with the laws and relations of *participation*.

By "prelogical," Lévy-Bruhl had in mind the notion that primitive thought as a collective representation (and I insist he was not *for the most part* referring to the issue of innate structures of the individual mind and brain) did not portray rules similar to those followed in modern logic – such as the laws of contradiction, and the rules of inference and proof. By "mystical" mentality Lévy-Bruhl meant beliefs in supra-sensible forces: since the "savage," he pointed out, had made no demarcation between a domain of nature as opposed to the supernatural, it was better to describe his view of certain beings, forces or powers as "supra-sensible" rather than as beliefs in "supernatural beings." He was only too conscious of the problem of translation and asserted that the thought of primitives proceeded "along a path in which it is very difficult to follow it."

Lévy-Bruhl put the problem this way in *How Natives Think (Les Fonctions)* (1910): Do the collective representations of primitive societies derive from higher mental functions that are identical with our own, or must they be related to a mentality that differs from our own?[5] Lévy-Bruhl's critique of Comte and his British followers went like this. Philosophical inquiry and applied science appeared to have raised Western thought to a commanding height from which the thought systems of others could be confidently measured. The aim of anthropology, many Victorians held, was to explain how the simpler peoples' erroneous conceptions had originated. "But it was at the same time desired to demonstrate," remarks Needham, "that the errors were reasonable ones, understandable in the circumstances, such as evolution naturally tended to correct and which could more speedily be eradicated as the savages copied European standards of observation and discourse."[6] The anthropologist's unquestioned task was to find out where and why the primitives had gone astray. Lévy-Bruhl proposed in place of this the idea that it was not that primitive thought was "irrational", or had misapplied the laws of thought, but that it had its own characteristic organization, coherence and rationality. This organization was the *"law of participation."*

It is the relations of *participation* then that deserve our closest scrutiny and our empathetic understanding, because I believe – and this is the theme of this chapter – that the doublet of concepts, *participation* versus *causality*, raises the issue of the two coexistent mentalities or two coexistent modes of thought and action in mankind, that in turn opens a window onto the enormous and pregnant, but clouded issue, of *science* versus *religion*.

Participation, according to Lévy-Bruhl, signified the association between persons and things in primitive thought to the point of *identity* and *consubstantiality*. What Western thought would think to be logically distinct aspects of reality, the primitive may fuse into one mystic unity.[7]

One of the most intriguing exegeses Lévy-Bruhl gave was the relation between the primitive personality and society. Primitive personality is much broader, because it incorporates the idea of *mana* emanating from the individual as suffusing his shadow, hair and nails, his clothes and his environment. On the other hand, primitive personality is much less differentiated than our conception of it and is less ample in content. "The notion of society, too, is entirely different for the primitive mind. Society consists not only of the living but also of the dead, who continue to 'live' somewhere in the neighborhood and take an active part in social life before they die a second time . . . the dead reincarnate in the living and, in accordance with the principle of mystical participation, society is as much merged in the individual as the individual is merged in society. Thus Durkheim's legend of an archaic society that transcends and absorbs the individual must be abandoned once and for all."

An Australian horde does not "own" in our terms of property ownership its hereditary land, for it cannot conceive separation from it. When a Bororo declares himself to be a parakeet he means precisely that: an inexplicable mystical identity of himself and the bird.[8] This sense of participation is not merely a (metaphorical) representation for it implies a physical and mystical union. The primitive mind, said Lévy-Bruhl, unlike our own notions of causality, is indifferent to "secondary" causes (or intervening mechanisms): the connection between cause and effect is immediate and intermediate links are not recognized.

Lévy-Bruhl discussed as examples of participation such familiar phenomena as taboos and avoidances, rites of intensification, rites of severance: in describing these events as showing a participation between the dead, especially the ancestors, and spirits and deities with the living, he made as much sense of them as Tylor or Frazer did. Moreover, the manner of the ritual handling of materia medica in ritual healing, where mystical relations were also implicated, was also no less plausibly handled in terms of his theory.[9]

What Lévy-Bruhl struggled to describe under the concept of participation was in fact carried further and clarified by his friend Maurice Leenhardt who, unlike Lévy-Bruhl, had a deep first-hand knowledge of Melanesian life. I shall come to Leenhardt later, but let me remark here in passing, that Lévy-Bruhl's concept of participation, which he strove to illustrate from missionary and travel accounts of primitive peoples, has been magnificently documented by Foucault in *The Order of Things*, in terms of that sixteenth-century European thought known as the "doctrine of signatures," in which the notion of "resemblance" played a key role in the relation between man and the phenomena of his cosmos.[10]

Now between 1910 and 1938, Lévy-Bruhl faced critical comments from his French colleagues, and from Evans-Pritchard, whose essays written in Cairo in the early 1930s, and his later *magnum opus, Witchcraft, Oracles and Magic Among the Azande* (1937), were in an important sense a dialogue with Lévy-Bruhl.[11] As a result Lévy-Bruhl modified his earlier views and also clarified his final position in *Les Carnets*.

The two most interesting assertions in the Lévy-Bruhl corpus in their final distilled state are as follows:

(1) The first is that the acceptance of notions of the psychic unity of mankind and of a "fundamental structure of the mind" everywhere does not put in jeopardy his thesis that the collective representations of different societies could be built upon cultural premises and categories very different from the modern scientific and mathematico-logical form of thought and knowledge, which also must be seen as a collective phenomenon. There is a further implication to this view, that there might be principles of thought in earlier or pre-modern socio-cultural contexts, that have internal connections and "logics" or coherences of their own and these thought systems were totalities, which differed from our dominant forms of modern thought to such a degree that our own cognitive theories and logical systems might be powerless to explain them. In short we are asked to face the possibility of other cultures, civilizations, or epochs presenting us with alternative categories and systems of thought, which would exercise to the utmost our powers of empathy and translation.

Now, as may be expected, it is not in the Anglo-Saxon world which is always uncomfortable with notions of "esprit," "mentalité," and "représentations collectives" that we would expect this Lévy-Bruhlian thesis to be taken seriously. It is to that remarkable French School of History, called the *Annales* School, that we should turn for the most significant applications in historical writing of this first thesis. Before I report on the discussions by Lucien Febvre and Marc Bloch, who acknowledged their debt to Lévy-Bruhl,[12] let me signal a parallel development.

Some decades later there would come into being from a different quarter a philosophical tradition that owes nothing in the way of inspiration to Lévy-Bruhl, but which would confront us again with the question of commensurability and intelligibility of other traditions in terms of modern notions of explanation. I am of course referring to Wittgenstein's provocative suggestions in *Philosophical Investigations* – particularly such notions as "forms of life," "language games," and so on, which have had momentous implications for the problems of relativity between cultures, the translation of cultures, and the understanding of cultural logics. A language game, he said, is "meant to bring into prominence that the speaking of a language is part of an activity, or a form of life." We shall return to Wittgenstein in later chapters.

A suggestive idea in Lévy-Bruhl's writings, which he did not systematically explore, but which the *Annales* School of History exploited, is the supposition that if collective representations are functions of, or integrally connected with, social structures, then as social structures vary collective representations will show concomitant variations. Lévy-Bruhl held that primitives do not probe causal connections in the scientific mode, not because of deficiencies in their individual mental structures, but because such examination is precluded or excluded by their social doctrines, and by the parameters of their systems of knowledge.

Lucien Febvre (1878–1956), the founder of the *Annales* together with Marc Bloch, expressly invoked Lévy-Bruhl in his famous book, *The Problem of Unbelief in the Sixteenth Century*, which was written to rebut Abel Lefranc's thesis, proposed in 1902, to the effect that the secret message of Rabelais's rich and ebullient writing was a thoroughgoing attack on Christianity.[13] Febvre set out to demonstrate that anti-Christian free thought, as a form of atheism, was impossible in sixteenth-century France given the contours and constraints of the prevailing collective mentality.

In order to establish that a break with Christianity was impossible in the sixteenth century, he documented in detail the dominating place of religion in men's lives. A Christian of that time lived out his entire life – private, professional and public – within the embrace of Christianity. "Today," said Febvre, "we make a choice to be a Christian or not. There was no choice in the sixteenth century."[14] Baptism, the sacrament of marriage, death rites, food prohibitions were orchestrated by religion. The mediation of saints was necessary for healing; pilgrimages and vows had to be made to cure plagues and epidemics; the church bells proclaimed "a succession of prayers and services from morning to evening at recognized hours."[15] Even academic degrees were not merely examinations but religious acts: a candidate gave his defense in front of the altar – even if he was a Lutheran – in a ceremony of great pomp, between a mass and a thanksgiving. "This religion, this Christianity, was like the mantle of the Madonna of mercy, which was so frequently depicted in churches at that time. All men of all estates were sheltered under her mantle. Did anyone want to escape? Impossible. Nestled in its maternal folds, men did not even feel that they were captives. For them to rebel it would first have been necessary for them to question."[16]

Febvre then settles down to some exquisite documentation to explicate "what clarity, comprehension and efficacy" man's thought was capable of in the sixteenth century. Febvre says words of the following kind were missing from the vocabulary of that century, and this lack from the point of view of modern philosophical thought would constitute an "actual inadequacy or deficiency of thought" – adjectives such as "absolute" or "relative"; "abstract" or "concrete"; "intentional," "inherent," "transcendental"; nouns such as "causality" and "regularity"; "concept" and "criterion"; "analyses" and "syntheses"; "deduction" and "induction," "coordination" and "classification."[17]

Even the word "system" came into usage only in the middle of the seventeenth century. "Rationalism" itself was not christened till very late in the nineteenth century. Similarly missing from the vocabulary of that time were all these -isms: "Theism," "Pantheism," "Materialism," "Naturalism," "Fatalism," "Determinism" (a latecomer with Kant), "Skepticism" (it began with Diderot) and "Idealism." "None of these words was, in any case, at the disposal of Frenchmen in 1520, 1530, 1540, or 1550 if they wanted to think and then translate their thoughts into French for other Frenchmen."[18] The words that presented themselves to sixteenth-century Frenchmen when they reasoned "were not words made for reasoning, for explaining and demonstrating." And although Frenchmen possessed Latin at that time, Latin too could not have served them to philosophize any better.

Rather than summarize Marc Bloch's main arguments in *The Royal Touch*, I prefer to return here to Trevor-Roper's discussion of the witchcraze of the seventeenth century. This eclectic and brilliant historian turns to Lucien Febvre's concept of *mentalité* to argue that this craze is understandable only when located within a total cosmology and a total mode of thought and action. To turn to Thomas Kuhn's terminology: Trevor-Roper seems to be saying that the witchcraze was part of a whole "paradigm' and there had to be a total shift in paradigm (or mentality) before a different kind of reason and rationality could come to prevail in Europe.

Trevor-Roper's interpretation of the European witchcraze makes two major points. The first is that the witch beliefs of that time have to be placed in their general context and this requires our seeing them as an integral part of the whole cosmology of the time and as part of deep-seated social forms, rooted in permanent social attitudes. Hence it is unsound to detach the witchcraft beliefs from their total embedding, and to ask how these beliefs could have been taken to be true given their manifest absurdities as seen by the "rational" standards of today. Trevor-Roper says it is misguided to regard the "reason" and "logic" of today as a self-contained, independent system of permanent validity. "We recognize that even rationalism is relative; that it operates within a general philosophic context, and that it cannot properly be detached from this context."[19]

The corollary of this holistic perspective is that the witchcraft beliefs and practices and excesses of the sixteenth and seventeenth centuries could not be dissolved or eradicated in isolation, but only if the whole context of those views was revised. Unless there occurred a social transformation, the social basis of the belief would remain, and unless there was a critical change in the whole cosmology, the beliefs would continue. To destroy the myth, to drain away the poisoned pool, the whole intellect and social structure which contained it and had solidified around it had to be broken. When the change came, therefore, at the close of the seventeenth century it was a total "philosophical revolution which changed the whole concept of Nature and its operations," initiating modern "rationalism" and rejecting biblical fundamentalism. The final victory that liberated nature from biblical fundamentalism came on the one side from German pietists and English deists (the heirs of the Protestant heretics of the seventeenth century), and on the other from Descartes and his universal "mechanical" laws of nature.

These interpretive methods that place Lucien Febvre, Marc Bloch (and the *Annales* school in general), the later Wittgenstein and recently Foucault, and even Frances Yates, in the same camp are to my mind crushingly antithetical to the kind of comparisons between African (and in general primitive) thought and Western thought that the anthropologist Robin Horton has engaged in, comparisons that do not rely on fine-grained linguistic analyses of intellectual constructs, and are not sufficiently sensitive to the issue of commensurability between different mentalities.

A comment on Robin Horton

Horton's essay[20] argues that "theoretical thinking" in our Western culture has its African equivalent, the difference being just that they are couched in different idioms. But there is a catch in the analogy that is ultimately detrimental not only to African thought but to all thought systems, other than the modern "scientific" one. Horton's idealized view of science closely follows Karl Popper, and is innocent of Kuhn. Horton's essay confronts us with the question of whether popular African cosmologies and Western specialized scientific systems are comparable or whether they are in a relation of "incommensurable exclusivity," to borrow a phrase from Bernard Williams.

Horton's thesis is as follows: African cosmologies have for their purpose the explanation of the vast diversity of everyday experience in terms of the action of a few kinds of forces. The forces in question are the personalized gods. Like atoms and molecules and waves in modern scientific theories, concepts clothed in an impersonal idiom, the gods clothed in a personal idiom in Africa are really theoretical constructs that stand for, or introduce, the constraints of order and regularity. The African theoretical idiom is in a personalized mode because for Africans social relations are the main source of concern, and of their sense of order, while the world of nature is alien and beyond their control. The modern Western scientific idiom is in an impersonal mode because the reverse is true – nature and its workings are better understood, and they provide the idiom of causation even with regard to social relations, for these are less understood and less predictable.

One is inclined to applaud the liberal conscience at work here, except that its sting is in the tail. Having established "analogically" their comparability, we are then told that all said and done, African theoretical thought is inferior to the Western scientific thought – that is to say African thought is not reflective or critical, is closed rather than open, it is unable to entertain alternative conceptions to its dogma, it is ignorant of the experimental method and the concept of chance and it resorts to secondary rationalizations to protect its premises, rather than face courageously the possibility of falsification. Horton would certainly have been chastened had he encountered Kuhn's presentation of the conventional stratagems employed by the practitioners of contemporary normal science in order to keep their thoughts intact.

In the light of my references to Febvre (and Trevor-Roper) and other painters of holistic mentalities, who are sensitive to the translation of concepts and resistant to partial comparisons out of context, I hope it is clear why Horton's comparison seems to me misplaced and misguided. (It is, as my chapter on Tylor should make clear, against the spirit of Tylorian ideas as well. Tylor saw an antithesis and irreconcilability between the idea of personalized supernaturals and the concepts of science. Therefore Horton's claim to be a good neo-Tylorian is also in question in the same way as his interpretation of Durkheim is partial and tendentious.)[21] Ultimately Horton has to be viewed as taking a type of Frazerian intellectualistic point of view – that in so far as African religion is devoted to the explanation and control of nature, it is misguided and fallacious. There is, however, an ironical contrast in that Frazer thought magic was the bastard sister of science, not religion, whose basis was in individual psychology. We may well ask of Horton whether Africans practice religion in order to theorize foolishly or whether they practice it in pursuance of their own values and interests.

(2) The second major legacy of Lévy-Bruhl's later thought was the postulation of two coexisting mentalities in mankind everywhere – the mystical mentality and the rational–logical mentality, though their relative weight and salience may differ from primitive to modern times. In *Les Carnets*, Lévy-Bruhl suggested that there was a mystical mentality present in every human mind, but that it was more marked and more easily observable among primitives than in our own times. This mystical experience was touched by a characteristic emotion, which was the sentiment of the presence and action of an invisible power, or contact with a reality other than the reality given by the actual or everyday circumstances.[22] He went on to argue that these experiences of participation have been progressively subject in Western thought to the demands of accounting for them in logical terms, a development that has led metaphysics into difficulties. But he affirmed and warned: "In every human mind, whatever its intellectual development, there subsists an ineradicable fund of primitive mentality . . . It is not likely that it will ever disappear . . . For with it would perhaps disappear, perhaps, poetry, art, metaphysics, and scientific invention – almost everything, in short that

makes for the beauty and grandeur of human life." It "represents something fundamental and indestructible in the nature of man."[23]

Now it is in relation to the alleged co-presence of two mentalities of man that we may meaningfully insert some points in Evans-Pritchard's dialogue with Lévy-Bruhl, conducted in 1934 some years before the publication of *Witchcraft, Oracles and Magic Among the Azande* (1937).[24] Echoing Malinowski's plea for an ethnography in the round, Evans-Pritchard pointed to the danger of double selection by which savages are described entirely in terms of their mystical beliefs, ignoring much of their empirical behaviour in everyday life, and by which Europeans are described entirely in terms of scientific rational–logical thought, when they too do not inhabit this mental universe all the time. Thus we should avoid caricatures of both primitive and modern mentalities, and should not represent Westerners as thinking scientifically all the time when scientific activity is a special one practiced in very circumscribed circumstances. One must compare like with like, our everyday thought with their everyday thought.[25] Moreover Evans-Pritchard charged Lévy-Bruhl with failing to separate the various levels and styles of thought among the social segments of modern Western societies, in which intellectuals think differently from the peasants and so on. We may note in passing that roughly the same criticism was levelled by E. P. Thompson against Keith Thomas's account of changes in ideas about religion and magic in the seventeenth century and later. Again, had Lévy-Bruhl also discussed the changes in European patterns diachronically, that is, the changes manifest in the same society at different points in its history, he might have avoided a too simplistic dichotomy.

All in all, Evans-Pritchard's critique, which the later Lévy-Bruhl had largely met, advanced two ideas, which were not so much original as timely, and added to a confluence of ideas from many directions. One is that mystical and scientific thought could best be compared as normative ideational systems in the same society, especially a contemporary one. The second is that we should be keenly sensitive to the situations – and this was a point driven home by Malinowski as well[26] – in which a person can in a certain context behave mystically, and then switch in another context to a practical empirical everyday frame of mind. (For example, a Nuer compound has shrine posts to ancestors – at a specified time these objects and their surrounding space become sacred and the spirits of ancestors are immanent in them; but outside the staging of rituals, the same objects are treated casually and in a matter of fact fashion.) Thus it appears that it is this context in which sacred attitudes are evoked and in which code switching occurs that remains for us still a major phenomenon to interpret.

Now the idea of two (or more) mentalities simultaneously present in man can be carried further. In order to do so it is preferable to substitute for "mentalities" the terms "multiple orientations to reality," or "orderings of reality" so as to avoid any undue stress on "innateness," and to include the social construction of meanings and systems of knowledge.

To do justice to this issue I have to cover quite diverse terrains of thought – such as the psychoanalytic ideas of Freud, the aesthetic theories of Suzanne Langer, the phenomenological speculations of Alfred Schutz, the feminist developmental psychological thesis of Carol Gilligan, comparison of Indian and Western processes of ego development by Sudhir Kakar, and the ways of worldmaking as portrayed by Nelson Goodman. This journey will indicate to us where certain convergences of thought have occurred, and perhaps even more importantly how much more we need to know before the riddle of man's faculties and the diversity of his orderings of reality can be appreciated.

It is undeniable that in terms of current prominent positions on the philosophy of science, on the properties of language (especially as enunciated by Chomsky), and on the nature of man's symbolizing operations, the ideas of Freud, Langer, and Schutz would have to be modified and reinterpreted, and the inadequacies of certain other authors exposed. This critical assessment, however, is best taken up after I adumbrate the views of these authors and point to the interesting convergences between them, and with Lévy-Bruhl's conceptions.

Freud's interpretation of dreams

Ruth Bunzel tells us that Lévy-Bruhl, who had met Freud at least once, could not have been ignorant of Freud's writings. She remarks: "In many ways Freud's thinking runs parallel to Lévy-Bruhl's with an emphasis on non-rational sources of behaviour, on the role of the unconscious in structuring the perception of reality, on the importance of the mechanisms of projection, introjection, and identification in channeling man's relation to the meaningful world about him . . ."[27]

Lévy-Bruhl, approaching the problem of psychic process from philosophy and anthropology, developed the concept of a pre-logical mentality suffused with emotion. Freud, approaching the problem of perceptions of reality from the practice of psychiatry, was evolving his concept of "primary process" – the non-rational thinking that underlies dreams. It is claimed that each has contributed to a deeper understanding of the way people – not only "natives" – think.

I think it is a worthwhile move now to go to Freud's classic *The Interpretation of Dreams*[28] and to see what comparisons can be made between Freud's notions of "primary" and "secondary" processes in mental functioning and Lévy-Bruhl's mystical and logical modes of thought.

Secondary processes, said Freud, are to be found in conscious thinking, which is discursive, verbal and conforming to the laws of formal logic. In direct contrast *primary* processes are characteristic of unconscious thinking, which is non-discursive, condensive, iconic and ignorant of the categories of space and time. In *The Interpretation of Dreams*, Freud describes the processes of dream formation and dream recall in terms of the concept of condensation, displacement, representability, secondary revision, and so on. It is the non-discursive and condensive structure of dreams that sets them apart most dramatically from the linear structure of logical analytical thought. The elements of dream thoughts, said Freud, are under the pressure of dream work "turned about, broken into fragments and jammed together – almost like pack ice." In other words dreams collapse logical relations, or rather they have no means at their disposal for representing logical relations between dream thoughts: relations such as "if," "because," "just as," "either-or," and relations of "causation," "connection" and "contradiction."

Therefore in dreams various presentational devices are resorted to in order to express relations between dream thoughts: *logical connection* may be suggested by simultaneity in time (e.g. contiguity in space is equivalent to contiguity in time: two things happening together implies their adjacency in space and vice versa). A *causal relation* may be expressed by various means. Here are two examples: (a) by introducing the dependent clause as an introductory dream and the principal clause as the main dream (e.g. "since this was so, such and such was bound to happen"); (b) one image in a dream, whether of a person or thing, is shown as being transformed into another. The notion of *contradiction* can be represented by a reversal (e.g. a piece of dream content is turned around the other way). *Identification* may be conveyed by having only one of the persons linked by a common element succeed in being represented in the manifest content of the dream. Conversely, a composite figure may be constructed to represent a new *unity* of features that are shared by a collection of members.

Now Freud is both intriguing and also controversial in his attempt to (loosely) link the unconscious processes of dreaming with the processes of symbolization in the creative arts. He mentions that "the plastic arts of painting and sculpture labour, indeed, under a similar limitation [to that of dream work] as compared with poetry, which can make use of speech." What Freud alludes to here has been elaborated by Gregory Bateson,[29] who draws a distinction between *verbal* (or digital) coding and *iconic* (or analog) coding, and relates this duality to the conscious and unconscious levels of the mind. Bateson argues that the messages and meanings communicated by art forms, such as the kinesic and motor movements of dance or the representations of painting, are achieved in part at least at an unconscious level, or at the interface between the conscious and unconscious levels. Bateson underscores the point made by Freud that the devices of propositional language and verbal discourse – such as tense, simple negatives, modal markers – are not available to iconic communications such as dancing. At the same time the art forms are able to communicate with intensity an experience that is ordinarily un-available to speech. This is vividly conveyed by Isadora Duncan's remark that

"If I could tell you what it meant, there would be no point in dancing it." I was therefore recently pleased to come across this self-conscious remark by perhaps the greatest artist of modern dance, Martha Graham: "I don't want to be understandable, I want to be felt."[30]

All this meaningfully, if not exactly logically, links up with Suzanne Langer's contrasting in her works, *Philosophy in a New Key* and *Feeling and Form*,[31] the discursive form of language with the presentational forms of the arts (dancing, music, painting).

Suzanne Langer in *Philosophy in a New Key* had this to say about the discursiveness of language: "Words have a linear, discrete, successive order; they are strung one after another like beads on a rosary . . . we cannot talk in simultaneous bunches of names." By comparison, visual forms – lines, colours, proportions, are just as capable of articulation – but in a manner altogether different from the laws of syntax that govern language. Visual forms "do not present their constituents successively, but simultaneously, so the relations determining a visual structure are grasped in one act of vision."[32]

We may well ask in what ways might Lévy-Bruhl's law of participation be similar to some of the representational processes of unconscious thought (such as identification, fusion and condensation) and of the presentational arts, as developed by Freud, Bateson and Langer? I am tempted to say that what Lévy-Bruhl was striving to characterize as the processes of participation and mystical orientation was concordant with the process of presentational and iconic coding as proposed by Langer, Freud and Bateson. Moreover, there is scope for further probing of this issue in certain other writings.

But before I do that it is necessary to evaluate critically the propositions of Freud and Langer in terms of linguistic and semiotic theories that have been formulated by their successors, and thereafter to salvage from that critique certain conceptions that can be sustained in a revised form.

A critique of Langer and Freud

With regard to Freud's conception of primary process, the question we have to raise is how we may meaningfully correlate the unconscious activity of dreaming with the predominantly, though not exclusively, conscious processes of artistic creation and the operations of linguistic discourse. Are the symbolization processes of dreaming similar to, or the same as, the symbolization processes of artistic creation? After all, the motivation for substitution and condensation in the dream work is "censorship" by the superego, while the motivation for artistic representation lies in the "enhancement" and "intensification" of emotive meaning and patterning. In what way does symbolization differ when it occurs, as it frequently does in art, consciously and creatively, and emerges as a metaphor, and when it occurs unconsciously under restraint and emerges as a dream image? It would seem that symbolization is a general mental capacity that is used both consciously and unconsciously, while awake or asleep, neurotically or creatively in speech and writing, in the arts and in the sciences, with or without insight into its possibilities and implications. Furthermore, even in the Freudian system, in much of our waking life the conscious and unconscious are dialectically related, even though only a part of our mental life is open to conscious articulation.

Both Langer's and Freud's characterization of language as being exclusively linear, and discursive, and conforming to the laws of logic is too narrow in conception. Though language in speech and writing unfolds in a linear manner, the syntactical (and grammatical) rules that generate speech acts and sentences are recursive, combinatory, and ordered hierarchically (as Chomsky has demonstrated). The structure of poetry as, for example, famously explicated by Roman Jakobson, can hardly be described in terms of the linear and discursive succession of discrete words. Jakobson reminded us that verbal communication has several functions, that there are two modes of arrangement used in verbal behaviour, *selection* and *combination*. Then asserting that selection is "produced on the base of equivalence, similarity and dissimilarity, synonymity and antonymity, while the combination, the build up of the sequence, is based on contiguity," Jakobson defined the "poetic function" as "projecting the principle of equivalence from the axis of selection into the axis of combination."[33]

Even the ordinary language of everyday speech, let alone the crafted pieces of literary writing, is not innocent of features which Langer attributed solely to presentational forms, and Freud solely to unconscious primary processes. Just as Freud was not fully appreciative of the conscious symbolization processes deployed in the creative arts, so did Langer excessively oppose the processes involved in the comprehension of discourses in speech and presentations in visual form.[34]

A sign system or medium can have multiple representational capacities and communicative functions. If one may at this point resort to Peirce's semiotics, especially his treatment of the triad of signs classified as symbol, icon and index and their intersections and combinations, we can make the clarification that a medium like language lends itself to *many kinds* of representational modalities and communicative functions; so can visual forms like paintings and graphic drawings. (Music, however, as an auditory art form, is primarily a "non-representational" medium and has its special capacities and patterning by which it makes its effects.) Finally, given their potentialities there are ways in which it is possible to *interrelate* these (and other) sign systems and media into complex wholes as in theatrical performances, in rituals, in scientific exhibitions, and in trade fairs.

The Peircean semiotic categories also permit us to arrange signs on a continuum according to their representational and communicative capacities. At one end we can place those signs or complexes of signs which are used in a particular context primarily in their *referential* capacity to transmit *information* in a scientific mode; at the other end we can place signs which are used for their capacity to communicate primarily sensory effects in a presentational or participatory mode. An account by a physicist reporting an experiment, or an argument set out by a logician are in the former mode; a poem or a fiction are in the latter mode. An engineer's drawing or model of Brooklyn Bridge is nearer the referential and iconic pole, while a painter's rendering it on a starry night is nearer the presentational and sensory pole. The dance form, music, a sculpture, a painting, the opera, lend themselves more to aesthetic, polyvalent, and participatory effects than to the unambiguity and transparency of informational and referential purposes. Hence I would like to introduce here the point, which I hope to develop further, that communication media or sign systems like speech, writing, music, song, dance, painting, sculpture, and communication channels that are auditory, visual, tactile, olfactory and gustatory, can be deployed singly and in combination to maximize different messages and effects, which for our purposes I would place at the two poles (of a continuum) – the referential, informational, "scientific," logical, causal pole and the sensory, polyvalent, presentational and participatory pole. Moreover, these effects and purposes may be better achieved according to the manner in which a communication system deploys and emphasizes the potentialities of auditory, tactile, temporal or spatial channels and media.

Having made these clarifications and revisions of Freud and Langer, and after suggesting that it is still possible to contemplate the possibility of two systems of communication or two discourses portraying different orientations to the world, the two systems being the two poles of a continuum, let me return to the examination of certain other writings that have as their central theme the positing of two or more mentalities, or modes of constructing or experiencing reality, or ways of world-making. These writings enable us to continue with the issues raised by Lévy-Bruhl.

The two voices of men and women

Let me, therefore, shift gears, and deal with a recent discussion by Carol Gilligan in *In a Different Voice*,[35] in which she speaks of two modes in which men and women describe their interpersonal relationships and moral concerns.

Why this discussion is pertinent for us is that Gilligan identifies what was previously spoken of as discursive, logical, competitive, instrumental rationality as not only the male voice but also the dominant ideology of the United States, and she identifies the morality of connectedness, and the expressive concern for relationships in terms of intimacy and care, as not only the female voice but also as the subordinate and suppressed ideology of our society. Gilligan thus proposes two voices within the same society, but this time differentiated by sex or gender.

Let us review Gilligan's submission. She criticizes the regnant theories in development psychology, which turn out to be formulations of male theorists. They have adopted the male life cycle as the norm of description. Freud, Piaget, Kohlberg and Erikson, all are charged with this bias. Freud built his theory of psychosexual development around the experiences of the male child that culminated in the Oedipus complex; women's attachment to their mothers and insulation from an Oedipal conflict and its resolution was regarded as a sign of their retardation in superego development and in their sense of legalistic justice. Women's failure to separate and individuate early in life is regarded by definition as a failure to develop.

Similarly, Piaget's conclusions from the study of the rules of the game among boys and girls gives the palm to boys, who earlier on become fascinated with the legal elaboration of rules and the development of fair and pragmatic procedures for adjudicating conflicts. Again Kohlberg remarked that "rather than elaborating a system of rules for resolving disputes, girls subordinated the continuation of the game to the continuation of relationships."[36] Finally Erikson's stages of psychosocial development put the accent on "individuation" in the development of identity in adolescence, and this celebration of individuation, autonomy, and separation puts the girl in an invidious, deprived position. Erikson's male-oriented thesis sees the male's identity as forged in relation to the world, while female identity has to await its awakening in a relationship of intimacy.

Gilligan, on the basis of her own research and other female psychologists' work, argues for an appreciation and therefore a positive characterization of woman's moral strength – of her overriding concern with relationships and responsibilities, and of her interpersonal involvement seen not as a lower stage in a sequence culminating in masculine individuation, legalism, and instrumental capacities, but as a mature orientation in its own terms.

Thus the two intellectual and moral orientations, male and female, can be characterized as contrastive but equally mature formulations in these terms.

To the male-accented "morality of rights", with its preoccupation with individuation and the definition of self through separation or autonomy can be counterposed the female "morality of responsibility" for which connectedness and relationships are primary.

The first orientation reflects "the logic of justice approach," and a hierarchical ordering of rules, whereas the second orientation reflects the "ethic of care and responsibility," that is sensitive to the potentiality of conflicts to fracture human relationships, and therefore attempts to preserve relationships rather than come down on the side of absolute judgments. This female stance which defines self through connection, and sees problems in terms of the network of relationships, is reluctant to generalize and categorize but has a sophisticated understanding of the nature of choice.

There are some problems inherent in Gilligan's book as it now stands. In the interests of clarity it is desirable to differentiate "ideology" from "innate propensities", and also to specify how "voice" relates to them. It is also not clear to me whether her male and female voices apply only to the United States – in which case the difference in gender attribution is partly at least a function of cultural, social, and politico-economic circumstances, socialization practices and so on – or whether they are general universal male–female sex differences, in which case there is an intimation of innate (genetically coded) differences and structures. Any blanket generalization, of course, puts in jeopardy much of the recent feminist claims to equality with men of skills and aptitudes, and therefore the just need for affirmative action, for it may be ironical as Gilligan says that "at a time when efforts are being made to eradicate discrimination between the sexes in the search for social equality and justice, the differences between the sexes are being rediscovered in the social sciences."[37]

Kristeva thinks that a Manichean position is not a happy one. If women say that they must appropriate "the logical, mastering, scientific, theoretical apparatus" of men and gratifyingly produce women physicists and theorists, then it is difficult simultaneously to defend the particularity of women.

In characterizing male and female differences in terms of two kinds of discourse, Kristeva describes the women's dilemma thus: A woman can fit herself "to the dominant discourse – theoretical discourse, scientific discourse – and on the basis of that find an extremely gratifying slot in society, but to the detriment of the expression of the particularity belonging to the individual as a woman. On the basis of this fact, it seems to me, that one must try not to deny these two aspects of linguistic communication, the mastering aspect and the aspect which is more of the body and of the impulses, but try, in every situation and for every woman, to find a proper articulation of these two elements . . . I think that the time has come when we must no longer speak of all women. We have to talk in terms of individual women and of each one's place inside these two poles. One of the gravest dangers that now presents itself in feminism is the impulse to practice feminism in a herd."[38]

Be that as it may, it is interesting for me to record that Gilligan ultimately proposes an ideal double passage in the development of the careers of men and women in which the male and female voices are restored in time for both. In the case of man, power and separation secure in him an identity through work but they leave him at a distance from others: intimacy then becomes the critical experience that brings the self back into connection with others. For this reason intimacy is the transformative experience for man through which adolescent identity turns into the generality of adult love and aligns it with work. Women on the other hand begin with their propensity to define their identity through relationships of intimacy and care; and they then face the problem that in order to secure their relationships they have to mask desire and conflict, and thereby face confusion about the locus of responsibility and truth. "The critical experience then becomes not intimacy but choice, creating an encounter with self that clarifies the understanding of responsibility and truth."[39] Thus the two disparate modes of experience are in the end integrally connected. Gilligan's rhetoric is moving: "While an ethic of justice proceeds from the promise of equality – that everyone should be treated the same – an ethic of care rests on the premise of nonviolence – that no one should be hurt."[40]

The inner world of the Indian and the outer world of the Westerner

As a comparativist and an Asian, my attention was caught when I came across a discussion by a sensitive native interpreter of Indian personality in a mode not far removed from Gilligan's own approach. In *The Inner World, A Psychoanalytic Study of Childhood and Society in India*,[41] Sudhir Kakar uses the terminology of Freud and Erikson to tell us that "In India the process of ego development takes place according to a model which differs sharply from that of western psychologists . . . The [Indian] child's differentiation of himself from his mother (and consequently of the ego from the id) is structurally weaker and comes chronologically later than in the West." The outcome is that "The mental processes characteristic of the symbiosis of infancy play a relatively greater role in the personality of the adult Indian."

In other words, the primary mental processes (in which thinking is representational and affective, relying on visual and sensual images rather than the abstract and conceptual secondary mental processes) loom larger, says Kakar, in the Indian than the Western "psyche." "Compared with western children, an Indian child is encouraged to continue to live in a mythical, magical world for a long time. In this world, objects, events and other persons do not have an existence of their own, but are intimately related to the self and its mysterious moods." Traditionally Indians have sought to convey abstract concepts through vivid concrete images. "Causal thinking has never enjoyed the pre-eminence in Indian tradition that it has in western philosophy." The Indian propensity is to enlarge the inner world (radically manifest in the yogi's meditation and the artist's *sadhana*) rather than act on the outer one. And the Indian's responsibility and integrating reality is in discourse transferred from the mother – on whom there is a prolonged dependence in early childhood – to the family at large and other social institutions. Thus in decision-making "the individual functions as a member of a group rather than on his own." By making social interactions predictable an Indian is encouraged to respond according to tried traditional patterns. Kakar also connects the Indian child's prolonged emotional dependence on the mother to the salience of the *bhakti* type of religious devotion and emotional orientations of protective care, dependence, awe and humility, which connote in the extreme cases of saints like Sri Ramakrishna a "religiously sublimated femininity."

I think I have reported enough to suggest the flavour of Kakar's writing. In a sense what Kakar characterizes as the primary-process-tinged Indian personality as distinguished from the Western personality dominated by abstract logical thought is an East–West cultural contrast. It is exactly paralleled by Carol Gilligan's male–female contrast within a single but vast Western country, the United States. This parallelism at two different levels and contexts of contrast makes one wonder whether the two accounts are compatible. Although Kakar lacks the assurance of Gilligan to defend the subordinated orientation as in fact mature and worthy of equal valuation, I think both writers are eventually suggesting that it is a balanced combination of the two modalities of "female voice" and "male voice", or Indian and Western processes of "ego development", that will deliver the exemplary human being, and that the causal and instrumental orientation to the world which enjoys dominance needs to be complemented and enriched by the participating and fusing mode.

A phenomenological account of multiple realities and finite provinces of meaning

A discussion from an entirely different genre, namely phenomenology, resonates with and complements Lévy-Bruhlian ideas concerning the dual, perhaps multiple ordering of reality by man. I take as my example the discussion by Alfred Schutz, whose ideas of immediate relevance to use have been summarized by Bellah as follows:

"Basic to Schutz's idea is that reality is never simply given, it is constructed. The apprehension of reality is always an active process involving subject and object. Multiple realities arise because of the varieties of needs of consciousness and schemes of interpretation that link the two. Schutz pointed out that besides the world of everyday life, which is the social world par excellence, there is the world of dreams, the world of art, the world of science, the world of religion. By showing that these worlds are partially autonomous and irreducible one to the other, Schutz gave another powerful argument for the openness and multiplicity of the human spirit."[42] Bellah used Schutz's notion of multiple realities to argue for the reality of religion. But before examining Schutz's usefulness for our purposes, let us first understand and view his map of consciousness and reality construction.[43]

Schutz's formulations concerning multiple realities are elaborated from earlier contributions on the subject by William James and Bergson. William James, in his *Principles of Psychology*, had stated that the origin of all reality is subjective, and that there were various orders or "sub-universes" of reality. William James identified the world of sense of physical things as the paramount reality, and pointed to other sub-universes into which man may step – such as the world of science, the worlds of mythology and religion, even the world of sheer madness. James said "Each world whilst it is attended to is real after its own fashion; only the reality lapses with the attention." Bergson's philosophy also adumbrated the view that our conscious life shows a number of different planes, ranging from the plane of action at one extreme to the plane of dream at the other, the former showing the greatest tension of consciousness and the latter the lowest.

So Schutz's thesis of multiple realities takes "the reality of the world of daily life" as the centerpiece, and treats the other realities as provinces situated around it into which one can step in and out. The world of daily life Schutz describes as "an intersubjective world, common to all of us, in which we have not a theoretical but an eminently practical interest."[44] The "pragmatic" attitude governs our "natural" attitude toward the world of daily life. "Working," that is action in the outerworld intentionally undertaken to complete a practical project, is its typical mode. "The world of working as a whole stands out as paramount over against the many other sub-universes of reality . . . By my working acts I gear into the outerworld, I change it." The working world is experienced under both schemes of reference, the prospective "in-order-to motives," and the retrospective "because" motives. The former is the teleology of purposes and the latter is the causality of motives.

Although we ordinarily live in the paramount reality of everyday life, we frequently abandon it when, for instance, we experience a specific shock which compels us to shift the reality of meaning to another one. "Some instances are: the shock of falling asleep as the leap into the world of dreams; the inner transformation we endure if the curtain in the theatre rises as the transition into the world of the stage play; the radical change in our attitude, if before a painting, we permit our visual field to be limited by what is within the frame as the passage into the pictorial world . . ."

With this introduction, Schutz advances to his main thesis. All these worlds – the world of dreams, the world of art, the world of religious experience, the world of scientific contemplation, etc. – are "finite provinces of meaning" that have their peculiar cognitive styles and specific accents of reality. That which is compatible with one province of meaning may be incompatible with another province of meaning. Hence the passing from one finite province to another can only be performed by a leap, and not by a formula of transition or transformation. Moreover, to the cognitive style peculiar to each province of meaning belongs a specific tension of consciousness, a specific *epoché*, a specific self-experience and form of sociality.

Now from our point of view what is of particular interest is how Schutz presents the domains of religion and science as shifts from the world of ordinary reality. Schutz regards the religious experiences, in all their varieties, as much a leap from the reality of everyday life as is the professional orientation and activity of the scientist, who makes the decision "to replace all passionate participation in the affairs of 'this world' by a disinterested contemplative attitude."[45]

In fact Schutz is particularly interested in clarifying "the relationship between the reality of the world of daily life and that of theoretical, scientific contemplation" (p. 208). His idealized account of the world of scientific pursuit is reminiscent of Karl Popper's and goes something like this. Scientific theorizing proper is concerned to observe and possibly understand the world, rather than to master it or to apply the knowledge to the invention of technical devices, for the use of applied science for worldly purposes is not an integral part of scientific theorizing itself.

Thus unlike the orientation to the world of everyday life in which acts of working are pragmatically geared into the outer world, the attitude of the "disinterested observer" is the pre-requisite of all scientific theorizing. This attitude is a "leap" into a special order of reality; it represents an openness to permanent revision of knowledge. The scientist "puts in brackets" his physical existence, and does not allow his personal problems to interfere with his scientific environment. Since the leap into the province of scientific theoretical insight obligates the individual to suspend his subjective point of view, the scientist may be said to be a taker of a role which only covers a part of his self. The practice of science, the entry into the world of science, implies the subjection to certain rules of epistemology and methodology, such as the requirement of consistency between propositions, the testing of them by observation, that is, by immediate experiences of facts within the world, and so on.

That is why the theoretical scientist puts his physical existence in brackets. In this sense "The theorizing self is solitary; it has no social environment; it stands outside social relationships."[46]

One may rightly wonder to what extent this Popperian account synchronizes with Kuhn's account of the practice of "normal science" by a "scientific community." Yet I think Schutz is making the important point that the activity of science is a circumscribed activity, undertaken in very special and restricted circumstances by partial selves of human beings, and that, therefore, this is a special ordering of reality, only one of several others.

Moreover, Schutz is suggesting that the practice of science cannot, or need not, cover all our mental life and space, for the same human being may participate in different finite provinces of meaning. In the last resort the multiple realities or, if you will, the order of religious experience and the order of scientific theorizing, are but "different tensions of one and the same consciousness, and it is the same life, the mundane life, unbroken from birth to death, which is attended to in different modifications."[47]

I must confess that I find problematic Schutz's postulation of the "paramount reality of everyday life" with its "pragmatic" orientation as a "natural" (culture- and society-free?) condition. Without accepting it and therefore placing it in brackets, I find his conception of "finite provinces of meaning" and "multiple realities" (if read as multiple "orderings" of reality) as suggestive and pertinent.

Precisely because he avoids the same difficulty, it is apposite in this context of discussion to refer next to Nelson Goodman's notion of "ways of worldmaking," a philosophical inquiry which he says is concerned with "the structure of the several symbol systems of the sciences, philosophy, the arts, perception, and everyday discourse."[48] Goodman has described his position as "a radical relativism under rigorous restraints"; he maintains that there are "multiple frames of reference" according to which the world can be described. Opting for the possibility of "many different world-versions" (and rejecting the existence of a multiplicity of worlds or "worlds-in-themselves"), Goodman states his anti-reductionist position thus:

The diversity of accounts of the world cannot be routinely transformed into one another. There is "no consolation of intertranslatability," "no ready rules for transforming physics, biology, and psychology into one another, and no way at all of transforming any of these into Van Gogh's vision . . ." The many different world-versions are of independent interest and importance, without any requirement of presumption or reducibility to a single base. The pluralist, far from being anti-scientific accepts the sciences at full value. His typical adversary is the monopolistic materialist or physicalist who maintains that one system, physics, is preeminent and all-inclusive, such that every other version must eventually be reduced to it or rejected as false or meaningless."[49] The argument leads to this conclusion: "So long as contrasting right versions not all reducible to one are countenanced, unity is to be sought not in an ambivalent or neutral *something* underneath or beneath these versions but in an overall organization embracing them"[50] – that is to say, the ways of worldmaking and their interrelationships are built through symbol systems.

For our purposes the important notions in Goodman's account of "ways of worldmaking" are as follows:

(1)   He accepts the sciences at full value as a frame of reference (as Schutz does).

(2)   He maintains that there is a basic difference between at least these two ways of worldmaking, or the two modes of referential function: *denotation* and *exemplification*. Denotation is typical of the scientific, literal, linguistic or mathematical description of the world (though analog instruments and the use of metaphor in measurement are not alien to science), while exemplification, the referencing "by what possesses to the property possessed," is typical of art forms and non-representational forms, which denote nothing, but "show much" and convey feelings.[51] "The worlds of fiction, poetry, painting, music and dance, and the other arts are built largely by non-literal devices such as metaphor, by such non-demonstrational means as exemplification and expression, and often by use of pictures or sounds or gestures or other symbols of nonlinguistic systems."[52]

(3)   Finally, Goodman would maintain that the "truth" of science that appeals to correspondence with a ready-made world is but one special frame of reference, and non-denotational forms and pictures embody a kind of aesthetic truth or rightness whose bases are syntactic and semantic density and pattern recognition, and processes of worldmaking such as composition, ordering, weighting, and so on.

Karl-Otto Apel in *Toward a Transformation of Philosophy*[53] postulates the duality of orientations that may be used to conclude our discussion of theorists of multiple realities and ways of worldmaking. Apel asserts: "in my opinion, genuine hermeneutic inquiry stands in a complementary relationship to natural scientific objectification and explanation of events. Both types of inquiry are mutually exclusive and yet none the less thereby supplement one another."[54] "As Peirce recognized, the natural scientists' community of experience always expresses a semiotic community of interpretation . . . Linguistic agreement concerning what one means and what one wants is complementary to objective science . . ."[55]

"It seems to me that man has basically two equally important but identical *complementary* cognitive interests:

1.   an interest that is determined by the necessity for a technical praxis as the basis of insights into natural laws;
2.   an interest that is determined by the necessity for social, morally relevant praxis.

The latter is directed towards agreement – one that is already presupposed by technical praxis – upon the possibility and norms of a meaningful human 'being-in-the-world'. This interest in the understanding of meaning is not only directed towards communication amongst contemporaries but also the communication of the living with the past generations in the manner of a mediation of tradition. It is indeed primarily through this mediation of tradition that human beings achieve that accumulation of technical knowledge and that deepening of enrichment of their understanding of possible meaningful motivation which gives them their superiority over the animal kingdom."[56] Apel's worlds serve as a prelude to my summation in terms of two orientations to the world.

Participation versus causality: two orientations to the world

I should like to conclude by proposing that from our foregoing discussions it is possible to separate analytically at least two orientations to our cosmos, two orderings of reality that woman and man everywhere are capable of experiencing, though the specific mix, weighting, and complementarity between the two may vary between individuals and between groups within a culture, and between cultures taken as collective entities.

These two orientations I shall label as *participation* versus *causality*. Causality is quintessentially represented by the categories, rules and methodology of positive science and discursive mathematico-logical reason. The scientific focus involves a particular kind of distancing, affective neutrality and abstraction to events in the world. Particularly in the so-called hard natural sciences cause and effect in space and time are conceived in terms of measurable impacts of energy and force, and by the progressive atomization of information, by which entities are progressively broken down from molecules to atoms, and atoms to sub-atomic particles, whose interactions then provide the image of causality.

I need not develop the philosophy and methodology of the prestigious sciences further here, but I do want to delineate at greater length the contours of participation as a mode of relating to and constructing reality. The notion of causality is much out of place, and that of participation is very much in place, when describing aesthetic or religious orientations. Lévy-Bruhl in his somewhat muddled way, Maurice Leenhardt in a more concrete way, Suzanne Langer in an imaginative way, were speaking of a holistic and configurational grasping of totalities as integral to aesthetic enjoyment and mystic awareness.

Let us pause for a while and digest how Leenhardt bears on the issue under consideration. Maurice Leenhardt, a missionary in Melanesia for some twenty-four years (1902–25), who later as a professional anthropologist occupied Marcel Mauss's influential chair at the *Ecole Pratique des Hautes Études*, elaborated and refined the notion of "participation" as the central feature of the "mythical sensibility" of the New Caledonians. By virtue of his prolonged and involved ethnographic experiment, Leenhardt infused the notion of participation with a realism and intensity, and gave it the kind of body and substance, that Lévy-Bruhl did not achieve.

Leenhardt saw Melanesian life[57] as a dynamic totalistic weaving of nature, society, myth and technology, and he saw the Melanesian village as the centre of a surrounding mythic landscape, where mountains, rocks, trees and animals were seen as familiar, and as endowed with the power of its ancestor-god and with totemic life. Such natural entities and phenomena were regarded as discrete presences in which the living were implicated. The landscape was a mediator between the invisible and the visible worlds, an area of "lived myth," and the life of each group was guarded by its totems and ancestors immanent in the landscape. The concept of participation conveyed to Leenhardt this felt relation between the self and person, and the phenomena of the mythic landscape; ultimately participation enacted the relation between man and the immanent and/or the transcendent.

Leenhardt's sense of "participation" in a mythic landscape or a sacred geography as a reality-orientation can be illustrated from several ethnographies of peoples other than the Melanesians. Here is an example from Morocco's maraboutism or the cult of the saints. Vincent Crapanzano[58] explains:

> Moroccans speak of visiting a saint's sanctuary as "visiting *the* saint," for they believe him to be alive in his sanctuary . . . In certain instances – for example, when [Tuhami, the informant in question] talks about going to "Moulay Idriss" – there is even greater ambiguity, for "Moulay Idriss" refers not only to the saint, and to his sanctuary but to the village in which his sanctuary is located, the village in which he resides.
>
> "Associated with the saints is a gamut of rituals, ranging from the communal recitation of supernumerary prayers and highly stylized trance dances to special massages with rocks endowed with *baraka*, baths in waters sacred to the saint, the removal of a handful of earth from the saintly sanctuary, or simply the circumambulation of the saint's tomb. Pilgrims frequently sleep in the sanctuary in

the hope of having a dream; such dreams are thought to be messages from the saint or even visitations. Some Moroccans, like Tuhami, claim that the saints are alive in their tombs. For them the saints resemble rather more the *jnun* than deceased human beings. There is belief in neither ghosts nor ancestral spirits in Morocco. The sanctuaries tend to be specialized, though never completely so. They may serve as a sacred arena for political and legal arbitrage or, like the churches in medieval Europe or the Buddhist shrines in Vietnam, as a place for political asylum. They are visited by pilgrims anxious for a cure for any ailment, ranging from a bout of rheumatism or menstrual cramps to demonic attack and spirit possession. They are visited, too, for poetic inspiration, acrobatic prowess, success in business or school, for the birth of a male child or the preservation of a marriage, or simply for those feelings of well-being that are associated with the gift of *baraka*. Most often, supplicant pilgrims promise to sacrifice something, a sheep, a goat, or perhaps a seven-colored chicken, or to give something, food, candles, or money to the saint, if he responds to their supplication. Such a pledge binds the supplicant to the saint, and failure to carry it out will result in great harm to him or his family: they will become vulnerable to the demons, for the saint will remove his protection if indeed he does not incite the *jnun* to attack.[59]

On the Hindu mode of participating in a sacred geography, Diana Eck has this to say:

Pilgrims circumambulate the whole of India as a sacred land, visiting the *dhan* at each compass point, marking with their feet the perimeter of the whole, bringing sands from the Southern tip of India at Ramesvaram to place in the Ganga [the Ganges river] when they arrive, and returning with Ganga water to sprinkle the *linga* at Ramesvaram. The network of *tīrthas* [fords, places or crossings] constitutes the very bones of India as a cultural unit.[60]

Eck refers to this conduct as "a sacramental natural ontology," in which the symbols constitute the whole (rather than the Holy).

Participation can be represented as occurring when persons, groups, animals, places, and natural phenomena are in a relation of contiguity, and translate that relation into one of existential immediacy and contact and shared affinities. (In the language of semiotics, humans on the one hand, and places, objects and natural phenomena on the other, are represented as mutually representing one another "iconically," and also as transferring energies and attributes "indexically"). When the Trobriand Islanders relate their myths of origins in terms of emerging from holes in the ground or being associated with primordial rocks; when the name of a peasant in the Kandyan highlands of Sri Lanka was a lexical string that successively denoted his village of origin (*vāsagama*), the ancestral house in that village (*gedera*) with which his family was associated, and finally his personal name, names which fused location, territory, residence, caste and family status, ancestry in a single composite identity; when in a Southern Italian Calabrian village of today grandparents speak of their ancient rootedness in farms and villages of origin; when Americans, young and old, terrified by nuclear devastation and industrial waste turn out in droves to protect their environment and their ecology, their flora and their fauna; when the Romantic poets, Wordsworth, Coleridge and Shelley, waxed eloquent in the presence of, and communion with, nature; when national monuments like the Lincoln or Jefferson memorials, or graveyards like the Arlington Cemetery, or battlefields like Gettysburg, are believed to enshrine a people's history or radiate their national glories – in all these instances, we have manifestations of "participation" among people, places, nature and objects. And people participate in each other as well: the bonding and relation between parents and children, between kinsmen by the ties of blood and amity; the transmission of charisma or *metta* through amulets and talismans between a Buddhist saint and his followers; or between Thai royalty and their subjects; the Indian concept of *darshan* of a deity whose eyes fall upon the worshippers as much as the worshippers view their deity – all these are intimations of participation. The connectedness between persons, the sense of being a part of an ensemble of relationships that Gilligan and Kakar have described, are also bridges to the reality of participation.

Although "causation" and "participation" may seem different or contrastive orientations to the world, the analyst must maintain that both are projected on the experiential and symbolizing capacities of the *same* sensory modalities of man – the modalities of touch, taste, hearing, seeing. While much of the discourse of causality and positive science is framed in terms of distancing, neutrality, experimentation, and the language of analytic reason, much of the discourse of participation can be framed in terms of sympathetic immediacy, performative speech acts, and ritual action. If participation emphasizes sensory and affective communication and the language of emotions, causality stresses the rationality of instrumental action and the language of cognition. But these are ideal type exaggerations, and neither can exclude the devices of the other.

It is possible to suggest that a meaningful way to contrast participation and causality is through a comparison of religion and science as contrasting and complementary orientations to the world. What our discussion so far has led to is the plausibility of at least two modes of ordering the world that are simultaneously available to human beings as complementary cognitive and affective interests, and which in the self-conscious language of reflexivity and analysis might be labelled as "participation" and causality."

That these two orderings of reality are simultaneously available to human beings points toward our increasing realization that people of all cultures and societies engage in different genres of discourse that are linked to and enacted in different contexts of communication and "practice" (as Bourdieu has defined it). According to occasion and context we invoke, deploy, and manipulate bodies of idioms and concepts, that are culturally available to us and tailored to suit different systems of knowledge, styles of reasoning and rhetoric, and modes of emotional experience. In this sense we are men for all seasons and engage in many ways of worldmaking. And although societies and cultures do differ in the variety of discourses they permit and encourage, certainly no society hitherto known is an impoverished practitioner of only a single orientation. The kinds of concepts and characteristics that we may attach to participation and causality are, as follows:

Some representations of "causality" and "participation"

Causality	Participation
Ego against the world. Egocentricity. Atomistic individualism. The language of distancing and neutrality of action and reaction. The paradigm of evolution in space and time. Instrumental action that changes matter and the causal efficacy of technical acts. The successive fragmentation of phenomena, and their atomization, in the construction of scientific knowledge. The language of "dimensional" classification (Piaget). Science and experimentation. The doctrine of "representation" (Foucault). "Explanation" (Wittgenstein). "Natural scientific objectification and explanation of events" (K. Apel).	Ego/person with the world, a product of the world. Sociocentrism. The language of solidarity, unity, holism, and continuity in space and time. Expressive action that is manifest through conventional intersubjective understandings, the telling of myths and the enactment of rituals. The performative efficacy of communicative acts. Pattern recognition, and the totalization of phenomena. The sense of encompassing cosmic oneness. The language of "complexive" classification (Piaget) dictated by contiguity relations and the logic of interaction. The doctrine of "resemblance" (Foucault). "Form of life" (Wittgenstein) and the totality of experience associated with it.

Some of the contexts in which discourses predominantly in the perspective of causality are enacted are: scientific laboratory experiments; professional meetings of scientists, engineers, doctors, where their research findings are reported; the promulgation by development economists of economic plans for growth, development, control of inflation; doctor–patient consultations conducted within a "bio-medical" paradigm of illness and cure; many kinds of pedagogic sessions at universities attempting to reduce complexity to elementary principles.

Some of the contexts in which acts predominantly in the wavelengths of participation are performed are: courtship and sexual union; certain occasions and ceremonies of family life, such as festive meals, rites of passage (birthdays, weddings, funerals, etc.); Buddhist meditation; church services and temple worship; collective festivals both religious and secular including those labelled as part of "civil religion" (Anzac Day, Remembrance Day, Labor Day, July Fourth); saints holding audiences for their followers; *bhakti* worship devoted to union with god; millenarian movements; football and baseball games.

I emphasize the word "predominantly" in the preceding two paragraphs to signal the obvious and incontestable fact that elements of participation are not lacking in scientific discourses, and features of causality are not necessarily absent in participatory enactments. Analytically separate, they are intertwined in many mixes, and I have pointed at contexts and discourses where one or the other mode predominates.

Although I have described participation and causality as contrasting and complementary and coexisting orientations to the world, perhaps best illustrated by complexes labelled as "religion" and "science," it is relevant to note that "participation" defined in *a special sense* has been assigned an important role in the scientific theory-making of a branch of modern physics. In that special sense, "participation" has become a part of, and incorporated into, the scope of "scientific rationality."

J. A. Wheeler's provocative essay entitled "Bohr, Einstein and the Strange Lesson of the Quantum,"[61] discusses the fundamental disagreement between Albert Einstein and Niels Bohr about the nature of the quantum, and indeed the nature of the world, whether it is a reality "out there" to be discovered by the observer or whether the scientist as observer and participant, by his choice of what he will look for, by the experiment he conducts and the equipment he employs, has an influence on the observations, and in that sense constructs a "participatory" reality. It would appear that Heisenberg's principle of "indeterminism" or "uncertainty" contributed to Bohr's formulation of the principle of "complementarity," which asserted that no elementary quantum phenomenon *is* a phenomenon until it is a registered phenomenon, and that this act of registration or recording has an inescapable consequence for what you can say about the electron. "We can install a device to measure the position of the electron or one to measure its momentum," but we cannot fit both measuring devices into the same place at the same time, and make measurements of position and momentum simultaneously. The implication for the wave and particle theories of light is that they are complementary: "we can devise an experiment that brings into evidence the particle character of light, or one that brings into evidence the wave nature of light. But we cannot devise an experiment that will bring both features into evidence at the same time."[62]

The manner in which the scientist as observer-participant influences measurement, and his role in the construction of a "participatory" reality seem to loosen the validity of seeing "participation" and "causality" as two exclusive and altogether different orderings of reality. However, it is relevant to note that Heisenberg's "uncertainty" principle and Bohr's principle of "complementarity" relate to the scope of observations within the perspective of a scientific rationality that is predicated on the replicability of observations by different observers conducting the same experiments, and orientated to seeking relationships between observations in a causal mode.

6

Rationality, relativism, the translation and commensurability of cultures

In this chapter, I will attempt to grapple with four interrelated themes:

(1) The delineation and implications of *rationality* as a mode of reasoning, and as a process of constructing knowledge. The dictionary (Shorter Oxford Dictionary) glosses rationality as "reasonableness," "acceptability to reason," "having reasoning power," and it describes rationality as "the distinguishing character of man."

(2) The question of *relativism*, in regard both to the psychic unity or diversity of mankind (human universals), the unity or diversity of cultures and societies, and indeed of the entire world we live in. The question of relativism also includes the senses in which we can or cannot accept the unity of the world and the diversity of its realities.

(3) The question of *translation between cultures* or societies, the means by which we "Westerners" or "moderns" may understand "them," "other cultures," translate their phenomena into our categories and concepts and how that understanding in turn acts upon our own understanding of ourselves.

The "translation of cultures" involves what we may call a "double subjectivity" that is characteristic of the social sciences as presently practiced, and which does not pertain to the physical sciences. This double subjectivity involves sympathy and empathy as well as distance and neutrality on the part of the observer, analyst and interpreter of social phenomena. She or he must first as far as possible "subjectively" enter into the minds of the actors and understand their intentions and reactions in terms of the actors' meaning categories, and then subsequently or simultaneously distance herself or himself from those phenomena and translate them into or map them onto usually *Western* language terms and categories of understanding. This in turn induces another process of self-reflexivity by which our Western understanding of ourselves, our own cultural valuations and presuppositions, are deepened and filled out.

(4) The translation of cultures overlaps with the question of the comparability and *commensurability* between "their" phenomena, concepts and

categories and "ours." The question of commensurability of social and cultural phenomena that have prevailed in the past or prevail today in different parts of our globe raises simultaneously the related issues of *translation, relativism* and *rationality*.

A clarification: human universals and the diversity of cultures/societies

One clarification that I would like to make at the outset is that the doctrine of *the psychic unity of mankind* or *human universals* and the doctrine of *diversity of cultures/societies* are not contradictory dogmas.

The doctrine of human universals is applicable to certain basic human capacities and operations, both physical and mental. (I leave out of this account, of course, malformed individuals with birth or acquired defects.) All humans have within a common range similar sensory and motor skills, the ability, for instance physiologically to see – or the possibility of being trained to discriminate – the same range of colors,[1] and to taste the same range of tastes (sweet, salty, bitter, astringent, sour, etc.), although the cultures/societies they belong to may label, classify or emphasize only some of these colors and tastes, and invest them with different ranges of meanings. All humans see the same colors but color may have different meaning and significance for them. Chomsky has argued for an innately programmed capacity for language, an argument that possibly gains support from the finding that the linguistic skill or intelligence is localized in most (right-handed) humans in the left hemisphere of the brain. Jakobson's phonological theory of distinctive features again implies a universal pattern in the use of sound contrasts to construct morphemes. There are cognitive structures and processes associated with learning and memory that are known to be universal, and others that can be or might be isolated in the future as universals: such as mental operations of the metaphorical and metonymical varieties.

Now, the doctrine of human universals or of the psychic unity of mankind in the above sense can without contradiction be held to be consistent with the diversity of cultures/societies as an empirical fact. The diversity of cultures can be accounted for on broadly two fronts:

(a) Man is from the beginning a social being, and societies/groups have creatively adapted and developed in space and time in an open-ended way, and the cumulative products of their different trajectories are a diversity of cultural configurations, and a range of social institutions.

In accepting the thesis of a diversity of cultures and societies, it is important to bury the nature–nurture, or nature–environment question, by holding that from very early on in man's history his biological and mental endowments have interacted with his socially manipulated ecological environment, and therefore there is no point at which we can say nature ended here and culture began there.[2]

(b) Secondly, a hallmark of man's history in society has been the flexibility in the uses of his so-called innate capacities. Man's brain development placing a reliance on learning capacities and memory storage, and enabling him to be reflexive, to indulge in meta-learning, and so on, has simply expanded his creative horizons. Again early technology, which began as an accessory to man's physical skills and signified a state when man adapted to nature, became capable as it became more complex and inventive, to progressively free man from certain physical and ecological constraints, such that man has ended up by adapting nature to his needs rather than by adapting himself to nature. It is such cumulative and spiralling advances of an exponential kind that make some of us want to repudiate the narrow biological determinism of the E. O. Wilson kind of sociobiology in favour of the Stephen Jay Gould kind of "potentialist" open-ended evolution or change.

Thus to try to extrapolate outwards in a deterministic mode from allegedly basic biologically motivated impulses, such as the achievement of inclusive fitness or the ensuring of reproductive success, to the elaborate and varied array of institutions of kinship and marriage in distinct human societies is a forlorn hope; and to take as given whole complexes of human institutions that have crystallized in certain times and places, and then select certain features and sub-complexes such as polyandry, or levirate and sororate, or polygyny, as if they exist in isolation, and to argue that they make "functional" sense in terms of inclusive fitness or reproductive success is a simple-minded re-ductionistic exercise. What the sociobiologists have not grasped is that human adaptation is an open-ended process that reacts to historical contingencies and circumstances; that the constraints human beings in groups or societies confront appear at several levels – not only at the biological, but also at the ecological once an ecology has been evolved in conjunction with a technology and a pattern of human cooperation, and then again at the institutional level, once a whole complex of political, religious, and social arrangements are in place. The institutional level encompasses the ecological, and that in turn the biological. There is no biological untouched by the social. Not only do constraints, many of them man-made, operate at various levels, but also while providing the limits of possibilities they do not *determine* the ongoing dynamic outcomes of open-ended history.

(c) The result of social man's production and living in diverse and different social realities and his commitment to diverse collective representations is that in some delimited domains of knowledge – such as technical and mathematical skills, abstracting and theorizing scientific skills, and so on – men in different societies are "unequal" in performance (even though their innate capacities are the same). But there are other domains of life, and frames of thought and action, especially the arts and crafts, music, dance, cuisine, ritual performance etc., that lie outside the provenance of mathematico-logical and scientific skills, and their distribution seems to have little integral connection with the level of achievement in science.

There is some sense in referring to certain fundamental "existential problems," and "fundamental anxieties" faced by all mankind, such as the consciousness of the possibility of death and having to cope with that finality in terms of after-death beliefs and mortuary rites and cults of the dead, but even here mankind's cultural constructions have been so profusely rich and varied that we are well advised to be circumspect about the prospect of isolating worthwhile generalities beyond the superficial. Again, the problem of the origins of evil and suffering ("theodicy") and the explanation of its distribution in the world, and the modes of coping with it, have, as any student of comparative religion well knows, produced diverse (and even incompatible) answers and institutionalized religious responses. The same argument applies to human languages. Human languages may share certain universal features, whether at the phonological level of distinctive features or at the syntactical level of grammatical categories, but these features do not exhaust or explain the character or achievements or uses, literary, poetic, rhetorical, oratorical, etc., of any particular language, and the linguistic productions over time of the people who have spoken that language.

(d) There is one last point that can be made about "the unity of the world." Science in its most restricted and carefully formulated sense implies a construction of knowledge that in principle is about the "objective" features of one kind of reality out there. Although one must take important recognition of the nature of scientific revolutions and the shifts in paradigms, and although one must accept the provisional nature of extant scientific knowledge, yet I think it is sensible to hold that in principle the laws of physics or chemistry have to be the same everywhere in this world. As Popper has put it, and no scientist will disagree, while there may be many "logically possible worlds," empirical science affirms only one world, the real world of experience.[3] Now this conceptual and mathematico-logical unity of the reality out there is, as Schutz insisted, only one ordering of reality, with its own confines and area of competence.

As my forays into the history of science have suggested, *modern* science is the eminent achievement not only of certain kinds of societies and civilizations, but also of only a narrow coterie of human beings inside them, namely the scientists. As Gellner puts it – and this quotation is only admissible within the limits I have placed on the kind of reality the physical sciences relate to – "Science needs one world. It does not need one kind of man within it. But one *kind* of man did make the single world. His historical situation may have been unique, his basic constitution was not."[4] But though this science has been the construction of a few culturally specific people, the "scientists," yet being a universal knowledge in principle science is potentially transmissible as a system of knowledge to every corner of the globe. The tribesman on Mount Hagen in New Guinea, the peasant in Northeast Thailand, the pastoralist in Afghanistan – all these, though not scientists now, can become scientists given the right educational circumstances; better still their children are even more easily transformed.

But as we shall see shortly in our discussion on the impact of Western science and technology on the different cultural contexts and social arenas of the Third World, the limits of the power of this universalizable scientific knowledge and technology to transform, or dissolve, the beliefs, representations and activities that are already in place is a complex issue, on which no easy answers can be given.

The contesting positions regarding rationality and relativity

I have in chapter 3 referred to Wittgenstein's scornful denunciation of Frazer for being insensitive to the inappropriateness of his judging primitive (magical) rites to be *mistakes*; and we also gained some idea of Wittgenstein's contrasting of "explanation" with "form of life" as different modes of understanding.

A number of modern philosophers since Wittgenstein have grappled with the related issues of rationality, relativism, the translation of cultures, and their commensurability.

The kind of rationality invoked by modern philosophers, such as Alasdair MacIntyre, Peter Winch, Donald Davidson, Bernard Williams, Charles Taylor, and Stephen Lukes, usually refers to logical rules, and to the constraints of "consistency," "coherence," "non-contradiction," as they are used to articulate or theorize in abstract terms from a disengaged perspective, or to spell out propositions and to specify the rules of inference, both deductive and inductive, or to judge the appropriateness of means used to reach stated objectives. This kind of "rationality" has been, everyone will assent, most self-consciously formalized and systematized in the West, and the comparative question relates to the grounds and contexts in which, and the social and religious phenomena to which, this conception of rationality can be used as a universal yardstick.

The problem of the relevant contexts, in which the modern Western philosophical-scientific conception of rationality can be applied, has evoked a disagreement among modern philosophers (and philosophically oriented sociologists and anthropologists), who in a rough and approximate sense fall into two broad schools. Let us label them as "unifiers" or lumpers versus "relativizers" or splitters. I see on the basis of family resemblance scholars like MacIntyre, Gellner, Davidson, Lukes as "unifiers," and Wittgenstein, Winch, Geertz, Barnes, Hacking as "relativizers." Let me simplify and report their contrasted positions in the form of a dialogue, as a prelude to a deeper and more nuanced discussion subsequently.

Unifiers/"lumpers"	*Relativizers*/"splitters"
(1) There can be only one *rationality* based on universally valid rules of logic and inference. Modern Western analytic rules and	(1) There can be multiple "rationalities," different "language games," "forms of life" (Wittgenstein) or "styles of

concepts provide the categories of understanding, even if "rational knowledge" as presently constituted is provisional. An external observer should be able to apply these criteria of rationality to the phenomena he studies.

(2) Transcultural and comparative judgments can be made as to the degree of rationality and irrationality manifest in a belief or action system. In principle, it is possible to grade these systems as superior or inferior, and the possibility of such judgment revolves on the eliciting or inducing of the proper *evidence*.

(3) The translation of cultures is possible, and the problem of relativism can be set up and decisively tested, because we must and can presuppose between cultures a base of agreement (Davidson), a bridge-head of commonly shared standards of truth, and inference, and a commonly shared core of beliefs and experiences whose meanings are fixed by the application of those standards (Lukes). It is the common agreement that makes translation at all possible, or allows us to set up the problem of relativism at all.

reasoning" (Hacking)[5] and some of these can be incommensurable activities. It is therefore necessary to postpone, and to hold back as long as possible, from a too hasty application of rationality criteria that may not be appropriate.

(2) Transcultural judgments of greater or lesser rationality are difficult to apply between cultures, and between earlier and later historical periods. There are the ever-present dangers of making "category mistakes" (Winch), and misplaced comparisons, and of the misapplication of rational canons to phenomena that are poetic, aesthetic and affectively charged, and therefore not amenable to judgments of rationality.

(3) Translation of cultures is difficult, but possible, provided a "careful" mapping of the other culture's understandings onto our understandings is done, with the proviso that our own "rational" categories can in turn be informed and modified by virtue of our cross-cultural experience. The preference for "thick description" (Geertz) and for first grasping the "experience near" data in their fullness before translating them into more abstract "experience far" concepts (Kohut) comes close to the spirit of this position.

As a sequel to this aerial view of the arena in which the disputes have been conducted – the disputants have not always understood one another in certain matters – let me now attempt to state and clarify the issues and to resolve them, if possible, from my point of view.

Rationality, translation and commensurability

We are at a stage now to delineate, differentiate as well as interrelate systematically three notions that have been repeatedly used in recent discussions by both philosophers and anthropologists. They are rationality, translation of cultures, and their commensurability.

These concepts were central to a dialogue and a controversy which began in the 1960s between two philosophers, Peter Winch and Alasdair MacIntyre, a controversy which began to engage the anthropologists as well, because it used Evans-Pritchard's ethnographic writings on the Azande and the Nuer as grist for its philosophical mill. The controversy is historic because (despite some howlers concerning the meaning of cattle to the Azande, which Gellner exposed with some relish)[6] it was an occasion when modern philosophers dipped into exotic anthropological ethnography to argue their philosophical positions. It no doubt helped to raise the philosophical consciousness of contemporary anthropologists concerning a cluster of classical issues that had already been of concern to Tylor, Durkheim, Lévy-Bruhl and others.[7] Interestingly Evans-Pritchard himself because of his equivocations was not claimed by Winch or MacIntyre, who each placed him as belonging more to the opponent's camp! It is relevant to note that Winch uses the ordinary language philosophy of the later Wittgenstein to think with and against Evans-Pritchard. While Evans-Pritchard did subscribe to the notion that there was a context-independent notion of "reality" (the "reality" whose truth "science" establishes) against which the rationality of Zande notions of witchcraft and magic and oracles could be judged and be found wanting, Winch held that there is no reality independent of the language games and forms of life of a given language community. MacIntyre drives a wedge into Winch's position by demonstrating that there is a dialectical and reflexive character to understanding and that the privileging of the natives' categories does not, and cannot, imply the abdication of the investigator's categories. But as we shall see, Winch, though corrected on the translation issue, has important things to say on relevant comparison.

Rationality

In a general sense many of the modern philosophers, be they logical positivists, or "ordinary language" philosophers, or of some other persuasion, share a conception of rationality that minimally identifies logical consistency and coherence as its distinctive feature. As Charles Taylor puts it: "Logical inconsistency may seem the core of our concept of irrationality, because we think of the person who acts irrationally as having the wherewithal to formulate the maxims of his action and objectives which are in contradiction with each other." Someone who has willed an end and then acts to prevent it from eventuating is guilty of a formal inconsistency on the principle that he "who wills the end wills the means." Thus rational understanding is linked to "articulation" and being able "to give an account."[8]

Donald Davidson puts it this way:

> If we are intelligibly to attribute attitudes and beliefs, or usefully to describe notions of behaviour, then we are committed to finding in the pattern of behaviour, belief, and desire, a large degree of rationality and consistency . . . Just as the satisfaction

of the conditions for measuring length or mass may be viewed as constitutive of the range of application of the sciences that may employ these measures, so the satisfaction of conditions of consistency and rational coherence may be viewed as constitutive of the range of applications of such concepts as those of belief, desire, intention and action.[9]

Jon Elster in *Sour Grapes* attempts a systematic discussion of *rationality* in these terms. He begins by giving a "thin" theory and a "broad" theory of rationality as formal features of *individual actions*:

"Consistency, in fact, is what rationality in the thin sense is all about; consistency within the belief system; consistency within the system of desires; and consistency between beliefs and desires on the one hand and the action for which they are reasons on the other hand."[10] This gloss is thin because it leaves unexamined the beliefs and desires that form the actor's reasons for logically consistent action.

The "broad" theory, therefore, goes beyond the formal requirements, and tries to stipulate that the beliefs and desires motivating consistent action be themselves rational in a more substantive sense: Thus "substantively rational beliefs are those which are grounded in the available evidence: they are closely linked to the notion of *judgment*."[11] Remarking that it is difficult to stipulate a corresponding notion of substantively rational desire, Elster remarks that "*autonomy* is for desires what judgment is for beliefs."[12] The broad theory would imply "that acting rationally means acting consistently on beliefs and desires that are not only consistent, but also rational."[13]

If these are the formal features of individual rational actions, how is rationality to be extended to the *collective case*? Elster formulates his view thus: "At this level rationality may either be attached to collective decision-making (as in social choice theory) or to the aggregate outcome of individual decisions. In both cases the individual desires and preferences are taken as given, and rationality defined mainly as a relation between preferences and the social outcome. A broader theory of collective rationality will also have to look at the capacity of the social system or the collective decision mechanism to bring the individual preferences into line with the broad notion of individual rationality."[14]

Now, these delineations of "rationality" in general terms and its relation to, and exhaustiveness for, "explaining" human action do face certain limitations.

(1) The first relates to the fact that although "intentionality" is a necessary component for explaining behavior, it is not *sufficient* by itself. And logically following from this, is the issue that if human action is also "caused" by factors working outside the frame of actors' intentions and beliefs, how are we to systematically relate "intentions" and "causes" and "outcomes", and where does explanation and causality in terms of rationality stop and fall short?

Donald Davidson has a clear sense of this problem. Though intentional action is by no means all the behavior there is, yet for the human species intentionality is conceptually central. At the same time, we have to admit that intentional human behavior (and therefore thought, desire and voluntary choice) cannot be brought under deterministic laws as physical phenomena can, because the "psychological" features we have to take account of have no counterpart in the world of physics.

Davidson seems to be saying that intentionality and rationality provide causal explanation, but do not cover the entire ground of causality: "Two ideas are built into the concept of acting on a reason (and hence, the concept of behavior generally): *the idea of cause and the idea of rationality*. A reason is a rational cause. One way rationality is built in is transparent: the cause must be a belief and a desire in the light of which the action is reasonable . . ."[15] But, concedes Davidson, the advantage of this mode of explanation is that *we can explain behavior without explaining too much*. Explanations by reasons avoid coping with the complexity of causal factors by singling out one of them.

But Davidson's somewhat cheerful acceptance of the limits of causal explanation in terms of rational intentions is justified if only "acting on a reason" provides the basis for explaining much, if not all, of behavior. Aside from that huge area of darkness signified by "unconscious" motivations and desires, which the net of "rationality" as hitherto defined does not catch, there is another formidable caveat that can be stated from inside rational choice's own space. As Elster puts it: "There are many cases in which rationality – be it thin or broad – can do no more than exclude alternatives, while not providing any guide to the choice between those remaining. If we want to *explain* behavior in such cases, causal considerations must be invoked in addition to the assumption of rationality."[16] From here again, the anthropologist and the sociologist could take over and point to extensive documentation and demonstration in their literature (1) of unintended consequences of action, unanticipated by-products that are not connected with the reasons of action, and "latent functions" of action (Merton); and (2) of the shaping, manipulation, and dictation of actors' choices by the structures of power, privilege and domination in place.

(2) A second issue, closely related to the foregoing question of the sufficiency of rational intentionality for exhausting causality, concerns the very adequacy of the criterion of individual preference itself as the guarantee of rational choice and of the consistency among the choices of an individual actor.

Elster asks this devastating question that points to a problem in the very foundations of utilitarian theory: "why should individual want satisfaction be the criterion of justice and social choice when individual wants themselves may be shaped by a process that preempts the choice?"[17] The main thrust of Elster's *Sour Grapes* is to ask why he should take account of individual preferences as the building block of rationality, if actors in fact tend to adjust, adapt, and over time, change their aspirations and preferences according to the possibilities and circumstances that they face. The very cause of the fox holding the grapes to be sour was his conviction that he would be excluded from consuming them. Hence it is difficult to justify the allocation of welfare by invoking the fox's preferences.

Elster examines the mechanisms and processes that constitute the phenomena of *adaptive* preference formation and change, of which sour grapes is an instance. Sour grapes is a way of reducing cognitive dissonance (a concept originally formulated by Leon Festinger) by rearranging the preferences. "Rationalization" is a kind of adaptive mechanism that by contrast shapes the perception of a situation itself rather than its evaluation. There are other processes which shape preference formation and question the utilitarian theory of choice: such as addiction, pre-commitment, and manipulation by dominant interests, and so on.

(3) A third consideration that might well modify the criterion of logical consistency as the hallmark of rationality is a system of rules of conduct that are *context-sensitive*. In so far as the requirement of consistency is interpreted as demanding that moral rules and judgments be consistent with one another such that they are "universalizable" and have general application, those rules are *context-independent*. But as is well known, feudal and caste-based societies usually have codes of conduct and privileges appropriate to, and "relative" to constituent status groups, and these groups in turn may have ranked preferences indexed to contexts. Such a system of "relativized" and contextualized moral rules and judgments does not spell anarchy or atomism, but could be consistent as a system of hierarchized wholes, as a collection of strategies open to individuals or collectives, as has been demonstrated so convincingly for Indian society.[18] It is only when the expectation is that a rule be applied on a universalistic basis, that a particularistic application of it is obviously a violation of the canons of consistency and of rationality.

Our last fly in the ointment, concerning the *philosophical justification* and tenability of a conception of rationality of the kind put forward by logical positivists and many of the "ordinary language" philosophers alike, is introduced by Hilary Putnam. Putnam labels as "a criterial conception of rationality" any conception which appeals to "institutionalized norms" to define what is and is not rationally acceptable. It is self-refuting to argue that rationality is "identical with or properly contained in what the institutional norms of the culture determined to be instances of it. For no such argument can be certified to be correct, or even probably correct, by these norms alone."[19] This philosophical objection does undermine all systems of rules and judgments that base their rationale on understanding shared by a community of practitioners, and it thereby also applies, as we shall see later, to the canons of scientific rationality as well. But such a criterial conception of rationality that appeals to institutionally shared norms need not inevitably lead to anarchism or total relativism or the impossibility of translation between cultures.

Translation

In the original debate between them, Winch and MacIntyre emphasized different centres of gravity in their positions. Winch, beginning with the prescription that the understanding of people should be in terms of their own concepts and beliefs, went on to emphasize the possibility of different "rationalities" and social logics, warned against the error of making "category mistakes" in comparing (or reducing to a common measure) phenomena whose points or foci of interests are different as "forms of life," and maintained that his principle of charity required that translation of another people's conceptions into the categories of one's own language be not regarded as a one-way street, for the true understanding of another should hold open the prospect that the other's conceptions may inform our own, and thereby extend and/or modify our own conception of rationality.

It seemed that MacIntyre's counterthrust scored some initial victories in respect of the question of what is involved when an anthropologist gives an "account" of another society in his own language, a task that involves translation and an unavoidable meeting and confrontation of the notions of intelligibility of that society's and the anthropologist's own. That is to say, an anthropologist's successful translation and account of another people's beliefs, norms and actions implies that there is some shared space, some shared notions of intelligibility and reasoning (rationality) between the two parties. Secondly, MacIntyre, while granting the force of Winch's insistence that the anthropologist's first task is to grasp from within their tradition the criteria and valuations governing the belief and behavior of a people, and that the anthropologist can only complete his or her task by filling in the social context of their use and application, insisted simultaneously that it is not possible to approach alien concepts except in terms of the anthropologist's own criteria. The anthropologist's probing of, and search for, another society's or culture's standards of intelligibility, implicit or explicit, or even their fuzziness and incoherence, necessarily invokes his or her own standards. And if the social scientist does this self-consciously he or she has a better chance of becoming aware of his or her own culture's limitations and distortions. In short, MacIntyre has argued, I think correctly, that to successfully describe the rules of use of another culture, the anthropologist (in practice a Westerner or one exposed to Western indoctrination) applies "standards of rational criticism" as developed in the contemporary West.

I think it is undeniable that any conscientious attempt at glossing and exegesis of the other society's linguistic concepts and practices, systems of classification, and contours of belief involves systematic questioning – both structured and open-ended – so as to separate out areas where there are no problems of meaning, from those where the meanings are implicit or embodied in phenomena not commonly transparent to the actors, and those in turn from areas where no clarity or coherence seems possible. Again when structural functionalists or Marxists probe the functional relations between phenomena, and their contributions and consequences (latent, manifest, and unanticipated), and make judgments about their "effects" with regard to harmony, conflict, or integration at various levels, they are employing a form of "rational criticism." And scientists of other persuasions and styles, structuralists, psychologists of various brands, and symbolists engage in their own exercises of systematization that move from local formulations to their meta arrangements and patterns.

Moreover, it is relevant to bear in mind that conceptions and beliefs and valuations have a "history," in the sense that they have or have had their salience in their present or past contexts; also in the sense that the significance and meanings attached to them may change through time; and, moving to a synchronic level, in the sense that in differentiated societies, they are capable of being differently understood, or valued, differently accepted or rejected, and these differences also constitute a form of "rational criticism" from the inside. Moreover, if there are internal criticisms and evaluations within a society, then its agents have to exercise some choice between alternatives and engage in debate about the "rationality" of their rules and conventions. These internal critiques help sensitize the anthropologist and orient him for his own task of intelligible translation and structural evaluation.

Let us leave MacIntyre here and probe further the intricacies of translation; but I also want to give notice that he has by no means said the last word, because we have yet to face the issue of the limits and scope of "rational criticism," and the limits of making intelligible "comparisons" and commensurations. As we shall see, Winch's strictures against "category mistakes" cannot so easily be buried.

Donald Davidson has amiably proposed some working rules for translation of cultures that perhaps cast more light than MacIntyre's polemical and sometimes cryptic assaults. Remarking that the correctness of an attribution of belief is no easier than interpreting a man's speech, and that in turn we cannot master a man's language without knowing much of what he believes, he proposes that "the problem of interpretation [and translation] therefore is the problem of abstracting simultaneously the roles of belief and meaning from the pattern of sentences to which a speaker subscribes over time."[20] Davidson proposes certain maxims of "interpretive charity" which in effect stress the "shared space" of rationality between the translator and his subject (and, as Putnam reminds us, that interpretive charity or "benefit of the doubt" *maximizes the humanity* of the person being interpreted):[21] "In the case of language, the basic strategy must be to assume that by and large a speaker we do not yet understand is consistent and correct in his beliefs – according to our own standards of course. Following this strategy makes it possible to pair up sentences the speaker utters with sentences of our own that we hold true under like circumstances. When this is done systematically, the result is a method of translation. Once the project is under way, it is possible, and indeed necessary, to allow some slack of error or difference of opinion. But we cannot make sense of error until we have established a base of agreement."[22] Davidson has stated elsewhere that "the only possibility at the start is to assume general agreement on beliefs," and that if the method of charity has as its purpose "to make meaningful disagreement possible, this depends entirely on a foundation – some foundation in agreement. Such charity is forced on us . . . if we want to understand others, we must count them right in most matters."[23]

From here Davidson makes what seems to be a "strong" conclusion: that interpretation of the patterns (syntactic and semantic) of verbal behavior and language use, and of the patterns of beliefs and social actions, is parallel to similar exercises in that we interpret the patterns "in accord, within limits, with standards of rationality . . . In the case of language, this is apparent, because understanding it is *translating* it into our own system of concepts. But in fact the case is no different with beliefs, desires, and actions."[24]

Now, the maxim "translating it into our own system of concepts" is not self-evident, nor does it easily guide us out of the woods. For one thing, there is a world of difference between establishing a *one-to-one correspondence* between a concept or practice in another culture and one in our own, and *mapping* a phenomenon in another culture onto one of our own. The latter involves establishing by a dialectical process the overlaps as well as the differences in their contours and their provenance, thereby raising the question of meaningful "comparison" and "commensuration." For another thing, Davidson's notion of "a base of agreement" (or other similar notions of "shared space" and "bridgehead of understanding") leave unspecified the *width* of the base of agreement, or the *amount of content* of the space that is shared, such that it also leaves open the prospect that a translation or mapping of the kind described may yet reveal that "the common universal rationality" that is shared as a lowest common denominator, is less significant than the differences that are not shared. In this case the rationality we have to seek to establish must try to fit the "relativities" into an encompassing framework of absolute truth and rationality, which is both contingent and open-ended (but not indefensible). And it is this more complex notion of the *possibility* of universal reason that Winch, the seeming relativist, was, I like to think, affirming in words to which many anthropologists, who have labored and striven to understand the other, and holding open the door to options to life other than that of the dominant West, sympathetically responded to. Stressing the dialectical implications of translation, Winch thought that "our standards" can be "extended and modified" by probing what intelligibility amounts to in the life we are investigating, and by bringing it into (intelligible) relation with our own conception. "That is, we have to create a new unity for the concept of intelligibility, having a certain relation to our old one and perhaps requiring a considerable realignment of our categories . . . Seriously to study another way of life is necessarily to extend our own."[25] And I do not think MacIntyre or Davidson would dismiss this ampler scope of human reason.

Inevitably then, we have to try and clarify the nature of the relation between translation of cultures and the concept of *commensurability*, which has been variously used and has been a source of some confusion.

The coin of "commensurability" seems to have begun to circulate with high visibility in the academic marketplace after Kuhn's somewhat spectacular use of it to characterize scientific revolutions and paradigm change. "The transition from a paradigm in crisis to a new one from which a new tradition of normal science can emerge is far from a cumulative process, one achieved by an articulation or extension of the old paradigms. Rather it is a reconstruction of the field from new fundamentals, a reconstruction that changes some of the field's most elementary theoretical generalizations as well as many of its paradigm methods and applications." The paradigm change is like a "gestalt switch," and the new paradigm is "incommensurable with the old, their conceptual networks are different, the data they assemble are different, and they propose different systems of relations."[26] In short, each paradigm has its own nest of commitments – conceptual, theoretical, instrumental and methodological.

Kuhn's assertion of "incommensurability" between the old paradigm and its successor has raised many problems regarding the "progress" of science, and the "history" of science. Kuhn has been less than clear on "progress." While he has said that it makes sense to talk of cumulative knowledge within "normal science" (that is, knowledge-making by scientists working within a paradigm), it is difficult to say so in the case of switches of paradigm. But he is also on record as saying that there is progress in science because a victorious paradigm not only accounts for all that the superseded one did, but also solves new issues and generates new puzzles to solve. The application of these criteria should differentiate earlier from later theories descended from a common stock and signify progress as a unidirectional and irreversible process: "accuracy of prediction, particularly of quantitative prediction; the balance between esoteric and everyday matter; and the number of problems it solved."[27] If the incommensurability thesis as propounded by Kuhn, and further deployed by Feyerabend, implies that terms used in a displaced or buried theory, or another culture different from ours, cannot be equated with any terms or expressions we possess, and if this thesis were really true, then Putnam objects that "we could not translate other languages – or even past stages of our own language at all ... To tell us that Galileo had 'incommensurable' notions and then to go on to describe them at length is totally incoherent."[28]

In order to clarify the question of whether translation schemes can succeed in capturing the "real" sense or reference, Putnam introduces a distinction between "concept" and "conception" which we may usefully adopt, for it serves to distinguish the issue of the possible lack of one-to-one correspondence in a variable number of concepts (terms, categories) between cultures from the issue of mapping and glossing and describing in detail the contours of one culture's concepts in the language of another culture, even if the latter does not possess the verbal concept in question. This after all is what anthropologists and Indologists have done a great deal of the time; the concepts of *nirvana, dharma, karma* and so on, familiar to students of Buddhism and Hinduism can be glossed and described in English, and much Indological scholarship is devoted to these translations that have no exact conceptual parallels in English, French and German. Quine's warning of indeterminacy of translation has not been a serious deterrent.

So Putnam's distinction between concept and conception formalizes what has been extensively practiced with success. Taking an example from the European history of science, he observes that the concept of "temperature" used in a previous historical period from ours can be mapped onto ours by special glosses and other devices. "But so doing is compatible with the fact that the seventeenth-century scientists, or whoever, may have had a different *conception* of temperature, that is a different set of beliefs about it and its nature than we do, different images of knowledge, and different ultimate beliefs about many other matters as well . . . we could not say that conceptions differ and how they differ if we couldn't translate." ". . . Interpretive success does not require that the translatee's beliefs come out the *same* as our own but it does require that they come out *intelligible* to us."[29] To apply the same argument to a more complex example involving two cultures and two languages, it is possible to take the concept of "god" in the Bible and of "deva" in a Hindu text in Sanskrit, treat them as roughly parallel concepts and by recursive glossing and describing, delineate their different profiles, and from there by progressive expansion explain how the Christian God in a monotheistic religion is embedded in a conception of religion that is so different from a polytheistic Hindu conception. Now, this whole operation is possible because although Christian "god" and Hindu "deva" are not the same concepts, we can still compare and plot their distinctive features because they share, or we assume they share, *some* commensurabilities, some amount of base agreement. Ultimately then the anthropological project of translation of cultures is committed to the maxim of interpretive charity which commits us "to treating not just our present time-slices, but also our past selves, our ancestors, and members of other cultures past and present, as *persons*; and that means . . . attributing to them shared references and shared concepts, however different the *conceptions* that we attribute."[30]

So, translation implies *some* measure of comparability, and comparability in turn implies *some* measure of *commensurability*. But this inference has brought us to the threshold of the thorny and contested issue of how we are to understand *commensurability* and *comparison*.

Scrutinizing the dictionary definitions of "commensurate" and "commensuration" I am tempted to say that while "measurement by comparison" is their shared meaning, this in turn divides into two modalities. One modality focuses on "reducing to a *common measure*, measuring by a *common unit*," and the other one "making proportionate, the act of proportioning." And "proportion" in turn is said to signify "the relation as to magnitude, degree, quantity or importance that exists *between portions or parts, a part and the whole, or different things.*" (In mathematics it signifies "an equality or identity between ratios".)

In anthropology there are two styles of comparison which can be associated with the two modalities listed above. They have enormously different implications. A debate between Berreman and Dumont as to how to characterize the caste system in India illustrates them well.[31] Berreman's method – which has precedence in much positivist, behavioristic and quantitatively oriented sociology – aspiring to comparison by common measures – would group Indian caste, together with systems of social class in the industrialized West, racial discrimination and domination in the United States, European feudalism, under the common rubric of *Social Stratification*, and then compare them according to their "similarities" with regard to measures of inequality, rates of social mobility, exercise of power, economic well-being, and so on.

For Dumont this method of comparison is anathema and violates the spirit and organizational principles of the Indian caste system as a total social phenomenon. His structuralist method aspires to delineate a system of relations, and is akin to the second mode of comparison by "proportioning." The Indian caste system is a "hierarchy" constituted in terms of differential valuation given to parts and functions according to their contribution to the whole; in this hierarchy *dharma* as morality, and the priestly function as "status," are superior to, and encompass *artha* as instrumental action and *power* as the function of the ruler/warrior. The unit of such a system is the group which takes priority over individuals. The post-capitalist and industrial Western class systems are constructed on different structural principles. Their basic unit is *homo aequalis*. Possessive individualism is the point of departure and is linked to the triumph of an economic ideology. The economic system of production and distribution and consumption relations (market relations) assigns individuals to class positions; society itself is seen as an aggregation of individuals serving their interests, and individuals take priority over the collectivity. Finally, the understanding of Indian hierarchy teaches the West about its implicit basis submerged by the claims of atomistic individualism.

In other words, if Berreman's sociological method executes comparison by a willingness to sever parts of larger entities, and subject them to common measures of quantitative variation, Dumont's method insists on first con-stituting the total design in terms of the valuations of the socio-cultural entity from within the tradition. This ambition towards totalization bears some similarities to the Maussian concept of "total social phenomenon," to the "collective mentality" of the *Annales* School, the structural–Marxist notion of "social formation," and the Wittgensteinian theme of "form of life." This approach, contrary to common misunderstanding, is *not averse* to comparison. Explicit comparison comes *after* the totalities have been constructed, and it entails the dialectical opposing of total designs, systems of valuations, and hierarchies of relations. It therefore reveals qualitative differences as well as similarities, and in highlighting the former is sensitive to civilizational options.

It is not sensible to declare one of these comparative frameworks true or valid, and the other false or invalid. Dumont's program is closer to the Winchian preference for first understanding a people in terms of their own concepts, valuations and ideologies, whereas Berreman's seeks to derive generalizations by moving to another level of context-independent general measures. But one can ask which method yields better understanding of the socio-cultural phenomena in question, in terms of their historical derivations and trajectories, civilizational preferences, and "developmental" directions. (My own preference, as should be evident from the previous chapters, is for the second mode of comparison by proportioning, by juxtaposing palimpsests of larger designs.)

The preference for the construction of totalities and forms of life in fact may lead us to the *limits* of comparison and commensuration, in that "the point which following the rules has in the society" (Winch), the emphases and centre of gravity of a culture, its total design, may in summation give a society or culture a *distinctiveness*, even perhaps a *uniqueness* as a special crystallization of components, such that a comparativist might conclude that it does not take you very far to strip it down and to denude it to a common measure *vis-à-vis* another entity equally distinctive and complex. This is the very edge of the divide to which the process of translation may lead us, the edge which is a situation of *incommensurable exclusivity* (Williams), and which is close to Winch's red signal of "category mistake" and misplaced comparison. So I am sympathetic to these sentences of Winch:

> It may be true, as MacIntyre says, that the Azande do not have the categories of science and non-science. But Evans-Pritchard's account shows that they do have a fairly clear working distinction between the technical and the magical . . . A much more important fact to emphasize is that *we* do not initially have a category that looks at all like the Azande category of magic. Since it is we who want to understand the Zande category, it appears that the onus is on us to extend our understanding so as to make room for the Zande category, rather than to insist on seeing it in terms of our own ready-made distinction between science and non-science.[32]

Kinds of relativism and universal claims

Relativism or its opposite are points of view that have adherents in many disciplines: cultural anthropology, ethics, philosophy and methodology of science, comparative religion, and so on. Useless as a blanket term, relativism and its denial, in the form of universalism or absolutism, must at least be examined in relation to different substantive domains – in relation to science, to moral or ethical systems, to religions, to art styles and so on. For our purposes, we may initially simplify and address the rival claims of relativism with regard to two domains, "culture" and "science," while keeping in mind that these rubrics are themselves capable of further differentiation.

In its strongest, and some philosophers might say its most vulgar, form *cultural relativism* implies these propositions:

(1)   That cultures or societies may have their own distinctive systems of morality and social practices.

(2)   That these systems are "right" for those cultures or societies in terms of their own contexts and their own functional interrelations.

(3)   That, therefore, it is a mistake to pass critical judgments of better or worse on a comparative basis between them, since each is acceptable in its own place.

In this extreme form this kind of cultural relativism is I think untenable. For one thing, proposition (3) above contains a logical contradiction in that it makes a non-relativistic general claim about a relativistic assertion: as Williams puts it, there is here an "unhappy attachment of a nonrelative morality of toleration or non-interference to a view of morality as relative . . . The central confusion of relativism is to try to conjure out of the fact that societies have differing attitudes and values an a priori non-relative principle to determine their attitude of one society to another; this is impossible."[33]

Hilary Putnam has argued in a similar vein that total relativism is inconsistent. The idea of relativism, says Putnam, in its "natural first formulation is that every person (or, in a modern 'sociological' formulation, every culture, or sometimes every 'discourse') has his (its) own views, standards, presuppositions, and that truth (and also justification) are relative to these." Quipping that "if all is relative, then the relative is relative too," Putnam gives a deeper account of relativism's implications, by pointing out that the relativist, in holding that x is true or justified relative to the standards and circumstances of a local culture, accepts this judgment as something "absolute." If a statement of the form x is true (justified) relative to a person, group, or culture is true absolutely, "then there is, after all, an absolute notion of truth." A *total* relativist would have to say that whether or not x is true *relative* to a person, group or culture "is *itself* relative."[34] Let me underscore this point since the philosophical inference has not always fully dawned on us anthropologists: if, as many anthropologists do, we are prepared to argue that on a certain issue societies or cultures A and B hold different views, and each in its context is justified, true or meaningful, we should be prepared to defend this judgment as having *absolute* validity for us, and provide the necessary proof.

There is no doubt an unwelcome entailment to an uncritical total relativism: we would be unable to criticize and condemn what are clearly barbaric and unacceptable violations against humanity, such as the Belsen and Buchenwald prison camps under the Nazis, or South African violations of the human rights of blacks, or the Prevention of Terrorism Act in force in Sri Lanka or the wanton killings there of civilians by armed forces and militants (terrorists). By the lights of the twentieth century one ought to be able to mark out a bottom line, such that United Nations declarations concerning human rights, freedom from hunger and so on become defensible and worthy of support.

Another difficulty could pose a formidable intellectual task. If two moral systems are "apparently" in conflict, the relativist should be able to explain why in fact they are not in conflict, and such an explanation of the problem requires that the relativist find a logical form which makes the two statements straightforwardly compatible, so that there is no problem accepting both.[35]

Speaking for myself I certainly reject a relativist or an anti-anti-relativist stance in any unqualified or total sense, because for the reasons already stated one is likely to cut the ground from under one's own feet when one makes absolute statements on behalf of unqualified relativism.

Does rejection of vulgar cultural or moral relativism necessarily require one to embrace a cultural or moral absolutism, which, in its extreme, and therefore equally vulgar, form declares on a priori grounds that all cultures and societies in their diversity are parts of an encompassing single world system, and in this sense *each* and *every* instance falls under the umbrella of a universal paradigm of "rationality"? Such a position entails its own difficulties if the con-temporary rationality of the West is held to be the sole universal yardstick. The danger is that when every piece of symbolic behavior is sought to be translated as a form of "proposition," a translation supposedly demanded by the notion of "rationality," then either the translation process resorts to various transformational "fictions" which may be as contrived as they are unconvincing, or the notion of propositional rationality itself is so weakened until it becomes a minimalist claim that is more vacuous that illuminating.[36] In regard to this issue, the universal rationalist should beware of too cavalierly underrating the difficulties that have to be surmounted in the process of translation between cultures, or of artificially overrating the status of the requirement that all discourse be reduced or transformed into the verifiable propositional format of logicians.

For these and other reasons I declare myself to be neither a relativist nor an anti-relativist in an absolutist or blanket sense. It is possible to take a more complex position between these extremes, and strive towards comparisons and toward general judgments wherever they are appropriate and possible, and to leave other matters in an unsettled state until better information and superior frameworks make comparative evaluations possible. Let me also assert as part of my plea for patient inquiry that to declare that two phenomena seem incommensurable in our present state of knowledge does not automatically put you in the relativist camp or deny the possibility of measurement at some future time.

It is possible and defensible to hold that in the case of moral systems (and moral philosophy), art forms (and aesthetics), religious systems (and com-parative religion), one could achieve a significant inter-translation between the entities in each rubric. One could also maintain that moral or religious systems address certain universal existential issues and human constraints, and yet hold that the systems in question are in important respects *different* in their emphases, commitments, styles and preferences, and in this sense they are meaningful and acceptable in their place.

A proponent of the above position which addresses moral systems, art styles, religions may simultaneously espouse a unitary philosophy of science which holds that in a certain core sense there can be only a "single science." This universalistic claim pertains, say, to such inquiries as physics (e.g. nuclear physics, quantum physics), genetics, molecular biology, mathematics, and so on, where all practitioners of a discipline in question share concepts, rules of the game, notions of relevant evidence and proof, and strive for unified consistent theories which are in principle correct for the time being. This is a notion of a non-relativistic science concerned with the workings of our world understood in relation to a shared *framework* for creating knowledge.[37] However, this sense of a "single science" in relation to physical, chemical and biological processes can and does coexist with different roles that science in this core and special sense can play in different societies. Societies, and indeed their scientific professions and establishments, can differ in regard to what substantive areas they wish to concentrate on (nuclear warfare, pollution control, AIDS, and so on), what claims "scientific" knowledge makes in regard to matters outside its special provenance (planning the "good" life), and what alliances scientists make with interest groups and wielders of power and affluence. And these differential emphases in the context in which science is conducted might dialectically and recursively reflect back on the kinds of "theoretical knowledge" being constituted in a particular epoch in the sub-disciplines of the hard sciences. Finally, the assertion that there can only be a "single science," exemplified by branches of physics, biology, and so on, pertaining to a "single world," does not logically rule out the possibility of the same single world possessing other "realities" or provinces of "meaning," outside the scope of the single science and capable of being understood in terms of other "frameworks."

Some exercises in meaningful comparisons and judgments

In the light of the foregoing discussion, it is my view that it is more profitable to set down as precisely as possible, firstly, under what conditions firm judgments can be made about the "rationality" (that is the coherence, consistency and verifiability) of one belief system or mode of action *vis-à-vis* another; secondly, under what conditions we can meaningfully compare two systems and pronounce them to be *truly relative*, and thirdly, under what conditions they are best treated as incommensurable. In other words there are three possible outcomes: comparison is possible – even in a partial way – and a judgment of the true/false, or superior/inferior is possible; comparison is possible but the phenomena compared are *truly relative* or alternatives of the *same standing*; thirdly, no meaningful comparison is feasible in our present state of knowledge, because the two phenomena in question have such narrow bases of agreement or shared space that they are better treated as distinctive configurations. In this sense they are better left in a state of *incommensurable exclusivity* rather than being subject to forced comparisons.

The ground rules might be stated more fully as follows:

(1) We have to agree with Donald Davidson that no comparison between two phenomena is possible, without establishing "a base of agrement" between them, from which meaningful disagreements or differences can be projected. This is a minimum condition for setting up the problem of relativism.

(2) Let us call the two phenomena or systems to be compared s1 and s2. The most straightforward case of comparison is where s1 and s2 exclude each other by virtue of proposing conflicting consequences or implications to the same issue or question, which constitutes their base of agreement.

(3) If there is some straightforward decision procedure by which the efficacy or truth of the positions of s1 and s2 can be decided, then relativism will have been banished, and either s1 or s2 can be declared to be superior or rational, and the other inferior and irrational.

(4) A truly relativistic outcome is one in which the formulations of both s1 and s2 are alternatives to the *same* problem, in that their formulations, implications and consequences in their own contexts cannot be shown to be untenable or implausible or inefficacious, such that neither side sees a necessity to abandon its position as inferior.

(5) When two phenomena should not be compared at all because their presuppositions are different, and they constitute two different "forms of life," then there is no basis for setting up the relativism question at all. In these circumstances spurious comparisons may be sought to be made by injecting from s1 a set of concepts and issues which are unthinkable in s2 at all. This is a case of "incommensurable exclusivity" (Williams).[38] In my view Robin Horton's attempt, which I described earlier, to see in African religions "causal theories" in a personal idiom ("causal" as theoretically understood in Western science) is an untenable comparison, a misplaced imposition of theoretical expectations upon the African religions he examines, and therefore a misplaced exercise.

It seems to me that Horton's comparison was misplaced for at least two reasons: Firstly, rather than concentrate on the favoured styles of "reasoning" of African religions and positively delineate their foci, Horton transposes theoretical issues appropriate to Western science to African phenomena. Moreover, African participation in animistic rites, or to switch to another example, the Azande witchcraft beliefs and practices, give no evidence that the African peasants in question were interested in general theoretical and abstract judgments, outside of how events take place in particular social contexts and in relation to certain circumstances. *Horton must be more rigorous and specific in his setting up the relativity test between West African religious beliefs and modern Western science.*[39]

In this set of ground rules it is number (4) above, allowing for a truly relativistic outcome, that is the most interesting and problematic for anthropologists and moral philosophers, because it seriously involves the vexed question of how to achieve a satisfactory translation between cultures in order to make a meaningful comparison.

In the physical sciences it is possible that there may coexist two alternative paradigms for explaining the same phenomenon, but nevertheless it is imagined that in due course the proper instrumentation will be devised and the appropriate evidence be elicited to make a preferential decision. (However, the question of commensurability and relativism does crop up in science in the context of Kuhn's version of scientific revolutions and changes in paradigm and perhaps also Lakatos's account of how a "progressive" research programme will in due course gain over a "degenerating research programme."[40] This issue touched on earlier is best continued later when I deal with modern science and its extensions.)

But in matters social and moral the question is not so easily decided, unlike the imagined examples of some armchair philosophers where the questions are made to look transparently clear, and the decidable evidence is optimistically taken to be within arm's reach. Can we really reduce to a logically testable form what an ordinary Roman Catholic holds about the "immaculate conception" of Mary or a Trobriand Islander about the male contribution to the conception of babies? Or what a doctor at a Rochester hospital means when he says a cure is "miraculous"? Be that as it may, let me now illustrate the kinds of comparative and translation problems anthropologists who have a realistic appreciation of the diversity of cultures and societies are likely to face.

Case 1

In Sri Lanka or in South India in the past smallpox was experienced as a sudden epidemic, and villagers attributed its occurrence to the anger of a named mother goddess (Pattini or Mariamma, *et al.*), because of moral lapses on the part of villagers. Annual festivals were held to appease the mother goddess, purify one's own moral lapses, etc., and thus keep the epidemic at bay.

After the Second World War Western medicine entered the scene and attributed the occurrence of smallpox to a germ theory of disease and managed to eradicate it by vaccination and regulate it by preventive action.

Clearly in this instance both systems of thought and action are *incompatible*, but because they occupy to a significant degree the *same space* – the cure or control of a disease that both Indian villager and WHO expert can recognize as smallpox from its somatic manifestations – modern science was clearly superior according to the criteria of efficacy that both parties can agree to (namely, cure), despite their incompatible explanatory theories. Thus here we can say one set of practices (modern medicine treating epidemics) has posed a challenge to a different interlocutor (the traditional Indian system), not indeed in the language of the interlocutor, but in terms which the interlocutor could not ignore.[41] In this case one can make a valid transcultural judgment of superiority in the treatment of smallpox in favour of Western medicine. The decisive evidence is that the cult of the smallpox goddess may die out, and indeed, has in these parts (though rituals to her of other kinds addressing other issues may continue).

The point of this example is that transcultural judgments of a very *specific* kind can be made, even of seemingly incompatible activities, provided they occupy at least in part the same *space* in the sense I have defined, and their claims can be put to the test.

And I think this example of transcultural judgment also occurs with the kind of assertion Gellner has made – and which we treated earlier – that one can subscribe to a "single unity of the world," provided we limit this to that portion of objective reality which modern physical sciences strive to construct, and whose constraints pertaining to that reality are potentially diffusable to all mankind.

Case 2

My second example concerns the possibility of a relativistic situation. It is related to the definition and understanding of particular kinds of mental disorder as viewed in certain formulations in, say, Western psychiatry and Indian Ayurvedic healing systems.

Both Western psychiatry and Indian *ayurveda* could conceivably establish this basis of agreement and shared space: that there are certain *mental states* that are labelled and are considered to denote some form of illness and ill health. And they may both agree that certain behavioral and somatic symptoms – such as withdrawal from social relations, a depressed emotional state, lack of appetite, and so on – are indices of mental ill health. But beyond this shared space, the Western and Indian cognitive perspectives may be truly incompatible, and there is no clear possibility of a rational judgment as to which is superior, based on results – for both seem to boast successes and admit failures under present circumstances.

Let us say for purposes of a sharp comparison that there exists a certain *Western* theory of the mental illness in question that is predicated on the notions of bounded self and atomistic individualism. Humans exist as separate bounded beings, who are self-centered, and society is only a collection of individuals, and society exists to promote the interests of these individuals. Such individuals extend a limited number of drawbridges which connect them with the outside. I have already referred in my last chapter to the fact that much of developmental psychological theory accents "individuation" as the key task in identity acquisition in adolescence. In such a theory it is natural to posit the *self* as the focal point of consciousness and desire (motivation). Desires, their frustrations, and their non-fulfillments, become the points of reference for considering mental illness. Accordingly therapy stems from this psychology of the individual and concentrates on the "internalized" and "interiorized" processes of the self. Thus a self encased in its subjectivity is seen as splitting into multiple smaller selves or parts, which become cut off from one another, a kind of failure of internal communication. (As we well know, in psychoanalytic theory the self consists of three internal levels – superego, ego and id and their mutual relations). Therapy in this Western paradigm may thus consist primarily of reuniting the "dividual" selves, accepting a coherent account of the alienated patient's biographic past, and of a more fulfilling future course of action to follow.

Let us compare this framework of ideas with an indigenous Indian counterpart. There is an increasing literature on the premises of Indian thought,[42] which it is said does not take as its point of reference the individualistic notion of bounded autonomous selves, but postulates a relational thesis by which the person is integrally connected with the cosmos. The Indian cosmos is seen as constituted of transactions, flows, interactions between various orders and levels: between communities and groups, between families, between persons, and finally within individuals, and between their internal parts. Or to translate it into Western terms, if we must employ these levels or orders of being – namely physical, psychological, social and metaphysical – then the boundaries between these orders in Indian thought are considerably more fluid. The empirical individual self is therefore seen as porous and open to outside influences all the time, and is therefore the residue rather than the motor, the final product and crystallization of diverse exchanges and contracts, rather than their activating cause or agent.

The Ayurvedic system we have in mind postulates that the constituents of nature and of man are the same, and that processes such as the ingestion of food and medicine and the excretion of bodily waste products are part and parcel of the flow of energies and potencies between man and nature. Physical illness is the result of imbalances that can be corrected by exchanges at various levels – by the ingestion of the right substances and diet, by exposure to or protection from climatic conditions, by maintaining proper relations with other persons – family, and kin, and the gods. The Indian conceptions of rasa (aesthetic emotion) and gunas (qualities) emphasize the sensory modalities of taste, touch, smell and hearing, and consider them as vital mediators in exchanges of all types. All in all the Western theory is predicated on a body–mind dualism, the Indian theory tends to be based on their non-duality.

Given these different sketches of basic formulations, it is to be expected that the Indian view of mental illness would be incompatible with the Western approaches. In the Indian shamanistic or spirit possession beliefs, mental illness may be admitted to be related to undue or unfulfilled desires, but the results of such unfulfilled desires are not internally split-off portions of the self but are externalized entities given phenomenal existence as demons and spirits. Hence the viewing of mental illness as caused by the attacks or intrusions by external agents is in line with the paradigm of flows and exchanges between persons, groups and collectivities. The therapy naturally addresses itself to the expulsion of demonic agents and to the orienting of the patient to having solidary relations with other significant persons. It does not, as Western therapy might do, attempt to raise the patient's level of internal consciousness, self-reflexivity, and memory of the past, nor to manipulate his or her feelings of guilt and shame in any conscious way.

It seems then that an Indian aetiology and therapy of mental illness that is "open" to the contributions of society, family, and nature to the internal balance of individuals would be not only incompatible but in certain respects "incommensurable" with that kind of Western paradigm that operates on the conception that body and self are bounded entities, and the basic source from which deviant states are generated. But if each system in its context is no more or less rational and efficacious than the other, then we are faced with the conundrum whether it is possible to delineate a single transcultural context-independent profile of mental states like hysteria or depression, or whatever, that is constructed from a common set of socio-psychosomatic components.

Perhaps the only way general transcultural profiles will become possible is when the Western and Indian systems make passages in opposite directions: if among Western patients it is shown that what are identified and conceived as internal affects and feeling states in fact are also simultaneously statements about their extra-individual, social and cosmic circumstances; and in turn the Indian patients' fears of the intrusion of external agents are demonstrated to have their internal affective and emotional sounding boards. It would be inaccurate on my part if I failed to mention that there have been distinguished Western theorists, such as G. H. Mead, C. H. Cooley, Harry Stack Sullivan, Gregory Bateson and Alfred Schutz, who have seriously and illuminatingly explored the self in its sociocentric, semiotic, relational and dialectical aspects. My stereotyped contrast between an alleged Western psychiatric perspective and an Indian Ayurvedic perspective was constructed to illustrate the conditions under which a relativistic judgment might seem plausible. It is also worth mentioning that aside from these "earlier" theorists there is much being achieved today in the developing field of medical anthropology in the way of larger and ampler theorizing about the concepts of self, person and individual in a comparative context and about issues relating to the translation between cultures that such comparison poses.

Case 3

In Case 1, I dealt with a situation where scientific knowledge and technology could be said to have decisively displaced a phenomenon which was incompatible with it, but which competed for the same space of explanation and remedial action. Smallpox vaccination did decisively kill the smallpox goddess.

But quite often the socio-cultural phenomena that anthropologists (and all social scientists) have to cope with are totalities in which instrumental and performative symbols and actions, causal logic and communicative logic, are intertwined and fused.

Here I draw your attention to the point I made in an earlier chapter: that for me one of the most significant issues that stem from Malinowski's work was how in Trobriand life magical or ritual acts and technical or practical acts were interlaced and interdigitated to constitute larger formations and amalgams which we can label Trobriand "yam cultivation" or "canoe building" and so on.

Not only among Trobrianders but life virtually everywhere manifests totalities in which technico-causal and expressive-performative features are linked, such that to translate these totalities as belonging *exclusively* to one or the other domain alone, leads to the desiccating Tylorian and Frazerian comparative judgments that magical and early animistic beliefs and acts are false "science" or irrational applications of thought. But at the same time, I have argued that the actors make shifts into and out of different orderings of reality, and that we have to recognize at least two modalities of thought and action – participation and causality – as potentially within everyone's reach. Take the case of rice agriculture in any Asian village – it combined, even before the epoch of pesticides and tractors, pretty advanced technical knowledge of soils and cropping techniques, with ritual action, during preparation of the fields, sowing, harvesting and storing the grain. In Northeast Thailand, to advert to a single instance, when the rice grains begin to mature on the plants, the villagers propitiate Maephosob, the goddess (or female spirit) of rice: they take cosmetic articles like a mirror, comb, face powder and beautify her; then at harvest time they solicit permission from her and lead her out of the fields before the heads of rice are cut. The rites are a kind of pregnancy rite. From one point of view the villagers, when asked, would say the ceremonies enable a good harvest. These same farmers also say that good agricultural techniques enable a good harvest. But the Maephosob rites are not only about a good yield, they are also recitations about the value of rice to the people, about its being the basis of their good life, enabling them to be good Buddhists, by enabling them to give gifts of food to the Buddhist monks (*dāna*) and so on, forming a thicket of entailments. The rites thus situate rice production in the larger contexts of life – its promises and values, and its meanings, both retrospective and prospective. In this sense they are an integral part of the ultimate meanings and the "substantive" rationality of action, though judged in terms of a narrow, formal, causal technological scientific rationality, they may well be declared by a neo-Tylorian to be a false technology.

In India in the past, craftsmen who were sophisticated technicians by anyone's criteria cleaned, propitiated and decorated their tools of trade at annual rites: an observer may say that the craftsmen are propitiating the spirit of the tools. Today in industrial factories Indian workers, though they know how the machines work and tend and repair them, may perform a similar rite of annual propitiation of the machines.[43] In Kathmandu in 1981 I witnessed during the Dassein festival several bus drivers, taxi drivers and garage mechanics sacrificing to their machines, daubing blood on them and decorating them with flowers. Thus Western technology and Western technological knowledge, which amplifies and extends traditional technological knowledge, does not necessarily drive out or displace ritual and magical acts which combine the purposive aims of better mechanical performance, or larger yields of rice, with the aims of a moral and prosperous social and religious life.

We are thus driven to ask, not so much why science and technology or causal thought does not displace such communicative and performative action, but why it in fact cannot stand alone and be complete unto itself. Must causality be complemented by participation, and must formal rationality recognize its limits of application and provenance? Did we not perceive from Schutz's reflections that science is a mode of reality consciousness that constitutes a specialized shift from the everyday world, and therefore by definition it cannot fill all the social and moral space around us?

The problem of commensurability and making transcultural judgments faces its biggest obstacles when it attempts to compare and evaluate different systems of morality. In a recent book, *Morality and Conflict*,[44] Stuart Hampshire discusses the difficulties in making transcultural moral judgments. His ruminations can also be said to bear on our discussion of why cultural traditions and forms of life do not lend themselves to simple comparative judgments, and also why the impact of Western science on Third World societies produces complex reactions. Hampshire's arguments conveniently recall many points that I have made earlier, and add new edge to the perspective stemming from the later Wittgenstein and his followers like Winch. It may also be taken as a statement on the limits of human *rationality* with regard to the choice and justification of moral systems.

Hampshire's critical and skeptical stance is built around a set of basic tensions and dualities: between the "two farces of morality," the rational and articulate side and the less than rational, the historically conditioned, imaginative, affectively charged and fiercely parochial; between the "natural" universal species-wide moral requirements and the "conventional," historically conditioned, diversity of moral systems. And in working through the implications and outcomes of these tensions Hampshire concedes that *some* moral injunctions and prohibitions can be explained and justified "by reference to unvarying dispositions and needs of human beings, living anywhere in any normal society: for example, the requirement not to cause suffering when this can be avoided."[45] I understand him as saying that particular customs may be criticized and faulted if they produce glaring and excessive injustice, pain and unhappiness, that is, if they violate truly universally sustainable standards of utility or justice. This, however, is a limiting judgment (rather than a maximal notion) that can apply to such things as wanton murder, robbery, abuse of children and so on. Hampshire's main arguments, however, are devoted to establishing that one definitive list of essential virtues, deducible from human nature, could not be drawn up; that any human species-wide constraints or requirements are compatible with many different conceptions of the good life, and that there are insuperable difficulties in the way of establishing a general theory of morality.

To place the issue in its grand philosophical background: Hampshire is arguing against any kind of general theory of morality that derives ultimately from Aristotle and proximately from Hume, the utilitarians (particularly J. S. Mill and G. E. Moore), the deontologists (such as Kant), and ideal social contract theorists (such as Rawls) – that implies firstly "that moral judgments are ultimately to be justified by reference to some feature of human beings which is common throughout the species," and secondly, "that a morally competent and clear-headed person has in principle the means to resolve all moral problems as they present themselves, and that he need not encounter irresoluble problems: the doctrine of moral harmony."[46]

The main arguments marshalled by Hampshire are of the following kinds:

(1) History and anthropology show that the natural constraints imposed by the common sexual and reproductive needs of the human species still allow for a wide area of diversity: "diversity in sexual customs, in family and kinship structures, in admired virtues appropriate to different ages and to the two sexes, in relations between social classes . . . and in attitudes to youth and old age."[47] The universal species-wide requirements, derived from basic human necessities are very *unspecific*; "they are very general restraints which are compatible with different conceptions of the good life for men."[48] There is an analogy between moralities and natural languages in respect of their diversity, plurality and historical specificity. In short, human nature, conceived in terms of common human needs and capacities, always *underdetermines* a way of life.

(2) The "doctrine of moral harmony" predicated by earlier philosophers is difficult to uphold, because "our everyday and raw experience is of a conflict between contrary moral requirements at every stage of almost anyone's life." Moreover, the recognition of reflexivity in human beings – that is, their capacity to reflect on their desires and interests and actions in their own distinct languages – opens up a duality between "nature" and "convention." It entails the recognition of human beings having to make rational choices between kinds of life and kinds of human excellence. Alongside the power to calculate and argue logically is the capacity to envisage conflicts between norms for a complete life. Hampshire is addressing here the limits put on *rationality* itself by virtue of man's reflexivity, and the inevitability of conflicts "between moral requirements of utility and justice, and moral requirements that are based on specific loyalties and on conventions and customs of love and friendship and family loyalty, historically explicable conventions."[49] These are conflicts *within* moral systems.

(3) The "no shopping principle" relates to another kind of limitation: that the choice of certain worthwhile moral ideals might exclude the pursuit of

other equally worthwhile moral ideals, and therefore entails the sacrifice of some orientations which are greatly admired elsewhere within other ways of life, but cannot be grafted to the original one.

(4) Finally, there are instances when the justification of a moral ideal or injunction cannot be found within a universal rational structure, which has utility and justice as its base, "but in the specification of a complex array of historical realities and causal relations of the kind which Kant called anthropological", that is, their justification is that they are essential elements in the subject's way of life, they "are part of an interconnected set of duties and obligations which, taken together, represent a particular and distinct moral ideal to be expressed in a distinct way of life."[50]

Hampshire warns that these considerations of the interconnectedness of practices and their powerful rootedness in conventional soil acting as their justification might raise moral issues which have no straightforward solution. "Argument might show that a custom does offend against some entirely general principles of fairness and justice, and this is a very strong ground for condemning it. But the custom might be one of a network of interconnected customary family relationships which could not be radically disturbed without undermining a whole valued way of life."[51] These cautions should be borne in mind when social scientists try to understand the attitudes of Muslims to the veiling of their women, of Hindus to the sacrifice of animals to Durga, of fundamentalist Mormons to polygyny, and so on.

7

Modern science and its extensions

In this concluding chapter I shall briefly outline the form and shape of modern science as a pursuit, and place it in its larger context, and probe how this larger context affects science and how, in turn, science affects it. Such an examination is particularly relevant because in contemporary Western civilization "positive science" is held to be the quintessential form of rationality.

In my first chapter I mentioned that the Western conception of science as a labelled, self-conscious and reflexive activity of experimentation, measurement and verification matured in the sixteenth and seventeenth centuries in Europe, that at this time there was a decisive separating off of Christianity (Protestantism) from science, and the repudiation of a third realm of activity as magic. I pointed out that the seeds of this denunciation of certain kinds of transactions as magic are to be found in early Judaism which marked off the monotheistic worship of YHWH from pagan idolatry. I also stated that a very critical precondition of modern science was the contribution of early Greece. According to the classicists it was in early Greece that the systematization of the rules of demonstration and proof was begun, and the marking off of nature as the domain of regular laws of causality was achieved.

From the writings of some eminent philosophers and historians of science, like Karl Popper and Thomas Kuhn and Imre Lakatos, one infers that modern science as a process of knowledge-making has a double axis, a vertical dimension and a horizontal dimension, if I may be permitted to describe it as such (see Figure 1).

The vertical axis is theoretical and philosophical, and is part of science's internal structure. It consists of the rules of logic and research operations, the rules of the game, and the methodology by which observations are tested against the objective "reality out there."

The horizontal axis is the scientific community at large, itself subdivided into specialisms and subcommunities with their distinctive problems and paradigms. This horizontal sociological axis of science as a profession, also part of science's internal structure, signals the fact that the scientific community to which the scientist belongs is the scientist's primary point of

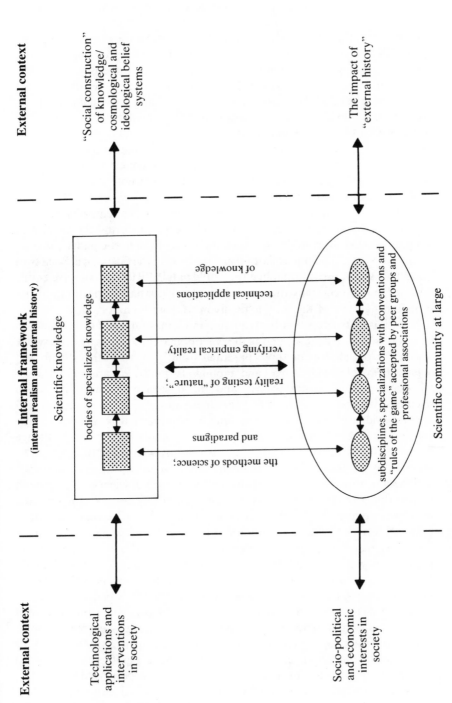

Figure 1 The logic and sociology of scientific inquiry.

reference. It is the social body that writes and enforces the rules of the game: what shall count as the relevant evidence, what constitutes proof and disproof, and so on. The scientific communities clearly highlight the problems most worthy of research, nominate the scientists whom they regard as most prestigious, and uphold certain of the practitioners and their achievements as exemplars. We do know for a fact now that the high profile that some theories enjoy over others is not unrelated to the persuasive and rhetorical skills employed by groups of scientists, to the publicity techniques and media they control or have access to, and other such transmission mechanisms which are necessary to propagate a point of view. It is relevant to note here that a recent book, interestingly titled *The Great Devonian Controversy, The Shaping of Scientific Knowledge among Gentlemanly Specialists*,[1] documents how the resolution of a geological controversy that occurred during the 1830s was integrally related to complex social interactions of the participants based on class, status, age, religious affiliation and position in the Geological Society of London. As an approving Stephen Jay Gould puts it: "Rudwick views scientific knowledge as a social construction, uninterpretable as nature speaking directly to us through bits of fact in a logic divorced from human context."[2]

Now, it is instructive that the regnant paradigms of normal science tend to function as "sets of beliefs" among the practitioners, in so far as the latter work within the parameters of those paradigms and seek to both validate and defend them against challenges and anomalous results. We are very aware of the "conventionalist stratagems" and the defensive measures by which scientists attempt to defend their paradigms in the face of anomalies and counter-evidence. But at the same time, it is important to underscore the convention that in principle science is a game without end, that its knowledge is regarded as provisional, and it accepts rules by which one theory is to be replaced by another if they are in competition. In principle it is these norms and their institutionalization that ensure "the growth of science." The growth of scientific knowledge may thus be seen as occurring through the repeated overthrows of pre-existing theories or paradigms – by intellectual revolutions (to use Kuhn's language) – or by the supersession of one research programme that is degenerating or has run its course, by another that is progressive and generates new puzzles to solve (to use Lakatos's language).[3] Thus, all in all, however convention-bound a scientist as a professional is, still it is the hallmark of a scientist that while he wears the scientist's badge so to say – perhaps his white coat – he is in a special way open to the provisional nature of his knowledge, and therefore to the possibility of changing current theories, much more than he, as well as we non-scientists are open to, indeed resistant to, changing our social conventions and religious paradigms. This is so because the mode of acquiring scientific knowledge, as specialized knowledge, is in some respects less ramified with all the other manifold features and values of our life – our politics, family life, leisure life and so on. It has been held by many theorists of science that a mark of the rationality of science is the commitment of its practitioners to seek a theoretical understanding from a disengaged perspective, an understanding sought from outside the immediate perspective of their goals, desires and activities. This same distancing was emphasized by Schutz in his discussion of different "provinces of meaning" (see chapter 5). Another way of saying the same thing is that science proper aspires to differentiate as a specialism out of the larger totality of our life and experience. An entailment of its specialist and partial character is that a Japanese, or Russian, or American, or Indian nuclear physicist or molecular biologist can and do agree on evidence and proof regarding their technical problems, and whatever their other differences, they can enter into a kind of "context for discourse" and share the conventions of an "internal realism" that is focused on their variety of reality testing. To launch a spacecraft or a missile or to cure cancer Americans and Russians have to pursue and use much the same science.

While we may accept that there exist these theoretical and professional features of a universal science, and that this universal science produces knowledge that is "internal" to it, there are many ways in which science is not merely affected by the outer or external context but also directly leaks into it. The precise dialectic between "the internal history" and "the external history" of Western science is a vexed question, on which the historians of science seem to take different views. I would draw the reader's attention to these points. On the one hand the larger social, political and economic context in which science is embedded affects its history and profile in critical ways. Scientific research is heavily dependent on funding by government, by foundations and by private industrial corporations and the like. This dependence directly affects what problem areas are investigated in preference to others. Nuclear energy may be researched but not solar energy. Military engineering, space research and weaponry (the "star wars" proposal is the latest instance) may take precedence over research into civil engineering, low-cost housing, pollution control, the AIDS disease, and the larger study of sociocultural dimensions of illness and disease.

On the question of how the wider context impacts on science Putnam observes that increasingly it is becoming evident to philosophers of science that "it is not possible to draw a sharp line between the *content* of science and the *method* of science; that the method of science changes as the content of science changes." "The hope for a formal method, capable of being isolated from actual human judgments about the content of science (that is, about the nature of the world), and from human values seems to have evaporated." Even an expanded notion of scientific method that incorporates a formalized psychology of an ideal rational human scientist cannot be constructed independent of judgments about aesthetics and about ethics. It was the belief that the scientific method was a formal method that after all undergirded the claim that "the scientific method would not apply to or presuppose beliefs about ethical, aesthetic, etc., matters."[4] In saying this one does not mean to deny the efficacy of the methodological maxims and procedures developed by scientists, or belittle the impressiveness of their backing their claims with successful predictions, and with remarkable instrumental and technological success. But clearly these maxims and tenets and successes do not define or exhaust rationality, or the scope of reason itself; indeed scientific method presupposes prior notions of rationality, and, as will become clear soon, the truth of ultimate value judgments cannot be scientifically verified by an instrumental logic limited to relating means to ends.

Max Weber on rationality

Among all scholars – social scientists and historians – of the twentieth century it was Max Weber who relied so much on, and was responsible for, the diffusion of "rationality" as an analytical concept, outside the realm of pure science itself.

Since most readers of this book will know something of Weber's writings I shall be brief when I introduce his twin concepts of *Zweckrationalität* and *Wertrationalität*. *Zweckrationalität* has been translated into English as "formal rationality" or "instrumental rationality" (Parsons), or, more cumbersomely but more meaningfully, as a "this worldly relativistic form of consequentialist reasoning." Roughly speaking, this formal rationality is best illustrated in terms of a means–ends schema. For instance, it is employed in neo-classical economics thus: given certain goals what are the relative costs and advantages of using the available (and limited) resources for attaining these goals; given certain means what outcomes are possible and how do they relate to the chosen goals? *Wertrationalität* has been translated as "substantive rationality" (Parsons) or as the "absolutist rationality" of ultimate ends. Here the commitment to the goal is absolute, there is no space for calculations about means and their payoffs. For example, a pacifist is absolutely committed to non-violence or to not engaging in warfare under any conditions. That is the bottom line. He doesn't change his mind if he has to go to prison.

Now Weber contrasted rational authority wherein actors were committed to the rationality of rules and procedures and charters with the authority of custom-bound traditional rulers, and the authority granted to charismatic personalistic leadership. And Weber, as we well know, gave an ideal type description of "capitalism" as a rational form of economic activity – whose distinctive features were calculation of inputs and profits, the use of predictable procedures and accounting systems, the adoption of standard prices, the systematic ploughing back of profits for purposes of increased production in the future, and so on. Weber's ideal type description of bureaucracy as rational organization focused on such features as the systematic delineation of offices, and their command structure and their competencies, the use of universalistic criteria for recruitment and of predictable rules for promotion, the adoption of affective neutrality in the performance of one's official duties, and so on. As a result of seeing Western industrial society as inexorably impelled to create rational structures in every sphere of life, and the powerful snowballing effect these tendencies had as they spread from Europe outwards, Max Weber coined the phrase "the process of rationalization as a world historical process."

Now many readers of Weber imagine that Weber stopped here, and that his delineation of rationalization was a panegyric to capitalism and Western civilization. But it is equally important for us to realize that Weber insisted that within Western civilization itself there was a continuous tension between certain absolutist and ultimate ethical values of the *Wertrationalität* order, and the instrumental manipulative logics of formal rationality. And he, with increasing despair and pessimism, saw that the processes of bureaucratization and consequentialist reasoning if carried too far would work against and turn inimical to some of the most cherished values of individual freedom, creativity, intimacy, and so on. For government bureaucracies and industrial corporations and party machines will in time become vested interests following their own goals to the detriment of the ordinary citizens, who will increasingly find themselves trapped in an "iron cage." Thus although Weber travelled a different route from Karl Marx, they converged in their darkest visions of Western civilization – Marx's theory of the "alienation" of Western man corresponded in part with Weber's notion of his progressive "disenchantment" with the world.

So I want to comment now at some length on how "pure science" and scientific knowledge, by virtue of Western civilization's according it a regnant and privileged position with regard to the understanding and manipulation of the world, has itself spread out into the larger economic and political environment, and is used and perhaps misused to make larger claims, which in the end may produce problems for our civilization. What I have to say on this are extensions first, from Max Weber's classic treatment, and second, from critiques made by the Frankfurt School, such as Habermas.

The extension of the Weberian exposition and critique of "rationality" and the "process of rationalization"

Great and illuminating as was Weber's discussion of rationality and of rationalization as a world-historical process, his analysis can be and has been extended, and carried to new heights.

In *One Dimensional Man*[5] Marcuse asserts that there is an *"internal instrumentalist character"* to modern *"scientific rationality,"* and that it is the consequence of developments such as the following. The quantification of nature and its explication in terms of mathematical structures was accompanied by the separation of science from ethics, of the true from the good, and of reality from ultimate ends. Science could no more conceive the objectivity of nature in terms of "final causes," and this in turn meant that morals and values were labelled "ideal" and incapable of verification by scientific method. As the ethical evaporated into the metaphysical atmosphere, the objective world constituted by the scientist in terms of quantifiable characteristics eminently lent itself to questions of "how," that is, to instrumental operations.

So even if the philosophy of modern science, such as that offered by Karl Popper, allows for only provisional truths and not ultimate certainties, yet science is viewed as marching towards the real core of reality, and there is an air of "practical certainty" associated with its manipulations of matter. In this vein the transformation of man and nature is seen as facing no objective limits save that offered by unmastered knowledge.

Marcuse in a sense takes the Weberian argument to its limits when he asserts that "the new scientific rationality was in itself, in its very abstractness and purity, operational in as much as it developed under an instrumentalist horizon." Science, by virtue of its *own method* and concepts, has projected and promoted a universe in which the domination of nature has remained linked to the domination of man – a link which tends to be fatal to this universe as a whole. Nature, scientifically comprehended and mastered, reappears in the technical apparatus of production and distribution which sustains and improves the life of individuals while subordinating them to the masters of the apparatus.

Marcuse sees the "instrumentalization of things" as also producing the "instrumentalization of men." Technology becomes the great vehicle of "reification," that is, man's feeling that he is subject to an objective rationality that is both uncontrollable and mysterious. Technology is invoked as providing the rationale for the organization of men's lives; technical criteria are said to determine the organization of life, and thus technological rationality protects the "legitimacy of domination" of those who control the productive uses of technology. In this sense "the process of technological rationality is a political process." This truth is larger and prior to the secondary truth that the rationality of pure science is value-free and that it does not stipulate any practical ends, and that technology *per se* could be put to different political services whether of capitalism, socialism or something else.

In an essay entitled "Technology and Science as 'Ideology'" Habermas clarifies Marcuse's critique of Max Weber: what Max Weber called "rationalization" has realized not rationality as such but rather, in the name of rationality, a specific form of political domination.[6] Marcuse has made the charge that the rationality of "science" itself, as a process of knowledge-making, has spill-over effects, and diffuses into other areas of life – such as the choice of appropriate techniques to solve problems, the kind of institutional structures that are built up to support science – in which interests of various kinds are at work, such that it cannot be maintained that some kind of "neutral" and "objective" knowledge is being deployed untainted by social interests and concerns. In so far as science either makes claims, or is used to legitimate claims, to regulate the larger socio-politico-economic-moral life, it is in fact an "ideology" in the double sense – of masking the interests that back it, and of legitimating those interests at the same time. The existing institutional structures and activities thus present themselves as the technically necessary form of a rationalized society. Marcuse's warning is therefore apposite: "Technology is always a historical social project: in it is projected what a society and its ruling interests intend to do with man and things."

Michel Foucault in his writings[7] has similarly maintained that forms of knowledge define certain fields of empirical truth, and that disciplinary heuristics generate areas of empirical knowledge, which in turn have action consequences. For example, bourgeois society had a "repressive" attitude toward masturbation in the eighteenth century and to homosexuality in the second half of the nineteenth. "In reality, however, this discourse (of repression) served to make probable a whole series of interventions, tactical and positive interventions of surveillance, circulation, control and so forth . . ."[8]

Foucault has also argued that every society has its "general politics" of truth: that is, the types of discourse which it accepts and makes function as true; the mechanisms by which it distinguishes true and false statements; the techniques and procedures to which it accords value in the acquisition of truth; and the status of those whom it charges with saying what counts as true. In societies like ours, says Foucault, the "political economy" of truth is characterized by five traits. "Truth" is centered on the form of scientific discourse and the institutions which produce it; there is a constant economic and political incitement to produce this "truth"; it is immensely diffused and consumed by circulation through the apparatus of education and information; it is produced and transmitted under the dominant control of a few prominent political and economic apparatuses such as the university, army, press, publishing houses, and the media; lastly, "truth" is the topic of political debate, social information and "ideological" struggles.[9]

I would describe the main trends in the forward march of science as follows:

(1) Science in earlier times, in the sixteenth and seventeenth centuries, in its theoretical and philosophical role, was not integrally or directly tied in with technology and applied science.[10] But increasingly in our time scientific research has direct applications, and in this sense the scientists themselves as a profession become actively allied to the cause of an ongoing systematic and unceasing transformation of the world (as Weber would say), or support a stance in favour of a self-sustaining economic growth (as Schumpeter would say). Some obvious examples of this thesis today are genetic research, genetic engineering, gene splicing and the formation of companies like Genentech and so on who want to capitalize on this knowledge; one may also point to the direct implications of nuclear physics for nuclear energy development and its

The scientific profession, its extensions and connections

Plate 5.1 Professors and students in a physiology laboratory at Harvard Medical School in 1905: a scientific community practicing "normal science."

Plate 5.2 The collaboration of lay benefactors and medical scientists and missionaries in the transfer of medical science from the West to the East: the China Medical Board of the Rockefeller Foundation took over in 1915 the Peking Union Medical College, hitherto run by the London Missionary Society, for its further development. The photograph shows the trustees of the PUMC: among them are John D. Rockefeller, Jr., with hat in hand and to his right, Dr. William H. Welch (of Johns Hopkins) and on the far left Dr. Francis W. Peabody, and Dr. Henry S. Houghton (of Johns Hopkins), Director of PUMC. This enterprise also involved Charles W. Eliot, President of Harvard, and Harry P. Judson, President of the University of Chicago, John R. Mott of the International YMCA (who later was made a Nobel Laureate for Peace), and representatives of the principal missionary boards working in China, including several medical missionaries.

148

Plate 5.1

Plate 5.2

applications. We are witnessing today how the development of computer science has immediate translatability into technical applications, profit-making and economic growth. (Witness the mushrooming success of Route 128 in Boston and Silicon Valley in California.) There is truth then in the assertion that *today the sciences are the leading productive force*. With the advent of large-scale industrial research, science, technology and industrial utilization have joined. As Habermas put it: Scientific-technical progress has become an independent source of surplus value, aside from simple labour power.[11] It is not that such developments are bad, dangerous, or immoral, but that their implications and ramifications – especially the intermeshing of science with society – be clearly seen for what they are.

(2) But there is an even more problematic – and this time even dysfunctional in its implications if it is carried too far – spill-over effect from the core form of scientific knowledge in the so-called 'hard sciences' onto other disciplines, particularly in the social sciences, the science of economics, the science of politics, the science of international foreign policy management, and others curiously called "policy sciences." The labelling of these disciplines as "sciences" is a testimonial to the accolade given the hard sciences as prototypical knowledge.

First of all, the science–technology marriage has immediately affected that domain of life which is labelled the *economy*, and it is in economic life that we witness the attempted vigorous application of "purposive rationality" as instrumental action to change the world. Its focus and rationale is the production and distribution of wealth. This purposive rationality is celebrated and canonized in neo-classical economics.

At the next remove – by a kind of centre–periphery process – other domains of action, indeed other disciplines, have been carved out in turn. An example is politics – it in turn differentiates into its sub-specialisms – whose focal subject of study is something called "power," its acquisition and distribution. Politics, as a systematic science, now attempts to apply "instrumental rules" and "calculating strategies" that it is hoped will show the way to optimum decision-making in, say, the game of balance of power, or the nuclear weapons game. What I have in mind are all those "technical skills" and "methodologies" that bear a family resemblance – systems theory, cost–benefit analysis, games theory and choice theory, minimax strategies, and so on. These methodologies underscore such things as gamesmanship, adversarial contests, bargaining, and maximization – that is, ultimately the operations of the market place are applied to politics. Thus we have the following diffusion (some might say contamination) process: science invades the economy, the economy invades politics, and now politics is alleged to inform us on morality, choice and the values to live by. And there's the rub.

I have in the first two chapters of this book discussed the processes of secularization and scientific advance as they developed in Europe, especially in the sixteenth and seventeenth centuries and onwards. In this chapter we have so far described what kind of ideological dominance with instrumental and secular claims the scientific "revolution" has exerted on the world at large. Now I am arguing that these processes in turn have had one major consequence, namely the increasing atomization of modern life into sub-systems and domains of purposive rational action. These differentiating domains hive off and promulgate their own logics of action, and the substantive goals they are called upon by destiny to pursue.

The consequences of *atomization* into disciplines are two: a massive contradiction and an enervating crisis.

On the one hand the process of diffusion of spill-over effects from the hard core of science to the several surrounding domains of life, which are now invested with distinct logics, results in their having the monopoly effect of filling all the moral or social space in which we live. This process of alleged scientific reasoning – alleged scientific moral reasoning and social optimiz-ation – is reluctant, even opposed, to admitting other modes of consciousness or other world orientations into any space it already occupies, for it imperialistically expands to fill all the space available.

At the same time this diffusion process creates a contradictory effect. The continuing pressure to carve out the wholeness of life into separate domains, with their independent substantive goals, their independent logics and skills, corrodes away any existing overall unifying cosmology, with the result that there seems no way to unite what we have progressively split off. The possibility of inquiring into what may be the unifying themes of purposive life recedes further and further away as the specialisms with their experts jostle and jockey for territory.

The end result is some sort of moral cul de sac. On the one hand we know that, say in international politics, it is not so much a war of nerves, or gamesmanship, or strategy of deterrence that will lead to nuclear disarma-ment by America or Russia. A way out of the war game is by accepting the force of the truth that only if we take a fundamental moral decision to ban war, or totally disarm or embrace non-violence, another kind of peace game becomes possible. Again, the limits of environmental protection in the face of private industrial development cannot be "scientifically" decided, for it is not scientific knowledge *per se* that is on trial, but a conflict of social interests (that can mobilize "science" and "expert" evidence to champion their causes). And a decision to protect the environment, to keep beaches and mountains and forests for human aesthetic and leisure-time enjoyment, can only be willed in terms of a prior absolutist value decision by a majority.

In sum what I am saying is that the "technical sciences" that we have allowed to proliferate may not be able to deliver the best moral rules we wish to live by. As Gellner appropriately remarks: The validity of the scientific view and its practical effectiveness cannot be identified as one and the same. "There is in fact no reason to suppose that effective science does increase the survival-prospect of the species which carries it. The self-destruction of humanity, through nuclear or other war or ecological disaster is perfectly possible and perhaps probable in the post-scientific age . . ."[12] It has been known by anthropologists and sociologists for a long time that while the validity of technical rules and strategies depends in the first instance on the analytical logic of their propositions and their empirical verification, the validity of social norms is grounded in the intersubjectivity of actors, whose mutual understanding of intention is secured by the general recognition of obligations stemming from their inter-connectedness.

At this point, I want to remind the reader that in chapter 5 I argued that the discourse of scientific "causality" was only one "ordering of reality" among many, only one of the possible ways of "world-making." Some of the entailments of that chapter are that the framework of causality does not exhaust rationality, and that we cannot discover and realize the values of the interconnectedness of persons, the aesthetic and sensory modalities of social communication, and the "ultimate" concerns of human life, if under a totalitarian subjection to "causality" we repudiate or block out all those other "orientations" which I have for rhetorical purposes grouped under the label "participation."

The alleged incompatibility between science and religion in the West, and the thesis of the inevitable secularization and rationalization of the world as a world historical process, make sense only if we see them as the accompaniment of the central energizing role of science and technology in the industrial West as the motor of history.[13] And the claims of scientific methodologies and decision-making as legitimate extensions of the claims of science proper, as the basis of wider knowledge construction, are understandable in historical terms.

But these same logics of measurement and calculation may be very much out of place in the study and understanding of societies and cultures in which science and technology, or more generally the technical and practical orders of life are subordinated to, contained and encompassed by, other institutional orders and values. Here the motor of history, or should I say the pillar of stability, the centre of gravity, lies elsewhere – in religious values and sacerdotal institutions, or in divine kingship and its polity, or political vassalage and fiefship, and so on.

Now it is when we transport the universal rationality of scientific causality, and the alleged rationality of surrounding moral, economic and political sciences with their claims of objective rules of judgment (which in fact are colored by special cultural and social presuppositions), and try to use them as yardsticks for measuring, understanding and evaluating other cultures and civilizations that we run into the vexed problems of relativity, commensurability, and translation of cultures, which I have signalled throughout these chapters.

Weber at the end of the road

I should like to conclude the Morgan lectures by returning to Max Weber, arguably the greatest comparativist sociologist of the twentieth century, and place before the reader what I take to be the most important conclusions that he arrived at after his massive and sweeping comparative study of what he called the "world religions," principally, Protestant Christianity, early Judaism, Hinduism and Buddhism, and Confucianism.[14]

At the end of his long and panoramic intellectual journey, Weber realized that all forms of rationality, in particular the "instrumental" and "absolutist" rationalities he had used as his compass points, were ultimately grounded in subjective values, whose sources and wellsprings were non-rational, charismatic, affective and intuitive. This applied not only to absolutist rationality, dedicated to the "ethic of ultimate goals" unmindful of the pragmatic calculations of means and consequences, but also with equal force to instrumental rationality on which modern Western society puts so much store. The ends of capitalist economic action or democratic politics, or of socialistic or communist political economy, are ultimately non-rational and "arbitrary" or "conventional." Their validity cannot be reduced to simple instrumental reasoning; they derive their legitimacy from value decisions whose ground is anterior to instrumental decisions.

In the same way, all the great charismatic world religious movements which have sketched the cosmic maps for many humans, such as Christianity or Buddhism or Islam, were founded in affective non-rationality, and originally preached an ethic of ultimate ends. Religious inspiration draws from the fountain of charisma, and religious revelations emerge from the seedbed of experiences that are not "rational" in any restrictive sense. But they are "meaningful" and address existential issues regarding suffering, theodicy and death. As orientations to the world it is not possible to rate the Confucianist orientation of harmony of man with the cosmos as more or less rational than the Christian's orientation of imperative transformation of a world considered imperfect, or the Buddhist orientation of a disenchantment with the world and the need to transcend it. These orientations are not the product of any direct and immediate cognitive adaptation to the constraints imposed by the world, and these orientations cannot be reduced to adaptive, or ecological or biological or any other "objective" interest. Man's creative freedom consists precisely in his ability to devise cultural perspectives and meaning systems in form and content that cannot be wholly and significantly understood in terms of any objective logic of adaptation.

But Max Weber also said something else about the great religions. It was that once they formed their premises and perspectives, they were historically subject in their own distinctive ways to a progressive systematization and rationalization by their religious specialists and reflexive elites, in regard to dogma, doctrine and practice. The great religious debates and schisms and sectarian movements are a witness to this. And this criterion enabled Weber to distinguish between the effects these religions had on action in this world. Moreover, he held that in the comparative study of religion, while necessarily accepting the authenticity and meaningfulness of the initial axioms and cosmological parameters of each religion, a student may thereafter use the yardsticks of coherence, consistency and so on to test each religion's systematicity in relation to the horizons it has chosen. But such measurement of rationality cannot in any way illuminate the inspiration for the religious life, and the sensibility by which a man or woman of religion apprehends the transcendental or the immanent or the supramundane. The metaphysical springs and conceptions of religion, while being meaningful, cannot be explained in terms of the positivist tests of truth and falsity. It has to be conceded, however, that Max Weber's comparative study of world religions and their ethics, while leading him to realize that there are "different types of rationalism and rationalization," "different spheres of life which can be rationalized," and "different carriers of rationalization," was nevertheless always pegged to the *uniqueness of modern Western rationalism* as "the starting and end point of such a comparison." Weber's central preoccupation was with a special form of rationalism and rationalization which posed for him "an historical problem of identification and explanation and thus demanded an adequate 'historical theory'."[15] It would be foolish for any comparativist to deny the dynamism and coherence of the historical processes associated with capitalism, modern science, and philosophical rationalism as Western achievements.

It is not my intention, therefore, that my discussion of modern science should be read as conveying an apocalyptic message and a blanket denigration of science. I have tried to place science in its internal and external contexts, and to probe the implications of the fact that the sciences too are practiced within communities of interpretation. We owe too much to science, its investigations and applications, its mode of reasoning, to belittle it. Coming from a Third World country, how can I not appreciate how applied science has helped to curtail malaria, eradicate smallpox, reduce infant mortality, enable double cropping and the green revolution? But neither can I at the same time be unaware of or insensitive to the fact that these same benefits have taken their toll of cultural and social costs and unanticipated dislocating effects?[16] Provided we do not reify science, and provided we are mindful that science can be used in the service of different ends, and that we who construct it have also the responsibility to regulate its use, science will unquestionably be deemed as indispensable to the human quest for freedom, creativity, prosperity and peace.

Notes

1   Magic, science, and religion in Western thought: anthropology's intellectual legacy

1 Lewis Henry Morgan, *Ancient Society* (New York: Henry Holt and Co.) 1877, p. vi.
2 See Bronislaw Malinowski, *Magic, Science, and Religion and Other Essays* (New York: Doubleday Anchor Books), 1954. The collection was first published in 1948 by The Free Press. The essay in question was first published in James Needham (ed.), *Science, Religion and Reality* (New York: Macmillan Company), 1925.
3 Michel Foucault, *Power/Knowledge, Selected Interviews and Other Writings, 1972–1977* (ed. Colin Gordon) (New York: Pantheon Books), 1980, p. 108. Again: "it's not so much a matter of knowing what external power imposes itself on science, as of what effects of power circulate among scientific statements, what constitutes as it were, their internal regime of power, and how and why at certain moments that regime undergoes a global modification" p. 113.
4 Wilfred Cantwell Smith, *The Meaning and End of Religion* (San Francisco: Harper and Row), 1978. We should note that Smith writes as a committed Christian, and that he proposes as a conclusion to his study that we drop the concept of "religion," and deal instead with "faith" and "tradition." These features of Smith's work are not relevant to our discussion here.
5 Smith, *ibid.* p. 38.
6 Yehezkel Kauffmann, *The Religion of Israel from its Beginning to the Babylonian Exile*, translated and abridged by Moshe Greenberg (New York: Schocken Books), 1972 . . .
7 Wendy O'Flaherty, *The Origins of Evil in Hindu Mythology* (Berkeley and Los Angeles: University of California Press), 1976.
8 *Ibid.* p. 378.
9 *Ibid.* p. 13.
10 J. G. Crowther, *The Social Relations of Science* (New York: Macmillan Co.), 1941.
11 Charles Singer, *A Short History of Scientific Ideas to 1900* (New York: Abelard-Schuman) 1955.
12 (London: Oxford University Press), 1959.
13 G. E. R. Lloyd, *Magic, Reason and Experience. Studies in the Origins and Development of Greek Science* (Cambridge University Press), 1979; also *Early Greek Science, Thales to Aristotle* (London: Chatto and Windus), 1970.
14 On some recent medical disasters see William Silverman's *Retrolental Fibroplasia: A Parable* (New York: Grune and Stratton), 1980.

15 Max Weber, *The Protestant Ethic and the Spirit of Capitalism* (New York: Charles Scribner's Sons), 1930.
16 R. K. Merton's classic study first appeared in *Osiris*, 1938, 4 (Bruges), under the title "Science and Technology in 17th Century England." Much of it was incorporated in two chapters in *Social Theory and Social Structure* (Illinois: The Free Press Of Glencoe), 1949. Chapter 14 is entitled "Puritanism, Pietism and Science"; Chapter 15 "Science and Economy of 17th Century England."
17 "Puritanism, Pietism and Science" in *Social Theory and Social Structure, ibid.* p. 329.
18 *Ibid.* p. 346.
19 *Ibid.* p. 333.
20 *Ibid.* p. 331.
21 *Ibid.* p. 336.
22 *Ibid.* p. 340.
23 *Ibid.* p. 345.
24 See *Social Theory and Social Structure, ibid.*, chapter 15, "Science and Economy of 17th Century England."
25 *Ibid.* p. 357.
26 See for example, Marshall Clagett (ed.), *Critical Problems in the History of Science: Proceedings* (Madison: University of Wisconsin Press), 1957, 1959; and Philip P. Weiner and Aaron Noland, *Roots of Scientific Thought: A Cultural Perspective* (New York: Basic Books), 1957.
27 Thomas Kuhn, "The History of Science," *International Encyclopaedia of the Social Sciences* (ed.) David L. Sills, vol. 14 (New York: The Macmillan Co., and the Free Press).

2   Anthropology's intellectual legacy (continued)

1 Arthur O. Lovejoy, *The Great Chain of Being. A Study of the History of an Idea* (Cambridge, MA: Harvard University Press) (1936), 1976.
2 Cited in Lovejoy, *ibid.* p. 76.
3 Lovejoy cites Albertus Magnus as saying in *De animalibus* that "nature does not make [animal] kinds separate without making something intermediate between them," and Nicolaus Casanis as asserting in *De docta ignorantia* that "All things, however different, are linked together. There is in the genera of things such a connection between the higher and the lower that they meet in a common point . . . in order that the universe may be one, perfect, continuous" *ibid.* pp. 79–80.
4 Lovejoy comments that the heliocentric theory, properly so called, is owed to Kepler not Copernicus – the center of the world for Copernicus was the center of the earth's orbit, and the sun though nearest to that position did not occupy it.
5 Cited by Marie Boas, *The Scientific Renaissance 1450–1630: The Rise of Modern Science* (New York: Harper and Brothers), 1962; see especially pp. 76–88.
6 Lovejoy, *The Great Chain of Being*, p. 105.
7 These lessons have been reiterated recently, and their implication further developed by Stephen Jay Gould. For example, see his *The Panda's Thumb* (New York: Norton), 1980; *Hen's Teeth and Horse's Toes: Further Reflections in Natural History* (New York: Norton), 1983. Also see Stephen J. Gould and Elizabeth S. Vrba, "Exaptation – A Missing Term in the Science of Form," *Paleobiology*, 8(1), 1982, pp. 4–15.
8 Keith Thomas, *Religion and the Decline of Magic* (New York: Charles Scribner's Sons), 1971.

9   *Ibid.* p. 50.
10 *Ibid.* p. 640.
11 *Ibid.* p. 657.
12 *Ibid.* p. 41.
13 *Ibid.* p. 42.
14 *Ibid.* p. 659.
15 Michel Foucault, *The Order of Things* (New York: Pantheon), 1970.
16 Hildred Geertz, "An Anthropology of Religion and Magic, 1" in *Journal of Interdisciplinary History*, vol. 6, no. 1, Summer 1975, pp. 71–89.
17 See *Midland History*, vol. 3, pp. 41–55.
18 *Ibid.* p. 50.
19 See Frances Yates's "The Fear of the Occult", *New York Review of Books*, vol. 26, no. 18, November 22, 1979, which is a review of Brian P. Copenhaver's *Symphorien Champier and the Reception of Occultist Tradition in Renaissance France* (The Hague: Mouton), 1978.
20 Frances A. Yates, *Giordano Bruno and the Hermetic Tradition* (London: Routledge and Kegan Paul) [1964], 1971. A subsequent work which carries forward the same line of thought is her *The Rosicrucian Enlightenment* (London: Routledge and Kegan Paul), 1973.
21 *Giordano Bruno*, p. 1.
22 *Ibid.* p. 2.
23 *Ibid.* p. 3.
24 *Ibid.* p. 6.
25 *Ibid.* p. 11.
26 *Ibid.* p. 17.
27 *Ibid.* p. 148.
28 *Ibid.* p. 149.
29 Peter French, *John Dee: The World of an Elizabethan Magus* (London: Routledge and Kegan Paul), 1973.
30 Yates, *Giordano Bruno*, p. 150.
31 Yates, *ibid.*, p. 154.
32 *Ibid.* p. 155.
33 *Ibid.* pp. 233–34.
34 See Frances A. Yates, *The Art of Memory* (London: Routledge and Kegan Paul), 1966. In this work, Yates describes how the classical art of memory goes back to the *Ad Herennium* of Roman times, which sets out a mnemonical system of attaching images to a series of places in a building to remind the orator of points in his speech. Yates carries forward the discussion of the art of memory to the Middle Ages, the Renaissance and its "memory theatres," including Bruno's applications and to Robert Fludd's Memory theatre which influenced the Elizabethan Globe Theatre.
35 Yates, "The Fear of the Occult."
36 Yates, *Giordano Bruno*, pp. 160–64.
37 *Ibid.* p. 156.
38 *Ibid.* pp. 155–56.
39 *Ibid.* p. 156.
40 Karl Popper, *Conjectures and Refutations* (New York: Harper Torchbooks), 1963, p. 37.
41 T. Kuhn, "Logic of Discovery and Psychology of Research" in Imre Lakatos and Alan Musgrave (eds.), *Criticism and Growth of Knowledge* (Cambridge University Press), 1970, p. 8.
42 *Ibid.* pp. 8–9.

3   **Sir Edward Tylor versus Bronislaw Malinowski: is magic false science or meaningful performance?**

1   Bronislaw Malinowski, *A Diary in the Strict Sense of the Term* (New York: Harcourt, Brace and World, Inc.) 1967, p. 140.
2   *Ibid.* p. 236.
3   J. W. Burrow, *Evolution and Society. A Study of Victorian Social Theory* (Cambridge University Press), 1966, p. 235.
4   *Ibid.* p. 236, quoted by Burrow from R. R. Marrett, *A Jerseyman in Oxford* (Oxford University Press), 1981, p. 84.
5   See Burrow, *Evolution and Society*, chapter 7, p. 235. Burrow speculates "it was perhaps easier and more tempting, particularly to men nurtured in a Protestant, even puritan atmosphere, to regard religion as the product of individual thoughts and fears", *ibid.* p. 239.
6   Edward Burnett Tylor, *Religion in Primitive Culture*, vol. 2 (Gloucester, MA: Peter Smith), 1970, p. 539. Vol. 1 in the same series is titled *The Origins of Culture*.
7   According to George Stocking, Tylor was not directly influenced by Darwin and he cannot be dubbed a cultural or social Darwinist in the strict sense. Besides Lyell's uniformitarian geology Tylor, like many other nineteenth-century comparativists, was impressed by the achievements of comparative philology. See George W. Stocking, *Race, Culture and Evolution* (New York: The Free Press), 1971, ch. 5.
8   Later in his book he provides a similar list: "special dress, special tools and weapons, special laws of marriage and property, special moral and religious doctrines" (Tylor, vol. 1, pp. 1, 7, 12). These groupings are as miscellaneous and arbitrary as the recent identification of packets of "culture gens" by the irrepressible socio-biologist E. O. Wilson.
9   These issues are central to Evans-Pritchard's *Witchcraft, Oracles and Magic Among the Azande*. The question of the sorcerer's sincerity is addressed by Lévi-Strauss in his essay "The Sorcerer and His Magic," *Structural Anthropology* (New York: Basic Books), 1963, chapter 14.
10 H. R. Trevor-Roper, *The European Witch-Craze of the 16th and 17th Centuries* (Harmondsworth: Penguin Books), 1969, p. 12.
11 See Burrow, *Evolution and Society*, p. 237.
12 It may be noted that Tylor also discussed the development of notions of "superstition" in sacrifice, that is, the giving of a part of a thing for the whole (*pars pro toto*) – a finger or a lock of hair for the whole body, etc. In a wide-ranging manner, Tylor discussed the progression from offering slaves in sacrifice, to animals, and finally to sacrificial effigies (wax beasts) or to ex-votos. This principle of substitution would later engage Evans-Pritchard. See his *Nuer Religion* (Oxford: Clarendon Press), 1956 in which he discusses Nuer sacrifice, and the logic of the substitution of a cucumber for an ox.
13 George Stocking, *Race, Culture and Evolution*, pp. 105–06.
14 It is therefore all the more puzzling that Evans-Pritchard at the end of his superb essay "The Intellectualist (English) Interpretation of Magic" (in the *Bulletin, Faculty of Arts*, Farouk University, Cairo, vol. 1, part 2, 1933) more or less accepts Tylor's distinction between magic and religion.
15 Thus following the treatment of "language" from lower "natural" forms to higher forms unconstrained by natural factors, so religion too as it develops becomes more metaphysical and ethical.
16 As Talcott Parsons put it, Durkheim held not so much that religion is a social

phenomenon as that society is a moral phenomenon. See Durkheim, *The Elementary Forms of the Religious Life* (New York: The Free Press), 1965, p. 464.

17 I may remark here that Robin Horton in his essay "African Traditional Thought and Western Science" (*Africa*, 38, vol. 37, nos. 1 and 2) repeats in a more elaborate way the Tylorian point made here, and is also guilty of not answering the question: What is the relation between Christianity and Science in the contemporary West?

18 I suggest that Robin Horton take account of this since he claims to be a neo-Tylorian.

19 Horton fails to notice this difference in Tylorian and Durkheimian positions, when he appropriates both Tylor and Durkheim as his patron saints and legitimators.

20 Evans-Pritchard, *Bulletin*, p. 29.

21 Frazer's productive writing period spanned the years 1884–1938. *The Golden Bough* in its first two-volume edition appeared in 1890, and in its thirteen-volume edition in 1937.

22 See Mary Douglas, "Judgments on James Frazer" in *Daedalus* (*Journal of the American Academy of Arts and Sciences*), Fall, 1978 (*Generations*), p. 152.

23 For example, in the Sri Lankan exorcism rites which Frazer would have to label as "magical," both propitiatory or intercessionary and coercive or manipulatory techniques are used in relation to the demonic agents. See Tambiah, *Culture, Thought and Social Action* (Cambridge, MA: Harvard University Press), 1985, chapter 4.

24 See *Culture, Thought and Social Action*, chapter 1.

25 J. G. Frazer, *The Golden Bough. A Study in Magic and Religion*, Part 1, vol. 1, *The Magic Art and the Evolution of Kings* (London: Macmillan, 3rd edn), 1911, p. 222.

26 See J. G. Frazer *ibid.* pp. 242–43.

27 See S. F. Nadel "Malinowski on Magic and Religion" in Raymond Firth (ed.), *Man and Culture. An Evaluation of the Work of Bronislaw Malinowski* (London: Routledge and Kegan Paul), 1960.

28 Frazer elaborated the idea that divine kings were frequently among simpler peoples both magicians and kings. It must be recorded that Frazerian ideas were fruitfully developed by Evans-Pritchard in his essay on *The Divine Kingship among the Shilluk of the Nilotic Sudan* (Cambridge University Press), 1948.

Evans-Pritchard however rendered highly suspect some of Frazer's conjectures: for instance, whether the king whose powers were waning was actually killed. Did the myth of his killing actually require a ritual enactment, as Frazer assumed?

29 Cited by James Boon in his review in *The New York Sunday Times Book Review* of Robert E. Ackerman's *J. G. Frazer, His Life and Work* (Cambridge University Press), 1987. This work appeared after I had completed my book, and I have not been able to consult it before this book was handed to the publisher.

30 A partial translation is contained in A. C. Miles and Rush Rhees, "Ludwig Wittgenstein's 'Remarks on Frazer's *Golden Bough*'" in *The Human World*, no. 3, May 1971, pp. 28–41. For this the translators used the original German version incompletely published in *Synthèse*, no. 17, 1967. Mary Douglas, in her "Judgments on James Frazer", seems to have made use of the Miles and Rhees translation.

Postscript: It was only recently in June 1989 (while I was proof-reading) that I came across Rodney Needham's "Remarks on Wittgenstein and Ritual" in chapter 7 of his book *Exemplars* (Berkeley: University of California Press), 1985. Needham provides information, previously not known to me, regarding the publication of a German text (1977), a French translation (1977), and a complete English translation

(1979 by Miles and Rhees) of Wittgenstein's remarks on Frazer (see pages 151, 228). Needham's own reading and discussion of Wittgenstein's remarks are rather different from mine.

31 When Wittgenstein started to write his remarks on Frazer in 1931, Malinowski had already published *Argonauts of the Western Pacific* in 1922 and also his essay "The Problem of Meaning in Primitive Languages" in *The Meaning of Meaning* by C. K. Ogden and I. A. Richards (London: International Library of Psychology, Philosophy and Scientific Method), 1923, pp. 451–510. His two volumes on *Coral Gardens and Their Magic* were published in 1935; in vol. 2, p. 60, he acknowledges his debt to G. A. de Laguna, *Speech, its Function and Development* (New Haven: Yale University Press), 1927.

32 Concerning this issue see Milton Singer's illuminating discussion "A Neglected Source of Structuralism: Radcliffe Brown, Russell and Whitehead," *Semiotica*, 1984, vol. 48, no. 1/2, pp. 11–96.

I have been fortunate in having access to the fuller translation made from the relevant portions of Cornell vols. 12, 88b and 89b by Kenneth Laine Ketner and James Lerio Eigsti, and entitled *Ludwig Wittgenstein, Remarks on Frazer's Philosophical Anthropology*. All my quotations are taken from this translation which is not yet published. Ketner and Eigsti have also translated from Cornell vol. 68 certain further notes on *The Golden Bough* written by Wittgenstein. I do not cite from these notes. I thank Dr. Ketner for so generously granting me permission to quote from his and Eigsti's translation.

33 Ludwig Wittgenstein, *On Certainty* (ed. G. E. M. Anscombe and G. H. von Wright) translated by Denis Paul and G. E. M. Anscombe (Oxford: Blackwell), 1969.

The quotations are taken from pp. 7, 84, 107, 162, 145, 387 of this translation.

4 Malinowski's demarcations and his exposition of the magical art

1 The following are Malinowski's principal works: *A Diary in the Strict Sense of the Term* (New York: Harcourt, Brace and World, Inc.), 1967; *Magic, Science and Religion and Other Essays* (New York: Doubleday Anchor Books), 1954 (Illinois: The Free Press of Glencoe), 1948; *The Foundations of Faith and Morals* (Riddell Memorial Lecture, Durham 1934–35 (London: Oxford University Press), 1936; *Coral Gardens and Their Magic* (London: George Allen and Unwin), 1935 (New York: American Book Co.), 1935. 2 vols.; *The Sexual Life of Savages in North West Melanesia* (London: Routledge and Kegal Paul), 1929; *Sex and Repression in Savage Society* (New York: Harcourt), 1927; *The Father in Primitive Psychology* (New York: W. W. Norton & Co.), 1927; *Myth in Primitive Psychology* (New York: W. W. Norton & Co.), 1926; *Crime and Custom in Savage Society* (London: International Library of Psychology, Philosophy and Scientific Method), 1926; "The Problem of Meaning in Primitive Languages" in *The Meaning of Meaning* by C. K. Ogden and I. A. Richards (London: International Library of Psychology, Philosophy and Scientific Method), 1923; *Argonauts of the Western Pacific* (London: Routledge and Kegan Paul), 1922.

2 Interesting and illuminating facts about Malinowski's biographical, intellectual and cultural antecedents are contained in these two essays that appeared in *Anthropology Today*, January 5, 1985: Ernest Gellner, "'Malinowski Go Home': Reflections on the Malinowski Centenary Conferences" (pp. 5–7); and Robert J. Thornton "'Imagine yourself set down . . .' Mach, Frazer, Conrad, Malinowski

and the Role of Imagination in Ethnology" (pp. 7–14). For a vivid account of the interpersonal aspects of Malinowski's career, see Helena Wayne (Malinowska): "Bronislaw Malinowski: the Influence of Various Women in his Life and Works," *American Ethnologist*, December 3, 1985; pp. 529–40.

3 Ernst Mach's ideas on this are contained in his *Erkenntnis und Irrtum* (1905), translated as *Knowledge and Error. Sketches on the Psychology of Enquiry* by Thomas J. McCormack and Paul Foulkes (Boston, MA: D. Reidel Publishing Co.), 1976.

4 Thornton, "'Imagine yourself set down . . .'" p. 9.

5 Thornton, *ibid.* p. 9.

6 Gellner, "'Malinowski Go Home'," p. 7.

7 Wayne, "Bronislaw Malinowski," p. 531.

8 See Edmund Leach's essay "The Epistemological Background of Malinowski's Empiricism" in *Man and Culture. An Evaluation of the Work of Bronislaw Malinowski* (ed.) Raymond Firth (London: Routledge and Kegan Paul), 1957, pp. 119–37. Leach also comments that what W. B. Gallie (in his *Peirce and Pragmatism*, 1952) says of William James also applies to Malinowski: That he was an individualist, interested in the experiences, perplexities, and satisfactions of individual souls, and "anything claiming to be more-than-individual he distrusted from the depth of his soul."

9 I am however skeptical of Leach's allegation that Malinowski imposed on the Trobriander the conscious distinction between the rational and metaphysical: "He himself found the conceptual distinction between the rational and the metaphysical self-evident; he insisted that it must be self-evident to the Trobriander also" (p. 128). I shall provide the evidence on which Malinowski based the distinction between "magical" acts and "technical" acts as in line with Trobriand conceptions.

10 See Raymond Firth (ed.), 1957. *Man and Culture*, pp. 1–14; *A Diary in the Strict Sense of the Term by Bronislaw Malinowski*, translated by Norbert Guterman, (New York: Harcourt, Brace and World, Inc.), 1967; also see Wayne, "Bronislaw Malinowski."

11 Firth, *Man and Culture*, p. 6.

12 One quickly sees that Malinowski's notion of profane is not exactly Durkheimian. See Emile Durkheim, *The Elementary Forms of the Religious Life*, pp. 52–57, where he sees the sacred and profane worlds as not only separate but antagonistic: "The sacred thing is *par excellence* that which the profane should not touch" (p. 55).

13 Durkheim's discussion contains these assertions: All known religious beliefs presuppose a classification of all things, real and ideal, into two classes or opposed groups – the sacred and the profane. The division of the world into two domains is "the distinctive trait of all religious thought." "Sacred things are those which the interdictions protect and isolate; profane things, those to which these interdictions are applied and which must remain at a distance from the first. Religious beliefs are the representations which express the nature of sacred things and the relations which they sustain, either with each other or with profane things. Finally, rites are the rules of conduct which prescribe how a man should comport himself in the presence of these sacred objects." *The Elementary Forms of the Religious Life*, pp. 52, 56.

14 Nadel in his critique of Malinowski's notion of science (in Firth (ed.), *Man and Culture*) sides with the Durkheim–Mauss view of magic as in some ways being the forerunner of a "theoretical science." But Malinowski would disagree because the essence of magic for him was that it was man-made, not that it represented or

stemmed from conceptions of an impersonal collective *mana*-like force, and protocausal connections. This is part and parcel of his anti-intellectualistic anti-mentalist pragmatic posture.

15 *Coral Gardens and Their Magic*, 1978, vol. 1, p. 477.

16 See *Man*, vol. 3, no. 2, June 1968, pp. 175–208; also *Culture, Thought and Social Action*, chapter 1.

17 An example is the recitation of the principal spell of Omarakana garden magic over the magical mixture by the magician (p. 216): "He prepares a sort of large receptacle for his voice – a voice trap . . . He moves his mouth from one end of the aperture to the other, turns his head, repeating the words over and over again, rubbing them, so to speak, into the substance."

18 Vol. 2, p. 234 of *Coral Gardens and their Magic*.

19 *Ibid.* pp. 234–35.

20 See especially my "Form and Meaning of Magical Acts" and "A Performative approach to Ritual" in *Culture, Thought and Social Action* (Cambridge, MA: Harvard University Press), 1985, chs. 2 and 4.

21 Kenneth Burke, *A Rhetoric of Motives* (Berkeley and Los Angeles: University of California Press), 1969, p. 41.

22 *Ibid.* p. 43.

23 *Ibid.* p. 44.

24 *Ibid.* p. 42.

5 Multiple orderings of reality: the debate initiated by Lévy-Bruhl

1 The best known books by Lévy-Bruhl relating to "primitive mentality" are: *Les Fonctions mentales dans les sociétés inférieures* (1920): translated as *How Natives Think* (1926); *La Mentalité primitive* (1922): translated as *Primitive Mentality* (1923); *L'Âme primitive* (1927): translated as *The "Soul" of the Primitive* (1927); *Les Carnets de Lucien Lévy-Bruhl* (1949): translated as the *Notebooks on Primitive Mentality*; this was published posthumously.

2 See Jean Cazeneuve's essay on "Lucien Lévi-Bruhl (1857–1939)" in the *International Encyclopaedia of the Social Sciences*, vol. 2, Part 1, 1934. Even more suggestive and illuminating is Georges Gurvitch's memorial, "The Sociological Legacy of Lucien Lévy-Bruhl," *Journal of Social Philosophy*, New York, 1939, vol. 5, no. 1, pp. 61–70.

3 In his earlier writings, such as *How Natives Think*, he sketched the transition from prelogical mentality to logical thought in terms of the occurrence of a distancing of subject in relation to the object, and the progressive separating off and personification of supernaturals. These developments portrayed the increasing importance of the cognitive aspect of thought. Even myth is a later development. Lévy-Bruhl did not think that this development was automatic and universal, for the transition did not take place in India or China.

As I shall report in due course, Lévy-Bruhl's later idea of a coexistence of the two mentalities in man everywhere modifies this thesis of transition.

4 As Gurvitch ("The Social Legacy," p. 62) explains, Lévy-Bruhl was not that kind of great mind, which settles early in life on a central theme of research and devotes its life to its development, and which also founds a school. He was the other kind of great mind that developed slowly and by stages, changing its field of research periodically, and within each domain varying its point of view. Of this second type of mind, Gurvitch comments: "Their development is a more dramatic one, also

more painful, but their conclusions are richer, the results more manifold and fruitful." Durkheim was the former type, Lévy-Bruhl the latter. The last seventeen years of his life were also his most fertile years.

5 See Rodney Needham, *Belief, Language and Experience*, (University of Chicago Press), 1972, whose detailed and illuminating commentary I am following here.

6 *Ibid.* p. 180.

7 See Gurvitch, "The Social Legacy," p. 68. See also Robert H. Lowie, *The History of Ethnological Theory* (New York: Rinehart), 1937.

8 As Lévy-Bruhl puts it in *How Natives Think* (New York: Washington Square Press), 1966, p. 62: "When Bororos say they are red *araras* (parakeets) it represents an actual identity or a participation which is represented in varied forms, "contact, transference, sympathy, telekinesis, etc."

9 See *How Natives Think*, pp. 54–81.

10 In *The Order of Things: An Archaeology of the Human Sciences* (London: Tavistock; New York: Pantheon, 1973), Foucault discusses the role of "resemblance" (as opposed to "representation") as having a constructive role in the making of knowledge in sixteenth-century Europe. The semantic web of "resemblance" is constituted of notions such as *convenientia* (similarity of adjacency), and *convenience* (resemblance at a distance). Sympathies between man and the phenomena of the world were seen as traversing vast spaces causing assimilations and minglings to take place. In a field of polyvalent relations man stood at the centre, and resemblances radiated from him to the world and back again.

The "doctrine of signatures" embodied a theory about language, especially how the names of things had an integral affinity with the things they labelled. The signatures of resemblance comprised an interlacing of both the verbal and non-verbal. This theory of names and how language is implicated in the world had a critical relevance for the use of language in magic and in the occult arts.

According to Foucault a new view of language as a conventional phenomenon which said that the relation between language and the world it described was one of representation only, a theory cultivated by the Port Royal School, represented a shift of episteme (or paradigm) from one mentality to another.

11 Evans-Pritchard, in certain essays he published in an obscure Egyptian journal, was the first to introduce the ideas of Lévy-Bruhl in a serious manner to Anglo-Saxon anthropologists. Malinowski bowdlerized and contemptuously dismissed Lévy-Bruhl's ideas, which deserved a better hearing.

See Evans-Pritchard's *Theories of Primitive Religion* and his essay "Lévy-Bruhl's Theory of Primitive Mentality," *Bulletin, Faculty of Arts, Farouk University*, Cairo, 1934, vol. 2, Part 2, pp. 1–36.

12 I may also indicate that the classicist Bruno Snell, in his *The Discovery of the Mind* (New York: Harper Torchbook), 1960, uses Lévy-Bruhl's distinction between prelogical and logical thought to describe the shift over time in Greek thought from the mythical mode to the logical mode. In mythical thought metaphors and similes are used as sensory images with metaphysical properties. The change to logical thought implies accurate descriptions and postulating natural causal connections which led to the scientific mode of thought.

Snell's account of a discontinuous shift is questioned by G. E. R. Lloyd in *Polarity and Analogy. Two Types of Argumentation in Early Greek Thought* (Cambridge University Press), 1966.

Lloyd says that the development of Greek logic shows a gradual recognition of logical principles implicit in archaic beliefs. Discovery of logic "merely rendered explicit certain rules of argument which were implicitly observed by earlier writers." See also my earlier discussion of Lloyd's later book.

13 Lucien Febvre, *The Problem of Unbelief in the Sixteenth Century. The Religion of Rabelais*, trans. by Beatrice Gottlieb (Cambridge, MA: Harvard University Press), 1982. The French title of the work is *Le Problème de l'incroyance au XVIe siècle: La religion de Rabelais*. Marc Bloch's perhaps equally famous work *The Royal Touch: Sacred Monarchy and Scrofula in England and France*, trans. by J. E. Anderson (London: Routledge and Kegan Paul), 1973, was devoted to constructing the *mentalité* that attributed healing powers to the King's touching with his hands.

14 *Ibid.* p. 331.

15 *Ibid.* p. 344.

16 *Ibid.* p. 351.

17 *Ibid.* pp. 356–57.

18 *Ibid.* p. 358.

19 Trevor-Roper, *The European Witch-Craze*, p. 105.

20 Robin Horton "African traditional thought and Western science;" see also "Ritual Man in Africa," *Africa*, vol. 34, 1964; and "Lévy-Bruhl, Durkheim and the Scientific Revolution" in *Modes of Thought*, eds. Robin Horton and Ruth Finnegan (London: Faber and Faber), 1973.

21 I am referring here to his essay "Lévy-Bruhl, Durkheim and the Scientific Revolution."

22 See Needham, *Belief, Language and Experience*, p. 131.

23 Quoted from *Les Carnets* by Needham, *ibid.* p. 166.

24 See in particular, Evans-Pritchard's "Lévy-Bruhl's Theory of Primitive Mentality." See also his *Theories of Primitive Religion* (Oxford: Clarendon Press), 1965. There are two other essays published at the same time that are relevant in order to appreciate the trends and tensions in Evans-Pritchard's thought. "The Intellectualist (English) Interpretation of Magic", and "Science and Sentiment: An Exposition and Criticism of the Writings of Pareto" in the *Bulletin*, 1933 (vol. 1, Part 2, pp. 282–311) and 1936 (vol. 3, Part 2, pp. 163–92) respectively.

25 Lowie, *The History of Ethnological Theory* (p. 221) makes the same critique independently, citing R. Thurnwald as his source:

> He [Lévy-Bruhl] establishes his contrast not by comparing civilized and primitive man, but, in Thurnwald's apt characterization, "The highest achievements of the modern intellect" – *nota bene*, only in its professional activites "with a rather vague 'primitiveness'."
> (The Thurnwald reference is *Deutsche Literaturzeitung*, 1928, pp. 486–94.)

26 Mary Douglas in her pious memorial to her teacher entitled *Evans-Pritchard* (Sussex: The Harvester Press), 1980, *overdoes* the comparison she makes between Evans-Pritchard's interpretive procedures and Wittgenstein's notions of language games, the viewing of language in terms of its social uses for achieving human ends, etc. While one does not grudge a possible convergence between these two scholars, it is only fair to point out that Evans-Pritchard is seriously deficient in not providing a pragmatic theory of language; such a theory was mostly importantly proposed by Malinowski. I would therefore say that Malinowski seems closer to the spirit of Wittgenstein's *Philosophical Investigations*. Evans-Pritchard was in some ways muddled trying to negotiate among the frameworks of Tylor, Lévy-Bruhl, and Pareto. See my "Form and Meaning of Magical Acts" first printed in Robin Horton and Ruth Finnegan, *Modes of Thought* (London: Faber and Faber), 1973.

27 See Ruth Bunzel's introduction to Lucien Lévy-Bruhl, *How Natives Think*.
28 See *The Interpretation of Dreams* (Book 2) in *The Basic Writings of Sigmund Freud*, trans. A. A. Brill (New York: The Modern Library, Random House), 1938.
29 Gregory Bateson, *Steps to an Ecology of Mind* (London: Intertext Books), 1972, especially the essay on "Style, Grace and Information in Primitive Art."
30 *The Sunday New York Times*, February 19, 1984.
31 Suzanne Langer, *Philosophy in a New Key* (New York: Mentor Books), 1942; *Feeling and Form. A Theory of Art* (New York: Mentor Books), 1953.
32 Langer, *Philosophy in a New Key*, pp. 65, 75. In certain respects Langer may have overdrawn the distinction. Recent work on visual perception shows that scanning procedures are at work and there is not instant configurational perception without scanning. Nevertheless there is a relative distinction to be made between the linear sequencing of speech utterances and written sentences and the confirugational perception of visual forms.
33 Roman Jakobson, "Closing statement: Linguistics and Poetics" in Thomas A. Sebeok (ed.), *Style in Language* (Cambridge, MA: The M.I.T. Press), 1960, p. 358.
34 Langer overdrew the distinction between the linear auditory reception of language and the simultaneous configurational character of visual perception in another way. The understanding of verbal communication, though auditorily received in sequence, involves recursive operations between parts and the whole.
35 Carol Gilligan, *In a Different Voice. Psychological Theory and Women's Development* (Cambridge, MA: Harvard University Press), 1982.
36 *Ibid.* p. 10.
37 *Ibid.* p. 6.
38 "Two Interviews with Julia Kristeva" by Elaine H. Baruch and Perry Meisel, in *Partisan Review*, 1, 1984, p. 123.
39 Gilligan, *In a Different Voice*, pp. 163–64.
40 *Ibid.* p. 174.
41 Sudhir Kakar, *The Inner World. A Psycho-analytic Study of Childhood and Society in India* (Delhi: Oxford University Press), 1978. The references are taken from pp. 104–12.
42 Bellah, *Beyond Belief*, p. 242.
43 My chief source is Alfred Schutz: *Collected Papers 1. The Problem of Social Reality*, ed. and introduction by Maurice Natanson (The Hague: Martinus Nijhoff), 1962, esp. pp. 207–59 "On Multiple Realities."
44 *Ibid.* p. 208.
45 *Ibid.* p. 231.
46 *Ibid.* p. 253.
47 *Ibid.* p. 258.
48 Nelson Goodman, *Ways of Worldmaking* (Indianapolis, IN: Hackett Publishing Co.), 1985. Also see his *Languages of Art. An Approach to a Theory of Symbols* (Indianapolis, Indiana: Hackett Publishing Co. [1976]), 1985.
49 Goodman, *Ways of Worldmaking*, p. 4.
50 *Ibid.* p. 5.
51 Goodman is careful to note that "Even if the ultimate product of science, unlike that of art, is a literal, verbal or mathematical, denotational theory, science and art proceed in much the same way with their searching and their building" (*ibid.* p. 107).
52 *Ibid.* p. 102.
53 Karl-Otto Apel, *Toward a Transformation of Philosophy*, trans. Glynn Adey and David Frisby (London: Routledge and Kegan Paul), 1980.

54 *Ibid.* p. 52.
55 *Ibid.* p. 53.
56 *Ibid.* p. 59.
57 See especially Maurice Leenhardt's *Do Kamo: Person and Myth in the Melanesian World,* ed. James Clifford (Berkeley: University of California Press), 1982, an unorthodox work in religious phenomenology. An illuminating biography and commentary on Leenhardt is James Clifford, *Person and Myth. Maurice Leenhardt in the Melanesian World* (Berkeley: University of California Press), 1982.
58 Vincent Crapanzano, *Tuhami, Portrait of a Moroccan* (Chicago and London: University of Chicago Press), 1980.
59 *Ibid.* pp. 16–17.
60 Diana L. Eck, "India's *Tīrthas*: 'Crossings' in Sacred Geography', *History of Religions,* vol. 20, no. 4, May 1981, p. 336.
61 John Archibald Wheeler, "Bohr, Einstein and the Strange Lesson of the Quantum" in Richard Q. Elvee (ed.), *Mind in Nature* (San Francisco: Harper and Row), 1982, pp. 1–30.
62 *Ibid.* p. 11.

6 Rationality, relativism, the translation and commensurability of cultures

1 The kind of colour tests administered by Brent Berlin and Paul Kay in *Basic Color Terms* (Berkeley: University of California Press), 1969, would establish the same visual discriminations. Also see Marshall Sahlins' "Colors and Cultures," *Semiotica,* 16, no. 1, 1976, pp. 1–22 for a statement with which I am in agreement.
2 This point has been forcefully argued by Clifford Geertz in *The Interpretation of Cultures* (New York: Basic Books), 1973, ch. 2.
3 Karl R. Popper. *The Logic of Scientific Discovery* (New York: Harper Torchbooks), 1959.
4 Ernest Gellner, "Relativism and Universals" in Martin Hollis and Steven Lukes (eds.), *Rationality and Relativism* (Cambridge, MA: M.I.T. Press), 1982, p. 200.
5 While Wittgenstein's conceptions of "language games" and "forms of life" are well known, it is worthwhile here to describe the expression "style of reasoning" which is exploited by Ian Hacking, who interestingly distinguishes "subjectivism" from "relativism." Identifying himself with the "anarcho-rationalist position," Hacking says his worry is that "whether or not a proposition is as it were up for grabs, as a candidate for being true-or-false, depends on whether we have ways to reason about it." The rationality of a style of reasoning may be built-in and self-authenticating in the sense that "The propositions on which the reasoning bears mean what they do just because that way of reasoning can assign them a truth value." The very candidates for truth or falsehood may have "no existence independent of the styles of reasoning that settle what it is to be true or false in their domain." The style of reasoning that we employ determines what counts as objectivity. (Ian Hacking "Language, Truth and Reason" in Martin Hollis and Steven Lukes (eds.), *Rationality and Relativism* (Cambridge, MA: M.I.T. Press), pp. 48–49.
6 The antagonists mixed up the Nuer, a Nilotic pastoral people, and the Azande, who have no cattle at all. Evans-Pritchard's monograph on the Azande was followed by one on the Nuer.
7 I shall not give here a blow-by-blow account of the controversy, but will allude to some of the issues it raised. The controversy is conveniently reprinted in *Rationality*

ed. Bryan R. Wilson (Oxford: Basil Blackwell), 1970. In this volume Peter Winch has a piece entitled "The Idea of a Social Science" which is abridged from his celebrated book by the same name published in 1958; and Alasdair MacIntyre also has an essay "The Idea of a Social Science" (originally published in 1967 in *Aristotelian Society Supplement*) which is his critique of Winch's book. Thereafter Winch's "Understanding a Primitive Society" and MacIntyre's "Is Understanding Religion Compatible with Believing?", which engage with Evans-Pritchard's work on the Azande, take the debate further.

There are subsequent edited essay collections that advance the examination of these issues, such as R. Horton and Ruth Finnegan (eds.), *Modes of Thought* (London: Faber and Faber) 1973; and Martin Hollis and Steven Lukes (eds.) *Rationality and Relativism*.

8 Charles Taylor, "Rationality" in Martin Hollis and Steven Lukes (eds.), *Rationality and Relativism*, pp. 86–90. This criterion, Taylor would admit, is unproblematic when the actor is conscious that he is frustrating his own goals, but more problematic when the actor is unconscious (or only has an implicit knowledge) of his goals and the consequences of his acts.

9 Donald Davidson, *Essays on Actions and Events*, ch. 12, "Psychology and Philosophy" (Oxford: Clarendon Press), 1980, pp. 236–37.

10 Jon Elster, *Sour Grapes. Studies in the Subversion of Rationality*, (Cambridge University Press; Paris: Maison des Sciences de l'Homme), 1983, p. 1.

11 *Ibid.* p. 2.

12 *Ibid.* p. 2.

13 *Ibid.* p. 15.

14 *Ibid.* p. 2.

15 Donald Davidson, *Essays on Actions and Events*, pp. 230–33.

16 Elster, *Sour Grapes*, p. 2.

17 Elster, *ibid.* p. 109.

18 Max Weber, principally citing the code of Manu, drew attention to the special codes of conduct allocated to the *varna* as status groups (see his *The Religion of India. The Sociology of Hinduism and Buddhism*, trans. H. H. Gerth and D. Martindale (Illinois: The Free Press of Glencoe), 1964). Louis Dumont's *Homo Hierarchicus. The Caste System and its Implications* (University of Chicago Press), 1980, is a monumental thesis about hierarchy which is organized in relation to the differential contribution of parts to the whole. Also see contextual morality and its underlying rules in McKim Marriott, "Hindu Transactions: Diversity without Dualism" in Bruce Kapferer (ed.), *Transaction and Meaning*, ASA Monographs, vol. 1, and Tambiah, "From Varna to Caste" in Jack Goody (ed.) *The Character of Kinship* (Cambridge University Press), 1973, pp. 191–230. A humorous and scintillating context-sensitive formulation of Indian conduct is A. K. Ramanujan's "Is there an Indian Way of Thinking?" as yet unpublished but originally written for a Seminar on Person and Interpersonal Relations in South Asia organized by the A.C.L.S. – S.S.R.C. Joint Committee on South Asia.

19 Hilary Putnam, *Reason, Truth and History* (Cambridge University Press), 1981, pp. 110–11.

20 Donald Davidson, *Essays on Actions and Events*, p. 238.

21 Hilary Putnam, *Reason, Truth and History*, p. 117.

22 Davidson, *Essays on Actions and Events*, pp. 238–39.

23 See his "On the very idea of a conceptual scheme," *Proceedings and Address of the American Philosophical Association*, 1973–74, 47, p. 19. In this essay Donaldson

also makes the point that any version of relativism that denies a common stock of non-relative observational truths which anchor communication also abandons "the attempt to make sense of the metaphor of a single space within which each (cultural) scheme has a position and provides a point of view" (p. 17).

24 Davidson, *Essays in Actions and Events*, p. 239.

25 Peter Winch, "Understanding a Primitive Society", p. 99.

26 Thomas Kuhn, *The Structure of Scientific Revolutions* (University of Chicago Press), 1962, pp. 84–85.

27 See Kuhn's "Postscript – 1969" in the second edition of *The Structure of Scientific Revolutions*, 1970.

28 Putnam, *Reason, Truth and History*, p. 115.

29 *Ibid.* p. 117.

30 *Ibid.* p. 119.

31 See Louis Dumont, *Homo Hierarchicus* (University of Chicago Press), 1980; "Caste, Racism, and 'Stratification'. Reflections of a Social Anthropologist" in *Contributions to Indian Sociology*, No. 5, October 1961, pp. 20–43; *From Mandeville to Marx. The Genesis and Triumph of Economic Ideology* (Chicago University Press), 1977; *Essays on Individualism* (University of Chicago Press), 1986. Gerald Berreman's views are collected in *Caste and other Inequities* (Meerut: Folklore Institute), 1979.

32 Peter Winch, "Understanding a Primitive Society," p. 102.

33 Bernard Williams, *Morality, An Introduction to Ethics* (New York: Harper and Row), 1972, pp. 21,23.

34 Hilary Putnam, *Reason, Truth and History*. The quotations are contained in chapter 5: "Two Conceptions of Rationality," especially on pp. 120, 121.

35 Bernard Williams, *Ethics and the Limits of Philosophy* (Cambridge, MA: Harvard University Press), 1985, ch. 9: 156–57.

36 Such seems to be the net result of Dan Sperber's position as for instance argued in his essay "Apparently Irrational Beliefs" in Martin Hollis and Steven Lukes (eds.), *Rationality and Relativism*. Sperber's resort to the notion of "a representational belief of a semi-propositional content" misses more than it explains with regard to many kinds of symbolic and performative discourses, etiquette, greetings and what Malinowski called "phatic" communication.

37 This conception of a shared framework and a unitary science has itself to be loosened up, as we shall see later.

38 I am particularly indebted to Bernard Williams's essay "The Truth of Relativism" (Chapter 11) in *Moral Luck. Philosophical Papers 1973–1980* (Cambridge University Press), 1981.

39 In my view this stricture by Peter Winch concerning the analysis of Zande data is wholly applicable to Horton's own discussion of his West African subjects: "Zande notions of witchcraft do not constitute a theoretical system in terms of which Azande try to gain a quasi-scientific understanding of the world. This in turn suggests it is the European, obsessed with pressing Zande thought where it would not naturally go – to a contradiction – who is guilty of misunderstanding, not the Zande. The European is in fact committing a category mistake." See Peter Winch, "Understanding a Primitive Society" in Bryan R. Wilson (ed.), *Rationality* (Oxford: Basil Blackwell), 1970, p. 93.

40 Imre Lakatos, *The Methodology of Scientific Research Programmes. Philosophical Papers*, vol. 1, ed. John Worrall and Gregory Currie (Cambridge University Press), 1978.

41 I am indebted for this wording to Charles Taylor. See his essay on "Rationality" in Hollis and Lukes (eds.), 1982, p. 102.
42 I am particularly indebted here to: McKim Marriott's concept of "dividualism" as stated in his various writings; Sudhir Kakar's *Shamans, Mystics and Doctors. A Psychological Inquiry into India and its Healing Traditions* (New York: Alfred A. Knopf), 1982: and Francis Zimmerman, "Remarks on the Conception of the Body in Ayurvedic Medicine, " presented at the A.C.L.S.–S.S.R.C. Seminar on Person and Interpersonal Relations in South Asia (University of Chicago Press), 1979.
43 See Milton Singer, *When a Great Tradition Modernizes* (London: Pall Mall Press), 1972, for a fascinating account.
44 Stuart Hampshire, *Morality and Conflict* (Cambridge, MA: Harvard University Press), 1983.
45 *Ibid.* p. 143.
46 *Ibid.* p. 144.
47 *Ibid.* p. 141.
48 *Ibid.* p. 143.
49 *Ibid.* p. 165.
50 *Ibid.* p. 5.
51 *Ibid.* pp. 167–68.

7 Modern science and its extensions

1 The author is M. J. S. Rudwick. The book was published by Chicago University Press, 1986.
2 *New York Review of Books*, "A triumph of historical excavation," February 27, 1986, p. 12.
3 See Imre Lakatos, *The Methodology of Scientific Research Programmes. Philosophical Papers*, vol. 1. See also Lakatos, "History of Science and its Rational Reconstructions" in Y. Elkana (ed.), *The Interaction Between Science and Philosophy* (New Jersey: Humanities Press), 1974.
4 Putnam, *Reason, Truth and History*, pp. 191, 192, 193.
5 All the quotations in the following paragraph pertaining to Herbert Marcuse are taken from chapter 6 ("Technological Rationality and the Logic of Domination") of his work, *One Dimensional Man* (Boston, MA: Beacon Press), 1964.
6 See Jurgen Habermas, *Toward a Rational Society*, trans. Jeremy J. Shapiro (London: Heinemann), 1971, ch. 6, "Technology and Science as Ideology," p. 82. Also his *Theory and Practice* (Boston, MA: Beacon Press), 1974, chs 1, 7.
7 For example, *Discipline and Punish. The Birth of the Prison* (New York: Vintage Books), 1979; *The Birth of the Clinic* (New York: Pantheon Books), 1972; *Power/Knowledge. Selected Interviews and Other Writings, 1972–1977*, ed. Colin Gordon (New York: Pantheon Books), 1980.
8 *Power/Knowledge*, pp. 119–20.
9 *Ibid.* pp. 131–32.
10 Thomas S. Kuhn remarks (in "The History of Science" in the *International Encyclopaedia of the Social Sciences* [ed.] David L. Sills [The Macmillan Co. and The Free Press], vol. 14), that some of the new historians of science have established that the radical sixteenth- and seventeenth-century revisions of astronomy, mathematics, mechanics and optics owed very little to new instruments, experiments or observations. If Galileo, Descartes, Newton saw things in a new light, the novelties were predominantly intellectual and included Renaissance

Neoplatonism, a revival of ancient Greek atomism and the rediscovery of Archimedes. Kuhn opines that if the main branches of science transformed during the sixteenth and seventeenth centuries are scrutinized – astronomy, mathematics, mechanics and optics – theirs was "a revolution in concepts." But in the seventeenth century there were other fields of intense scientific activity – such as the study of electricity and magnetism, of chemistry and of thermal phenomena – whose roots were not in the learned universities but often in the established crafts, and they were critically dependent on the new program of experimentation which craftsmen helped to introduce. These fields were not so much pursued in universities – except occasionally in medical schools – as in the new scientific societies by loosely assembled amateurs, and it is these latter that were the institutional manifestations of the Scientific Revolution. This new branch was the primary source of the scientific achievements of the late eighteenth and nineteenth centuries.

11 Habermas, *Toward a Rational Society*, p. 104.
12 Ernest Gellner, "Relativism and Universals," p. 191.
13 Habermas, *Toward a Rational Society*, pp. 92–93.
14 For this discussion I am particularly indebted to these essays: T. A. Tenbruck, "The Problem of Thematic Unity in the Works of Max Weber," *The British Journal of Sociology*, 1980, vol. 31, pp. 313–51; D. Kantowsky, "Max Weber on India and Indian Interpretations of Weber," *Contributions to Indian Sociology*, N.S., 1982, vol. 16, pp. 141–74; David Little, "Max Weber and the Comparative Study of Religious Ethics," *Journal of Religious Ethics*, 1974, vol. 2, pp. 5–41. Also see Guenther Roth and Wolfgang Schluchter, *Max Weber's Vision of History, Ethics and Methods* (Berkeley: University of California Press), 1979.
15 See Wolfgang Schluchter, *The Rise of Western Rationalism. Max Weber's Developmental History* (Berkeley: University of California Press), 1981, pp. 11–12.
16 For a recent sensitive documentation of both the benefits and destabilizing effects of the Green Revolution involving among other things double cropping, and the use of machines for plowing and harvesting in a Malaysian village and its region in Kedah, see James C. Scott, *Weapons of the Weak. Everyday Forms of Peasant Resistance* (New Haven and London: Yale University Press), 1985.

Bibliography

Apel, Karl-Otto. *Toward a Transformation of Philosophy*, trans. Glynn Adey and David Frisby (London: Routledge and Kegan Paul), 1980.
Baruch, Elaine H. and Perry Meisel. "Two Interviews with Julia Kristeva," *Partisan Review*, 1, 1984.
Bateson, Gregory. *Steps to an Ecology of Mind* (London: Intertext Books), 1972.
Bellah, Robert N. *Beyond Belief* (New York: Harper and Row), 1970.
Berlin, Brent and Paul Kay. *Basic Color Terms* (Berkeley: University of California Press), 1969.
Berreman, Gerald. *Caste and Other Inequities* (Meerut: Folklore Institute), 1979.
Bloch, Marc. *The Royal Touch: Sacred Monarchy and Scrofula in England and France*, trans. J. E. Anderson (London: Routledge and Kegan Paul), 1973.
Boas, Marie. *The Scientific Renaissance 1450–1630: The Rise of Modern Science* (New York: Harper and Brothers), 1962.
Boon, James. Review of Robert E. Ackerman's *J. G. Frazer, His Life and Work*. (Cambridge University Press), 1987 in *The New York Times Book Review*, 1988.
Burke, Kenneth. *A Rhetoric of Motives* (Berkeley and Los Angeles: University of California Press), 1969.
Burrow, J. W. *Evolution and Society: A Study in Victorian Social Theory* (Cambridge University Press), 1966.
Cazeneuve, Jean. "Lucien Lévi-Bruhl (1857–1939)" in *International Encyclopaedia of the Social Sciences*, vol. 2, Part 1, 1934.
Clagett, Marshall (ed.) *Critical Problems in the History of Science: Proceedings* (Madison: University of Wisconsin Press), 1957.
Clifford, James. *Person and Myth. Maurice Leenhardt in the Melanesian World* (Berkeley: University of California Press), 1982.
Crapanzano, Vincent. *Tuhami. Portrait of a Moroccan* (Chicago and London: University of Chicago Press), 1980.
Crowther, J. G. *The Social Relations of Science* (New York: Macmillian Co.), 1941.
Davidson, Donald. "Psychology and Philosophy", ch. 12 of *Essays on Actions and Events* (Oxford: Clarendon Press), 1980.
de Laguna, G. A. *Speech, its Function and Development* (New Haven: Yale University Press), 1927.
Douglas, Mary. *Evans-Pritchard* (Sussex: The Harvester Press), 1980.
    "Judgments on James Frazer", *Daedalus* (*Journal of American Academy of Arts and Sciences*), Fall, 1978.

Dumont, Louis. *Essays on Individualism* (University of Chicago Press), 1986.
  Homo Hierarchicus. The Caste System and its Implications (Chicago: University of
    Chicago Press), 1980.
  From Mandeville to Marx. The Genesis and Triumph of Economic Ideology (Chicago
    University Press), 1977.
  "Caste, Racism, and 'Stratification,' Reflections of a Social Anthropologist,"
    Contributions to Indian Sociology, no. 5, October, 1961.
Durkheim, Emile. *The Elementary Forms of the Religious Life* (New York: The Free
    Press), 1965.
Eck, Diana L. "India's *Tīrthas*: 'Crossings' in Sacred Geography," *History of
    Religions*, vol. 20, no. 4, May 1981.
Elster, Jon. *Sour Grapes: Studies in the Subversion of Rationality* (Cambridge
    University Press; Paris: Maison des Sciences de l'Homme), 1983.
Evans-Pritchard, E. E. *Nuer Religion* (Oxford: Clarendon Press), 1956.
  Theories of Primitive Religion (Oxford: Clarendon Press), 1965.
  The Divine Kingship Among the Shilluk of the Nilotic Sudan (Cambridge University
    Press), 1948.
  "Lévy-Bruhl's Theory of Primitive Mentality," *Bulletin, Faculty of Arts*, vol. 2, Part
    2 (Cairo, Egypt: Farouk University), 1934, pp. 1–36.
  "The Intellectualist (English) Interpretation of Magic," *Bulletin, Faculty of Arts*,
    vol. 1, Part 2 (Cairo, Egypt: Farouk University), 1933, pp. 282–311.
  "Science and Sentiment: An Exposition and Criticism of the Writings of Pareto,"
    Bulletin, Faculty of Arts, Vol. 3, Part 2 (Cairo, Egypt: Farouk University), 1936,
    pp. 163–92.
Febvre, Lucien. *The Problem of Unbelief in the Sixteenth Century. The Religion of
    Rabelais*, trans. Beatrice Gottlieb (Cambridge, MA: Harvard University Press),
    1982.
Firth, Raymond (ed.) *Man and Culture. An Evaluation of Malinowski* (London:
    Routledge and Kegan Paul), 1957.
Foucault, Michel. *Power/Knowledge. Selected Interviews and Other Writings,
    1972–1977*, ed. Colin Gordon (New York: Pantheon Books), 1980.
  Discipline and Punish. The Birth of the Prison (New York: Vintage Books), 1979.
  The Order of Things: An Archaeology of the Human Sciences (London: Tavistock;
    New York: Pantheon Books), 1973.
  The Birth of the Clinic (New York: Pantheon Books), 1972.
Frazer, J. G. *The Golden Bough. A Study in Magic and Religion*, Part 1, vol. 1, *The
    Magic Art and the Evolution of Kings* (London: Macmillan 3rd edn), 1911.
French, Peter. *John Dee: The World of an Elizabethan Magus* (London: Routledge and
    Kegan Paul), 1973.
Freud, Sigmund. *The Interpretation of Dreams* (Book 2), *The Basic Writings of
    Sigmund Freud* (trans. A. A. Brill) (New York: The Modern Library, Random
    House), 1938.
Geertz, Clifford. *The Interpretation of Cultures* (New York: Basic Books), 1973.
Geertz, Hildred. "An Anthropology of Religion and Magic, 1," *Journal of Inter-
    disciplinary History*, vol. 6, no. 1, Summer 1975, pp. 71–89.
Gellner, Ernest. "'Malinowski Go Home': Reflections on the Malinowski Centenary
    Conferences," *Anthropology Today*, January 5, 1985, pp. 5–7.
  "Relativism and Universals" in Martin Hollis and Steven Lukes (eds.), *Rationality
    and Relativism* (Oxford: Basil Blackwell), 1982 (Cambridge, MA: M.I.T. Press),
    1982.

Gilligan, Carol. *In a Different Voice. Psychological Theory and Women's Development* (Cambridge, MA: Harvard University Press), 1982.

Goodman, Nelson. *Language of Art. An Approach to a Theory of Symbols* (Indianapolis, Indiana: Hackett Publishing Co. [1976]), 1985.

Ways of Worldmaking (Indianapolis, Indiana: Hackett Publishing Co.), 1985.

Gould, Stephen Jay. *Hen's Teeth and Horse's Toe. Further Reflections in Natural History* (New York: Norton), 1983.

The Panda's Thumb (New York: Norton), 1980.

"A Triumph of Historical Excavation," *New York Review of Books*, February 27, 1986.

Gould, Stephen Jay and Elizabeth S. Vrba. "Exaptation – A Missing Term in the Science of Form," *Paleobiology*, 8(1), 1982, pp. 4–15.

Gurvitch, Georges. "The Sociological Legacy of Lucien Lévi-Bruhl," *Journal of Social Philosophy*, New York, 1939, vol. 5, no. 1, pp. 61–70.

Habermas, Jurgen. *Theory and Practice* (Boston, MA: Beacon Press), 1974.

"Technology and Science as Ideology," ch. 6, *Toward a Rational Society*, trans. Jeremy J. Shapiro (London: Heinemann), 1971.

Hacking, Ian. "Language, Truth and Reason" in Martin Hollis and Steven Lukes (eds.), *Rationality and Relativism* (Oxford: Basil Blackwell), 1982 (Cambridge, MA: M.I.T. Press), 1982.

Hampshire, Stuart. *Morality and Conflict* (Cambridge, MA: Harvard University Press), 1983.

Horton, Robin. "Lévy-Bruhl, Durkheim and the Scientific Revolution" in *Modes of Thought* (eds.) Robin Horton and Ruth Finnegan (London: Faber and Faber), 1973.

"African Traditional Thought and Western Science", *Africa*, vol. 37, nos. 1 and 2, 1967.

"Ritual Man in Africa", *Africa*, vol. 34, 1964.

Jakobson, Roman. "Closing Statement: Linguistics and Poetics" in Thomas A. Sebeok (ed.), *Style in Language* (Cambridge, MA: M.I.T. Press), 1960.

Kakar, Sudhir. *Shamans, Mystics and Doctors. A Psychological Inquiry into India and its Healing Traditions* (New York: Alfred A. Knopf), 1982.

The Inner World. A Psycho-analytic Study of Childhood and Society in India (Delhi: Oxford University Press), 1978.

Kantowsky, D. "Max Weber on India and Indian Interpretations of Weber," *Contributions to Indian Sociology*, N.S., 1982, vol. 16, no. 2, pp. 141–74.

Kauffman, Yehezkel. *The Religion of Israel from its Beginnings to the Babylonian Exile*, trans. and abridged Moshe Greenberg (New York: Schocken Books), 1972.

Kuhn, Thomas. "Logic of Discovery and Psychology of Research" in Imre Lakatos and Alan Musgrove (eds.), *Criticism and the Growth of Knowledge* (Cambridge University Press), 1970.

"Postscript – 1969" in *The Structure of Scientific Revolutions*, 2nd edn (University of Chicago Press), 1970.

"The History of Science" in David L. Sills (ed.), *International Encyclopedia of Social Sciences*, vol. 14 (U.S.A.: Macmillan Co. and The Free Press), 1968.

The Structure of Scientific Revolutions (University of Chicago Press), 1962.

Lakatos, Imre. *The Methodology of Scientific Research Programmes. Philosophical Papers*, vol. 1, eds. John Worrall and Gregory Currie (Cambridge University Press), 1978.

"History of Science and its Rational Reconstructions" in Y. Elkana (ed.), *The Interaction Between Science and Philosophy* (New Jersey: Humanities Press), 1974.

Langer, Suzanne. *Feeling and Form. A Theory of Art* (New York: Mentor Books), 1953.
   Philosophy in a New Key (New York: Mentor Books), 1942.
Leach, Edmund. "The Epistemological Background of Malinowski's Empiricism", in *Man and Culture. An Evaluation of the Work of Bronislaw Malinowski* (London: Routledge and Kegan Paul), 1957.
Leenhardt, Maurice. *Do Kamo: Person and Myth in the Melanesian World* (ed.) James Clifford (Berkeley: University of California Press), 1982.
Lévi-Strauss, Claude. *Structural Anthropology* (New York: Basic Books), 1963.
Lévy-Bruhl, Lucien. *Les Carnets de Lucien Lévy-Bruhl* (Paris: Presses Universitaires de France), 1949; translated by Peter Rivière as *Notebooks on Primitive Mentality* (Oxford: Blackwell), 1973.
   L'Âme primitive (1927) (Paris: Alcan); translated by Lilian Clare as *The "Soul" of the Primitive* (London: Allen and Unwin Ltd.), 1927.
   La Mentalité primitive (1922) The Herbert Spencer Lecture (Oxford: Clarendon Press); translated by Lilian Clare as *Primitive Mentality* (Oxford: Clarendon Press), 1923.
   Les Fonctions mentales dans les sociétés inférieures (1920); translated by Lilian Clare as *How Natives Think* (New York: Washington Square Press), 1966.
Little, David. "Max Weber and the Comparative Study of Religious Ethics," *Journal of Religious Ethics*, 1974, vol. 2, pp. 5–41.
Lloyd, G. E. R. *Polarity and Analogy. Two Types of Augmentation in Early Greek Thought* (Cambridge University Press), 1966.
   Magic, Reason and Experience. Studies in the Origins and Development of Greek Science (Cambridge University Press), 1979.
   Early Greek Science, Thales to Aristotle (London: Chatto and Windus), 1970.
Lovejoy, Arthur O. *The Great Chain of Being: A Study of the History of an Idea* (Cambridge, MA: Harvard University Press) [1936], 1976.
Lowie, Robert H. *The History of Ethnological Theory* (New York: Rinehart), 1937.
Mach, Ernst. *Erkenntnis und Irrtum* (1905); translated as *Knowledge and Error: Sketches on the Psychology of Enquiry* by Thomas J. McCormack and Paul Foulkes (Boston, MA: D. Reidel Publishing Co.), 1976.
Malinowski, Bronislaw. *A Diary in the Strict Sense of the Term* (New York: Harcourt, Brace and World, Inc.), 1967.
   Magic, Science, and Religion and Other Essays (New York: Doubleday Anchor Books), 1954; (Illinois: The Free Press of Glencoe), 1948.
   The Foundations of Faith and Morals (Riddell Memorial Lecture, Durham 1934–35) (London: Oxford University Press), 1936.
   Coral Gardens and Their Magic (London: George Allen and Unwin), 1935; (New York: American Book Co.), 1935, 2 vols.
   The Sexual Life of Savages in North West Melanesia (London: Routledge and Kegan Paul), 1929.
   Sex and Repression in Savage Society (New York: Harcourt), 1927.
   The Father in Primitive Psychology (New York: W. W. Norton & Co.), 1927.
   Myth in Primitive Psychology (New York: W. W. Norton & Co.), 1926.
   Crime and Custom in Savage Society (London: International Library of Psychology, Philosophy and Scientific Method), 1926.
   "The Problem of Meaning in Primitive Languages', in C. K. Ogden and I. A. Richards, *The Meaning of Meaning* (London: International Library of Psychology, Philosophy and Scientific Method), 1923.
   Argonauts of the Western Pacific (London: Routledge and Kegan Paul), 1922.

Marcuse, Herbert. "Technological Rationality and the Logic of Domination," ch. 6 of *One Dimensional Man* (Boston, MA: Beacon Press), 1964.

Marriott, McKim. "Hindu Transactions: Diversity Without Dualism" in Bruce Kapferer (ed.), *Transaction and Meaning*, A.S.A. Monographs (Philadelphia: I.S.H.I.), 1976, vol. 1.

Merton, R. K. "Science and Technology in 17th Century England," *Osiris* (Bruges: St. Catherine Press) 1938, 4.

Social Theory and Social Structure (Illinois: The Free Press of Glencoe), 1949.

Miles, A. C. and Rush Rhees. "Ludwig Wittgenstein's 'Remarks on Frazer's *Golden Bough*'," *The Human World*, no. 3, May 1971, pp. 28–41.

Morgan, Lewis Henry. *Ancient Society* (New York: Henry Holt and Co.), 1877.

Nadel, S. F. "Malinowski on Magic and Religion" in Raymond Firth (ed.), *Man and Culture. An Evaluation of the Work of Bronislaw Malinowski* (London: Routledge and Kegan Paul), 1960 (first printed: 1957).

Needham, Rodney. *Belief, Language and Experience* (University of Chicago Press), 1972.

Exemplars (Berkeley: University of California Press), 1985.

O'Flaherty, Wendy. *The Origins of Evil in Hindu Mythology* (Berkeley and Los Angeles: University of California Press), 1976.

Popper, Karl R. *Conjectures and Reflections* (New York: Harper Torchbooks), 1963.

The Logic of Scientific Discovery (New York: Harper Torchbooks), 1959.

Putnam, Hilary. *Reason, Truth and History* (Cambridge University Press), 1981.

Roth, Guenther and Schluchter, Wolfgang. *Max Weber's Vision of History, Ethics and Methods* (Berkeley: University of California Press), 1979.

Rudwick, M. J. S. *The Great Devonian Controversy. The Shaping of Scientific Knowledge* (Chicago University Press), 1986.

Sahlins, Marshall. "Colors and Cultures," *Semiotica*, 16, no. 1, 1976, pp. 1–22.

Schluchter, Wolfgang. *The Rise of Western Rationalism. Max Weber's Developmental History* (Berkeley: University of California Press), 1981.

Schutz, Alfred. *Collected Papers 1. The Problem of Social Reality* (ed. and introduction) Maurice Natanson (The Hague: Martinus Nijhoff), 1962.

Scott, James C. *Weapons of the Weak. Everyday Forms of Peasant Resistance* (New Haven and London: Yale University Press), 1985.

Silverman, William. *Retrolental Fibroplasia: A Parable* (New York: Grune and Stratton), 1980.

Singer, Charles. *A Short History of Scientific Ideas to 1900* (New York: Abelard–Schuman), 1955.

Singer, Milton. "A Neglected Source of Structuralism: Radcliffe-Brown, Russell and Whitehead," *Semiotica*, 1984, vol. 48, no. 1/2.

When a Great Tradition Modernizes (London: Pall Mall Press), 1972.

Smith, Wilfred Cantwell. *The Meaning and End of Religion* (San Francisco: Harper and Row), 1978.

Snell, Bruno. *The Discovery of the Mind* (New York: Harper Torchbook), 1960.

Sperber, Dan. "Apparently Irrational Beliefs" in Martin Hollis and Steven Lukes (eds.), *Rationality and Relativism* (Cambridge, MA: M.I.T. Press), 1984.

Stocking, George W. *Race, Culture and Evolution* (New York: The Free Press), 1971.

Tambiah, Stanley J. *Culture, Thought and Social Action* (Cambridge, MA: Harvard University Press), 1985.

"Form and Meaning of Magical Acts" and "A Performative Approach to Ritual" in *Culture, Thought and Social Action* (Cambridge, MA: Harvard University Press), 1985.

"From Varna to Caste" in Jack Goody (ed.) *The Character of Kinship* (Cambridge University Press), 1973, pp. 191–230.

Taylor, Charles. "Rationality" in Martin Hollis and Steven Lukes (eds.), *Rationality and Relativism* (Cambridge, MA: M.I.T. Press), 1982.

Tenbruck, T. A. "The Problem of Thematic Unity in the Works of Max Weber," *The British Journal of Sociology*, 1980, vol. 31, pp. 313–51.

Thomas, Keith. *Religion and the Decline of Magic* (New York: Charles Scribner's Sons), 1971.

Thornton, Robert J. "'Imagine yourself set down . . .' Mach, Frazer, Conrad, Malinowski and the Role of Imagination in Ethnology," *Anthropology Today*, January 5, 1985, pp. 7–14.

Trevor-Roper, H. R. *The European Witch-Craze of the 16th and 17th Centuries* (Harmondsworth: Penguin Books), 1969.

Tylor, Edward Burnett. *Religion in Primitive Culture, vol. 2* (Gloucester, MA: Peter Smith), 1970.

Wayne, Helena. "Bronislaw Malinowski: The Influence of Various Women in His Life and Works," *American Ethnologist*, December 3, 1985, pp. 529–40.

Weber, Max. *The Protestant Ethic and the Spirit of Capitalism* (New York: Charles Scribner's Sons), 1930.

The Religion of India. The Sociology of Hinduism and Buddhism, trans. H. H. Gerth and D. Martindale (Illinois: The Free Press of Glencoe), 1964.

Weiner, Philip P. and Aaron Noland. *Roots of Scientific Thought: A Cultural Perspective* (New York: Basic Books), 1957.

Wheeler, J. A. "Bohr, Einstein, and the Strange Lesson of the Quantum" R. Q. Elvee (ed.), *Mind in Nature* (San Francisco: Harper and Row), 1981.

Williams, Bernard. *Ethics and the Limits of Philosophy* (Cambridge, MA: Harvard University Press), 1985.

Morality. An Introduction to Ethics (New York: Harper and Row), 1981.

"The Truth of Relativism", ch. 11 of *Moral Luck. Philosophical Papers 1973–1980* (Cambridge University Press), 1981.

Wilson, Bryan R. (ed.), *Rationality* (Oxford: Basil Blackwell), 1970.

Winch, Peter. "Understanding a Primitive Society" in Bryan R. Wilson (ed.) *Rationality* (Oxford: Basil Blackwell), 1979.

Wittgenstein, Ludwig. *On Certainty*, eds. G. E. M. Anscombe and G. H. von Wright; trans. Denis Paul and G. E. M. Anscombe (Oxford: Blackwell), 1969.

Yates, Frances. "The Fear of the Occult," *New York Review of Books*, vol. 26, no. 18, November 22, 1979.

The Rosicrucian Enlightenment (London: Routledge and Kegan Paul), 1973.

Giordano Bruno and the Hermetic Tradition (London: Routledge and Kegan Paul) [1964], 1971.

The Art of Memory (London: Routledge and Kegan Paul), 1966.

Zimmerman, Francis. "Remarks on the Conception of the Body in Ayurvedic Medicine." A.C.L.S.–S.S.R.C. Seminar on Person and Interpersonal Relations in South Asia (University of Chicago), 1979.

Index